(Un)Bound, Together:

A Journey to the End of the Earth (and Beyond)

Amit Janco

ISBN (book): 978-1-9990182-0-7
ISBN (e-book): 978-1-9990182-2-1

Content design/layout: Joanne Haskins. Thinkcom.ca
Editing: Shelley Kenigsberg. Editinginparadise.com
Art direction: Amit Janco
Cover art: Pip Holmes
Author photo: Xiaofang Su (Suskita)

For author queries or order information, visit https://amitjanco.com/books/

Author's Note

To write this book, I relied upon my photographs, journal notes, MP3 audio recordings, researched facts, snippets of conversation—and a diary from my youth. My memory, albeit imperfect, filled in the rest. Several names and details have been altered to preserve anonymity. *Mea culpa* for any errors, oversights, or faulty Spanish grammar.

In memory of Jules 'Ticu' Janco, whose spirit, light and love still reside in the mist.

Bucharest 1896–Montreal 1985

Caminante, no hay camino, se hace camino al andar.
Wanderer, there is no path, the path is made by walking.
~ Antonio Machado, *Campos de Castilla*

כל העולם כולו גשר צר מאוד, והעיקר – לא לפחד כלל
Kol ha'olam kulo gesher tzar me'od, veha'ikar lo le'fached klal.
The whole world is a very narrow bridge, and the
important thing is not to be afraid.
~ Rabbi Nachman of Breslov

I wish no living thing to suffer pain.
~ Percy Bysshe Shelley, *Prometheus Unbound*, 1820

Contents

Prologue

"You're a walking miracle," said Dr. Gutman, shaking his head in disbelief while scanning the accident and medical reports. "Each one of these injuries could have killed you." He should know, I thought to myself. Exhaling slowly, I silently counted off the multiple bone fractures and nerve damage I'd sustained after falling ten meters through a defective bridge in Cambodia a few months earlier. After logging more than two decades as an ER physician, there was little in the way of trauma cases that he hadn't seen.

Dr. Gutman's words planted a seed. If I'd come this close to death, I was in no position to take for granted my capacity to walk. Gratitude trumped all else. Whereas I once jogged, cycled, trekked, played tennis, swam, trained, and competed in dragon boat races, I was now mentally crossing off that whole slew of rigorous activities. With a reconfigured body, my options had whittled down considerably.

Over the course of a year, with an intensive rehabilitation jammed with physiotherapy, osteopathy, swimming, acupuncture, and gentle yoga, I never deviated from my walking routine, weaving its healing-juice through everything else. Within a few months, I graduated from limping along with a four-legged assistive device to hobbling on crutches; from using a cane to relying solely on my own two legs. Eventually freed from all contraptions, I was getting antsy. My rehab regimen needed a boost. I had to push myself, see how far my body could carry me.

Why not walk to the end of the earth? I could start off with a goal of 1000 kilometers, give or take. Granted, it was a pittance compared to the 7-month, 21,000-mile walk that journalist John Salopek had just embarked on. After all, Salopek was famously trekking around the world, with National Geographic tracking his every move, while I was merely planning to traipse across Spain. But never mind the details. My mind was set: I was going to walk the Camino.

This epiphany wasn't the first time I'd entertained the notion of a walk of this magnitude; the seed had been planted long before.

More than a decade earlier, unemployed and newly arrived in Toronto from Montreal, I was looking for work—and meaning. With time on my hands, I accompanied an acquaintance to a networking conference, where I heard a woman talk about her experiences walking hundreds of kilometers along the medieval pilgrimage route known as the Camino Santiago de Compostela. Sue Kenney spoke about how she sought solace in adventure and nature after being dumped from a high-paying corporate job—by walking the Camino, and laying stones along the way. The connections she made and friendships forged provided the sustenance she had long sought and craved. My curiosity was piqued: I could use a dose of nature and nurture. At the end of the day, Sue and I sat down for coffee.

Though I wasn't very spiritual back then, nor am I Catholic, Sue's story—revealing humanity's deepest instinct and primal desire for nature, and how its inspiring and forgiving elements help us heal—struck a chord deep inside of me. Her narrative resonated on many levels; through a sharpened lens, I saw that my life too had reeled and roiled, through times of misery and depression, few work prospects, failed or non-existent relationships, and plenty of stagnation. After hearing Sue speak and reading her book, my gut and lungs were knotted. I ached for air. By the time we parted ways, a few hours later, the question wasn't if I would walk the Camino, but when.

My serendipitous meeting with Sue and our subsequent correspondence—even after my accident, she bolstered my confidence—laid the groundwork. Then, Dr. Gutman has his say—and the idea birthed buds.

Two years after plummeting off that unsafe Cambodian bridge,

I was still on a journey of recovery and healing. Returning to the South Asian country with its own grim history, I revisited the bridge of my accident and sought out those who saved me. Then, while visiting a friend in nearby Malaysia, I was urged to take a short detour to Indonesia—or more precisely to the resort island of Bali, a centuries-old locus of traditional healing. Before landing, I pictured a tropical isle coated in pristine beaches and wide open lush green fields. Beyond the verdant tiered rice paddies, I anticipated finding large swaths of land where, rain or shine, I could walk far and unimpeded. But, my expectations quickly evaporated. Besides a couple of yellowed and neglected "football" fields in my new hometown of Ubud, green parks and playgrounds did not exist.

The prospect of walking freely around the town of Ubud also soon evaporated—its increasing traffic and broken sidewalks swiftly dampening my enchantment. As one local writer has pointed out: "If you live in Ubud, walking anywhere is out of the question. If you walk, you are very likely to be killed in the traffic—quickly, by a schoolchild on a motorbike, or slowly by asphyxiation from bus fumes. Even walking through the rice fields, leaves you at risk of being hit by a motorbike, not to mention sunstroke, snakebite, getting lost, and above all, fatigue."

A few months of dodging bikes, fumes and gaping chasms later, I decided to seek out greener walking pastures. Even the heady allure of rice paddy walks, initially so appealing, was wearing thin. How often can you tiptoe along raised beds of earth bordering flooded fields before your teetering no longer feels like leisure?

That's when I went in search of a labyrinth. Surely Ubud, renowned as a center of healing (its original name, Obad/Oboed, translates to medicine) would feature at least one labyrinth, a set of circular paths that, in modern times, have been repurposed for walking meditation. Imagining that I'd discover a crop of them dotting the island, I looked online and asked around. Neither Balinese locals nor longtime expats had even heard of a labyrinth. Which compelled me to create one myself—at a silent meditation retreat center, far off the beaten track and in the shadow of Bali's sacred volcanic mountain, Mount Agung. Over the course of a year, the project provided me with an abundance of space, breathable air, respite from the hubbub of Ubud, and a closely shaved pate of green on which to walk.

During one of my meditative strolls around the labyrinth, the notion of a walk of unimaginably long proportions re-surfaced and sprouted wings. I could no longer ignore the imperative: Gotta walk. Slow. Long. Far. As far as possible.

Clearly, the time had come for me to walk the Camino. But did I even fit the profile of a bona fide pilgrim? Who knew? Google helped sort me out.

I learned that the main pilgrimage routes—to Jerusalem, Rome and Spain—had been popular with Christians ever since the 4th century A.D.; and that pilgrims had been travelling to Santiago, to visit the (alleged) tomb of Saint James, the country's patron saint, for over a thousand years. I had lived in Jerusalem and I'd toured Rome; I had even traveled through Spain—Madrid, Andalusia, and the Costa del Sol (by way of which I had acquired a passable though spotty comprehension of basic Spanish). But Galicia and Santiago were unexplored terrain; one more reason to walk a trail paved with history.

In the 10th century, a French bishop was one of the first pilgrims to make the journey to Santiago. At the height of the pilgrimage's popularity in the 11th and 12th centuries, over half a million Catholic pilgrims are said to have traveled the Camino Frances each year, from the southern reaches of the Pyrénée mountains to Spain's remote northwestern region of Galicia; staying in pilgrim lodgings (known as hospitals) along the way.

Despite a gradual decrease in the numbers of pilgrims walking to Santiago over the centuries, the past few decades were marked by a resurgence. But 21st century pilgrims often walk for non-religious reasons and causes; wellbeing and self-enlightenment, to lose weight, to recover from a failed relationship, to raise funds, for an outdoor adventure, to meet new people from around the world, or to see Spain from a different perspective than the interior of a tour bus.

I too had no religious justification for charting this particular path. The motivating factors were few and simple: Crank up my body's healing. Discover life in Spain's remotest villages. Meet other wanderlusters. Improve my Spanish. Nestle into nature. Celebrate my 50th birthday. Escape from everyday intrusions: noise, traffic, pollution, a jungle of tattooed bodies—and the crush of social media. Apparently, with the criteria now extensively relaxed, as an explorer, seeker and trauma survivor, I too would qualify. Hallelujah.

Which is how I—a Buddhist-leaning, *savasana*-practicing, re-formed lawyer and lapsed Jewess—came to embark on one of Catholicism's holiest pilgrimage routes.

❦

Chapter 1: Getting in Gear

Travel was in her DNA. During family road trips through New York, Virginia Beach and Vermont, the girl rattled off country names and played "I Spy" with her sisters in the back seat of the station wagon. Overseas travel meant bulky suitcases, passports and a prized teddy bear in tow. It meant sandy beaches, high dives into hotel pools, exotic foods, shopping, room service and dancing on the tips of her father's shoes long past sunset, to the sounds of tuxedoed crooners whose slick hair glistened under the wilting heat of tropical spotlights.

***

Over the months leading up to my departure, I am obsessed. While most wannabe-pilgrims in online forums ask about backpacks and hiking boots; thermal underwear and wicking socks; laptops or tablet (or both?), I have more pressing matters in mind.

How would my gear move itself from one town to another? Ever since my accident, I had become unable to carry any heavy items. This new normal ruled out the possibility of me carrying my own backpack. Short of finding a way to teleport my clothes and toiletries, I needed a walking partner-and-carrier. A personal hauler. Perchance, a butler. Heck, I'd even settle on a Spanish sherpa.

I had conjured up a few options. A camel sounded like a good idea. In 1977, Robyn Davidson had trudged across nearly 3,000 kilometers of the Australian outback with four camels lugging her gear. My guess was that a camel could be recruited quite easily as it would be covering a fraction of Davidson's distance, carting considerably less stuff. I'd ridden a camel a few years before, in Germany, and assumed Spain had its share of dromedaries. It could be a walk in the parque. E-mails were sent.

"Does anyone know if and where I might find a CAMEL (*sí, uno camello*) in Spain?"

"Sorry, the only camels in Spain are in zoos and on islands as tourist attractions."

"What about an alpaca or llama?"

"Impossible. It's not legal for them to carry gear."

"How about a donkey?" I wrote to sanctuaries and farms all around Europe.

No takers. No givers. No lenders. No way. Nada.

There was also the small matter of my... umm, rear end. The triangular-shaped sacrum at the base of the spine is one of the hardest bones in our body. It takes a heck of a whopping to split it into bits. Mine got whopped and shattered in a few places—most prominently, in the neighborhood of L4-L5. My pelvis and the whole left side of my body took the biggest brunt of the fall; my leg was crushed and shortened from impact, its spindly toes banged up, still today loath to straighten out, flatten. A cluster of muscles and fascia were dented and damaged. A bundle of nerves originating in the sacral region, weaving down and through my left leg to the tip of my toes, were struck numb. In short, my body, bum included, took a pummeling.

Here is what I learned: If your derriere gets banged up from landing on rocks, you may develop an inability to sit. Chairs, benches, hard surfaces of any kind, make me cringe. I adapt. Kneel. Squat. Crouch. Lean. Lie down. Cushions, sofas, chaise longues, beanbags, and yoga mats are allies. They have my back.

In light of (and despite) my sitting disability, I forged ahead with plans, which included launching a crowd-sourcing campaign—to raise funds and awareness about invisible illnesses, injuries and impairments. The love and cash poured in. I was edging closer towards the starting line.

Packing light was a priority—even if I wasn't going to do the heavy lifting. I borrowed a weathered backpack from my brother-in-law. A collapsible *carrito* (luggage trolley) from my parents. A green lightweight daypack from my niece. Weather-beaten and well-worn hiking boots from my Himalayan trek a few years earlier were pulled out of storage, now buffed up with sturdy orthotic inserts. And a last-minute splurge on Teva trekking sandals—just in case.

With the specter of chronic pain spiking if I carried too much load, weight restrictions were a key consideration. Fracture dislocation with displacement results in significant disc disruption and loss of load-bearing capacity. Every milligram counted. I skimmed down to the essentials: A (near-weightless) map, a (near-weightless) list of *albergues* (hostel-like accommodations for pilgrims), a (near-weightless) notebook, pen, pair of prescription eyeglasses. Even my toy-like Nokia cell phone, limited to messages and calls, felt lighter than air. Then, I took my research to the supermarket; lifting bags of white sugar and whole wheat flour in varying weights. The 500g bag was a little light and the 2kg bag so heavy, it tugged my whole body downwards. The 1kg bag was on the lighter side. With the 1kg bag in one hand and the 500g bag in another, I strolled the aisles (ignoring puzzled looks of onlookers) and, like a latter-day Goldilocks, hit my target.

In preparation, I also read stories about unusual modes of doing the Camino. "Almost anyone can walk, ride, or cycle a Camino," wrote South African co-author Sylvia Nilsen, about pilgrims setting out with different levels of ability. Nilsen's book introduced me to an unknown species: Backpack trolleys. "If you prefer to cart your own pack," she writes, "you might consider pulling a backpack trolley which will leave your hands free." Examples included the Dixon Roller Pack, the Dutch-made Wheelie 111 and the Australian-designed Trackmate.

But my ultimate swoon was reserved for the Swiss-engineered, ergonomically-designed Carrix and its custom-made harness. I fantasized about navigating the one-wheeled trolley with my backpack behind me—on my own. A stroke of luck landed me on the front steps of a former pilgrim; Charly had a Carrix and he invited me to take it out for a spin. Strapped in, I tried to lift the Carrix. Even without a single item placed onto its frame, the damn thing wouldn't budge. Which is when all my quixotic ideas of walking solo across Spain, the cool-looking Carrix trailing behind me, came crashing down. I left Charly's house bereft.

I cannot do this alone.

As my departure date approached, the search for my sherpa reached a new level of urgency. Taxi services that ferry backpacks from one village to the next village were not a viable option; pre-arranging a drop-off point was impossible due to unforeseen fluctuations in pain. If I couldn't reach the taxi's target destination, I might be left without a change of clothes and toiletries. And no one should be forced to sleep next to a foul-smelling pilgrim.

My new goal entailed tracking down another pilgrim, flexible enough to accommodate my slower pace and peculiarities. On the verge of canceling, I found some hope one morning in an e-mail, as if strapped to wings.

A German tour guide and seasoned pilgrim had gotten wind of my plans and predicament. Otto proposed that I join him for a week, after which he would locate someone to carry my gear the rest of the way. It sounded too good—and auspiciously timed—to be true. Due diligence flew out the window and I leapt at the offer. I was in too deep; there was no turning back now.

Chapter 2: The Pamplona Connection

Early on September 19th, 2013, one week after my 50th birthday, I wake up in Pamplona, Spain. I switch on my cell phone, impatient to hear from Otto. Hours later, my phone finally beeps, while I am exploring the park around the renowned Ciudadela fortress.

"Hello Amit," it reads, "welcome in Spain. We will be the 20th more or less at noon in Cizur Menor. A little village 5 kilometers behind Pamplona on the Camino. We can't go through Pamplona with the donkeys."

Yes, of course, the donkeys. He is taking a pair of burros on a trial run; I am not alone in requiring detours and accommodations. But it seems odd that these four-legged creatures should be prohibited from crossing through Spain's cities and towns. After all, it was the esteemed Spanish writer Miguel de Cervantes who conjured up Don Quixote (a.k.a. The Ingenious Nobleman Sir Quixote of La Mancha), the legendary literary figure who roamed the countryside on a donkey, running into challenges and windmills along the way. So why would Pamplona authorities allow enraged bulls to run amok through crowds of bystanders during its annual Fiesta Fermin, but bar a couple of lazy burros from ambling through?

"Can you come to Cizur Menor by taxi?" Otto asks. "Or you go by foot and we organize the transport of your luggage."

Most pilgrims who set out on the Camino Frances, embark from the French side of the Pyrenées, just north of the Spanish border. But I, balking at the prospect of negotiating such steep mountain passes—and unaware that uphill hikes would eventually track me down—pinpointed Pamplona as my starting line.

I'd arrived the day before, on a train from Madrid—where I had overnighted in one of the city's trendiest neighborhoods. Elena, the mother of friends living in the southern city of Granada, had invited me to stay the night, find my bearings, shake out jet lag. We strolled through the neighborhood, stepping into a little shop around the corner. A chalkboard was illustrated with a globe and a phrase written in Spanish: *Que Tus Suenos Sean Mas Grandes Que Tus Miedos.* May your dreams be larger than your fears. *I hear you.*

***

The girl's life was a patchwork of Polaroid moments, a kaleidoscope that brimmed with dreams. Hers was the quintessential family unit, warm, tight-knit, loving. Frozen in time.
***

Early the next morning, Elena escorted me to the train station. Hours later, Pamplona beckoned—one more city to add to the multitudes I'd explored around the world: Moscow and Singapore and Yangon and Berlin and Paris and Prague and New York and Tel Aviv and nearly unpronounceable ones like Tsetserleg and Nyaung Shwe, too.

Standing in front of a door with my thumb hovering above the bell, a wave of self-conscious regret overwhelms me; my backpack sits low to the ground, attached to the carrito, rather than glommed onto my back like a temporary appendage—the sign of a pilgrim. What will my host think when he sees me without a heavy pack ON my back? Fraud art thou.

My insecurities and self-doubt evaporate as soon as the door swings open, revealing a young man hobbling around with a crutch and a bum leg. Iranian-born Messoud greets me warmly, and welcomes me into his modest apartment. We exchange anecdotes about our respective accidents and injuries: A panic attack averted.

Early the next morning, under an overcast sky and slight chill, I head out to explore Pamplona—and track down bulls. Two elderly women are perched on stools in front of a bar, each one nursing a pint of beer. A mass of placards, haphazardly affixed to building façades and windows fronting abandoned shops, read: *Al Vende*. For sale. Or: *Alquilar*. For rent. Signs of Spain's economic crisis are prominent.

Drinking señoras. Vacant homes and stores. Even the bulls run wild here.

Spain's recession is fraught with contradictions. Locals congregate in the old town to catch up on gossip, walk their dogs, or drive the infirm around in their wheelchairs. After sunset, when the sky takes on a rosy glow, crowds head to the *jugeteria*—for toys; the *pasteleria*—for cakes; the carteria—for stationery; and the *heladeria*—for ice cream. Young couples congregate in cavernous smoke-filled bars sunken halfway into the ground, crowding around upturned barrel-tables, where they drink and dine on tapas. Crisis be damned, *la vida pura y loca!*

No word yet from Otto. I'm stuck in limbo. After picking up my *credencial* (pilgrim's passport), I stroll around town, this time strategizing about how to meet Otto and his furry beasts in the little village "behind Pamplona." A reconnaissance mission to Cizur Menor is in order—to gauge the distance, scope out the bus schedule and a meeting place. Sounds easy enough. Except for one thing: What sort of place will accommodate donkeys?

I set out in sandals, carrying a bottle of water, my daypack, and little else. Reaching the local university campus, I cross paths with students and pilgrims, all of whom carry backpacks of varying size; the students' version comparatively smaller than the pilgrims' bulky loads. My Shrek-colored daypack dangles behind me, setting me apart from the others. I'm neither a tourist, nor a student, nor, apparently, a pilgrim. Who am I?

***

The girl walked with her family, sometimes upwards of 20 kilometers in one day, to raise money for a cause, but mostly so she could cross the finish

line and score an engraved and much-coveted medal that hung from a
ribbon and that she would proudly collect and display for many years.

***

The first group of pilgrims that passes me looks determined in their staccato strides; their gazes, collectively fixed on a point far beyond the horizon—as if in hot pursuit of arrival. In comparison, I suddenly feel so inept, so physically in-able. A simmering trickle of self-doubt rises again. Where do I fit into this chain of able-bodied beings who wake up every day to walk long—and fast?

Bill Bryson comes to mind. The travel writer's words remind me that I require only "a willingness to trudge." I have the will—even though it may falter.

Reaching the outskirts of Pamplona, another wave of impotence hits me. What a crazy idea! What was I thinking? Fields stretch out ahead and on either side of me as I walk along a two-lane highway. I've clearly miscalculated. What was to be a short and leisurely stroll has morphed into a trudge gone too long and wrong. Siesta is at hand: Everyone is napping. I really should have packed a lunch.

At midday, with the day's heat beating me down, Pamplona fades into a hazy blur behind me. Up ahead, Cizur Menor is a Spanish hamlet fast asleep. Not a soul or car in sight. The only sound from any direction is a gentle breeze rustling through the leaves. There is a *rotonda* (traffic roundabout) with a bus stop; looks like el centro. After noting the location of an albergue across the road, I return to Pamplona feeling tired, sweaty, and miserably triumphant. Drifting off to sleep, I toy with the last-resort-option of throwing in the towel.

By the next morning, my misgivings have all but dissipated. I pack a vegetarian sandwich, and stuff extra lettuce into a bag—consolation for a couple of donkeys on detour.

"*Buenos días*," I text Otto. "I walked to Cizur Menor yesterday. Just 2 look around. I will try to take the bus 2 get there. Do u want to meet near the rotonda?"

"Choose a bar," he replies, "and send us the name."

A bar? Strange choice for a meeting place—until I remember that this country's bars are not just for booze; the locus of village life, they double as meeting places for locals and pilgrims—and breeding grounds for gossip. Which, when you're jobless or otherwise down on your luck, is a pretty harmless way to pass the time.

But the mystery remains unanswered: Are donkeys welcome in Spanish bars? Not likely.

"Otto. Change of plans," I write. "Meet me at Albergue Maribel."

Inside the front entrance of the albergue, I lean against a wall and wait. Though it is only mid-morning, sweat-drenched pilgrims plod in, a steady horde groveling for showers and beds. Unhooking themselves from enormous backpacks, they scan their new surroundings and the faces of other pilgrims. Looking for what, signs of fatigue? I feel tired just looking at them.

One by one, pilgrims shake off the day's heat, refill water bottles, register, and sign in. *Hospitaleros* greet them cheerfully, assign rooms, answer questions. They are a calming presence, these albergue-volunteers; rarely rankled by even the most persistent or unkind person. Pilgrims themselves, hospitaleros are quick to empathize with the many frustrations that land on their doorstep.

"Where are the cafés and bars?"

"Where can I find laundry or shops?"

"What time is check-out tomorrow?"

"Can I stay more than one night?"

Pilgrims lay out cash and credencials. They drag backpacks to rooms. Claim beds. Strip and shower. Collapse. Eat. Drink. Plan.

In the middle of the albergue's lush courtyard, a small bale of turtles surrounds an algae-filled pond while others glide under the water's surface, their colors camouflaged, barely seen. One pair slowly inches up a plank set diagonally from the water up to the pond's edge. The duo slithers over to a dry spot in the sun, and each one withdraws into its respective shell. I can relate; I'm about ready to hide away myself.

The faint sound of hoofs scratching against gravel summons my attention away from the timid turtles. I peer out the entrance, past an ominous-looking sculpture of a farmer who seems to have lost his upper torso. The sun's rays pelt down, firing up the day and the pavement and all creatures big and small.

One of those big creatures leads the caravan. A heavyset man in a dark, sweat-stained t-shirt, khaki shorts, and hiking boots lumbers up the road towards me with great effort, his head hanging low. A mop of stringy gray hair partly covers his face, already sticking to his forehead from the morning heat. A rope dangles behind him, its far end tied to a reluctant donkey. It is hard to visualize this man leading others (human or beast) along this route, when he barely seems able to move his own bulk.

Trailing behind, unexpected company: a young woman, decked out in hiking boots and a bright orange jacket tied around her waist. She plods along, her gaze fixed on the gravel underfoot. She grips the end of a rope that leads to a smaller-sized donkey, no more enthusiastic than the first.

Both burros are weighed down with gear. Given their fabled penchant for laziness, Otto doubted the donkeys could be coaxed into schlepping heavy loads for any length of time. He'd give them a week to prove their mettle and gauge their readiness to cooperate. I was to be part of the experiment. (Oh-oh.)

Barely out of the starting gate, the approaching quartet already looks exhausted. Bringing up the rear while scampering between everyone's legs, is a little mutt named Santi. Otto's charge.

By the looks of it, my entourage has arrived. Willing trudgers. But just barely.

When the burly fellow reaches me, his face pulsates and flushes red.

"Hi, are you A-mitt?" I'm not entirely surprised at his mispronunciation of my name. Most people do the same.

***

The girl was the middle child of three daughters of a Romanian-born engineer and an Israeli-born musician who shelved her career to become a full-time mother. The girl's name was unfamiliar in her hometown and school; a Hebrew name, difficult to pronounce, reserved exclusively for boys, making her the butt of jokes. Years later, the girl, now a woman, traveling in Nepal, would learn that her name was also a Hindi name—for boys only.

***

"Yes, I'm Amit." I say, pronouncing my name slowly: *Ahhh-meet.* "*Hola* Otto."

At a safe but friendly distance from the dripping-wet figure, I reach out to shake his hand.

Introductions are swift, their accents German. Otto's friend—girlfriend, apparently—is Klara. There is a glint of dismay or disinterest in her eyes, as if she has not been told that I will tag along. The prospect of traveling as a trio—animals excluded—strikes me as a smart move. No pressure, no expectations.

Otto introduces me to the burros. They are both a dirty shade of grey, with long manes and longer legs. They're well-equipped, with saddle pads, bridles, halters, and all manner of equine-friendly gear. Each one is also bogged down with saddle bags and tubular stuff sacks.

The taller, older creature is Sancho—presumably named after Sancho Panza, the mythical sidekick of Don Quixote. But my assumption is upended when I later learn that the Camino was re-routed in the 11th century, under the orders of a medieval king known as Sancho the Third (a.k.a "el Grande"). A donkey elder with ties to Spanish royalty? Why not.

On the heels of Sancho, an almost identical, but timid-looking Popeye trudges along. Dangling from a red thread tied to his saddle pad is a scallop shell, stamped with the distinctive red Cross of Saint James—similar to the scallop shell that hangs from my Shrek-pack, with the words Healing Pilgrim written across it in Sharpie. Popeye also has a small, orange, rear-reflecting light affixed to the back of his saddle pad; a puzzling add-on, seeing that we are not slated to walk after dark.

Otto hoists my backpack onto Sancho and slips my now-collapsed carrito under the ropes that prevent Popeye's load from toppling off. The big man then maneuvers and redistributes the rest of the gear—to ensure that neither donkey loses balance and tumbles into a ditch. I cringe, with remorse. We may have only just met, Sancho and I, but I'm already feeling inklings of guilt, arising from the knowledge that my involuntary in-abilities are adding to his burden.

"*Santi! Bei fus!*" Otto bellows in German, calling out to his dog: Heel. Now.

Then he turns to me, changing his tone.

"*Buen Camino!*" he calls out—which roughly translates to "good road"—offering me the common greeting that is exchanged among pilgrims on the way. I return the same in kind. Then, without fanfare, errant bulls from Pamplona or friends to wave us off, the six of us—two-and four-legged creatures all bound together—walk on, heading west.

Chapter 3: Meeting Mani

Falling into step behind Klara and Popeye, I walk at a bona fide donkey's pace—much slower than most other pilgrims, and certainly much slower than the cyclist who speeds by so noiselessly that Santi, caught unaware, flees into the neighboring field. Popeye, ignoring the commotion, has his eye on nature's wild edibles; steering me off-course and wading into greener pastures at the sound of a sheep's bleat.

We are a motley crew: A robust German tour leader, his puny pup and wannabe-girlfriend; two seemingly reluctant donkeys (are there any other kind?)—and me. Through untended expansive wild spaces, we walk while the sun's relentless rays bear down on our caravan. Trudging for hours along trails edged with huge dried-out fields, I am merely a spectator, watching closely as Otto and Klara struggle to nudge the asses up steep inclines. The donkeys rebel, dig in their hooves, and bray.

As I acclimatize to the rhythm of donkeys, it dawns on me that our routine will differ significantly from those of other pilgrims; we will be tied to these four-legged creatures, their every movement, their escapades, their needs for grub, drink, and rest. Hail to the animals.

After walking past soaring bales of hay that rise at our side, we reach an albergue in a tiny hillside hamlet, with the virtually unpronounceable name of Zariquiegui. Otto disappears through the narrow front door, seeking the owner. Through the opening, I hear him query the man, hidden inside. "Do you have any food for two donkeys, maybe a loaf of stale bread?" This question precedes all others, because donkeys get first dibs. As my body gravitates towards a couch or bed upon arrival at each village, Otto organizes a feast and paddock for his furry entourage.

Otto and Klara unload their gear from the donkey duo, temporarily placing it in piles beside the entranceway. After we sign in, Otto lifts my heavy backpack, wobbles for a moment under its bulk, and trudges up the stairs. I follow close on his heels with my carrito, Shrek-pack, and small bag of food in hand, unable to shed the gnawing feeling that I should be offering to help—even if I cannot. The stairs creak and groan under our combined weight.

***

There was nothing the girl could not do; not a sport that she would not attempt. She pushed herself to the limit: outran classmates, built higher towers, dug deeper sand pits, served from the line and played harder. She swam and dived and held her breath under the water longer than she thought possible.

***

Otto gently lowers my pack onto the floor of an empty room with three untouched sets of bunk beds—standard sleeping fare in albergues—and a fogged-up window. "*Gracias,*" I say, nerves curdling inside, as the instinct to offer him a tip wells up inside of me. But I restrain myself, because his offer to help me out came with no strings attached. "See you later," he says. I close the door, unpack my sleeping bag and crumple into the far, dark corner of the lower bunk. In the silence of the room, amplified by the hush of Zariquiegui, I discover that there is no way to completely stifle a cry.

When the tears dry up, and my normal breath returns, I lay the carrito on top of my backpack, and head downstairs. Stepping outside, I spot Otto and Klara leading Sancho and Popeye up the hill. Soon enough, I will learn about the daily donkey rituals: After pouring water into a collapsible container on the ground, Otto leads Popeye and Sancho into a field in which they are cordoned off by a pad-dock-like enclosure, complete with white strips running all around mimicking electrically-charged tape. It's a temporary space made to simulate their familiar fenced-in grounds at the farm where they live, and to train them to keep their distance from the perimeters.

Watching the spent donkeys being led away, I again entertain the idea of ditching this whole endeavor. As grateful as I am for their strength and prowess; and as awed I am by their ability to carry such loads on their back, my conscience insinuates itself into every other thought: How do I reconcile their strength and abilities with the weight we place on them? Just because they are pack animals, do we have the right to use them so? If I treat them well, brush their manes, disentangle burrs, stop regularly for water and shade along the way; if we give them enough rest and show them love, will that mitigate the burden—and appease my guilt?

While resting again in the empty dorm room, the door only slightly ajar, I hear voices wafting up the staircase and into the cor-ridor, then trailing off and disappearing behind closed doors down the hall. Suddenly, one of those disembodied voices stops outside the door. A knock follows. "Come in," I say. A young woman pokes her head inside, her short dark brown hair and fogged-up eyeglasses framing a pale-skinned, weary face.

"The other room is too busy, so many people, so much noise, laundry hanging everywhere," she says, her English tinged with a German accent. "I want to be where it is more quiet. It's ok if I stay here with you?"

"Yes, of course," I say, gesturing to the large uninhabited room, "take your pick."

She opens the door fully, revealing an enormous backpack hanging off her shoulders, which she dumps on the floor. She is on her own, a pilgrim walking solo. She is fully independent. She can take off at a moment's notice. She doesn't need anybody's help. She is so lucky.

Only five years earlier, she was me. Or I was her. The memory is almost palpable; the tug, the bend at the knees, the big heave, the twist, the swivel, the straps, the groaning, the *oyyyy!*—as I hoisted a fiendishly heavy pack of twenty to thirty kilograms onto my back; walking with it for miles at a time in Myanmar; trekking with it on my back for kilometers at a time, at high altitude in the Himalayas; heaving it onto trucks in Thailand and Laos; stuffing it into buses in Vietnam and Cambodia, all clattering with chickens, children and Chinese laborers.

But then, in one of those split-instances that forever change the course of a life, my body, for years astonishingly tough, flexible, nearly infallible, turned, then twisted, and toppled from grace.

***

In early 2009, the Cambodian railway system was in shambles. A French company was brought in to repair the network of bridges, deemed unsafe for travel. In the country's second-largest city, Battambang, bright red panels were affixed to either end of an iron train track, preventing passage over the Sangker river. Inconvenienced locals took matters into their own hands, re-opening the panels to lay rotting planks of wood onto the track, facilitating unstable and unsafe passage to the other side. For locals, it was a godsend. For anyone caught unaware, their lives hung in the balance. Locals had an explanation for unsuspecting foreigners who tumbled off the bridge towards injury or death; the river spirits were calling them.

Apparently, the river spirits had it in for me; they stood by as I catapulted off and over the handlebars, leaping off the bridge, tumbling down ten meters, head-first and helmetless, until I landed on the rocky riverbank below. In the twilight of my plummet, I blacked out. Splayed on the ground, I roused suddenly and for a few moments. A crowd gathered around me and on the bridge above. On the ground in front of me, I watched a man armed with a video camera capture my distress on film. I waved him off: "What are you doing? Get away from here!!"—then slipped out of consciousness once again.

When I came to, the glare of bright fluorescent lights seeped through my eyelashes, as white robes scurried by me in every direction. My arms were tied to tubes that kept guard over me, sustained me, kept me alive.

**

But with this solo pilgrim's arrival that re-awakens long-suppressed memories, I feel untethered; from the sensual immediacy and cool taste of freedom, from an independence borne of, and nourished from, lugging around a pack of one's own. Being entirely responsible for, and answerable to, nobody but myself. How was I to let go of that sense of liberty, even as it had already faded? How could I detach from the knowledge of my body's strength, physical endurance, the remembrance of things past? How do I ask for help?

Manuela, a thirty-something social worker from Germany, has just quit her job, ended a long-term relationship and, although she has not yet traveled solo, decided to walk the Camino on her own. But, below the brave and determined exterior, her face is also daubed in shades of self-doubt and fear. Perhaps remnants of a downpour or other obstacle. After a long, cold, and muddy day spent hiking over the Pyrénées from France, under heavy rains, Manuela's immediate desire is this simple: a hot shower and warm bed.

In the late afternoon, long after Otto and Klara have returned to the albergue, I amble uphill to check on the donkeys. They are placidly chewing away on wildflowers and shrubs. Glancing around to ensure that no other humans are within earshot, I lean in.

"*Muchas gracias, burros!*" Even if my words of gratitude fall on tuned-out pointy ears, I feel compelled to speak them out loud.

Turning away from the paddock, I take in the last vestiges of a setting sun, sheathed in shades of orange and red. I scan the hamlet's landscape. A rough count of houses confirms my hunch that they are fewer in number than the letters in Zariquiegui. *Pueblo pequeno*; a seriously small village.

Back in the room, Manuela is rested and more cheerful. She invites me to share her dinner. I readily agree, grateful for the company and certain that Otto and Klara will prefer to dine tête-a-tête. The albergue owner has already offered to cook dinner with the ingredients that Manuela carried in her backpack—all French imports. We sit down to a basic pilgrim's meal: pasta, cheese, tomato and carrots; Otto and Klara join us after all. With an abundance of food, wine and subjects to discuss—the Camino, above all—conversation flows, and shifts effortlessly between German to English.

Manuela is my only roommate that night. In lower bunks across from each other, our sleep is sound and undisturbed by the blowing winds outside. My last thoughts before slumber takes over are of the donkeys, high up on the hill, hopefully immune to the chill.

The next morning, the window is glazed in frost. As I'm packing to leave, Manuela's head emerges tentatively from her sleeping bag, like a child awakened by the Saturday morning scent of blueberry pancakes. Squinting against early morning rays streaming through the window, she uncorks an earplug.

"*Buenos días*," she mumbles, "can I join you today?"

An hour or so later, our original herd—plus Manuela, now abbreviated to the less formal Mani—sets out, heading up-slope, towards the renowned monument of Alto de Perdón (Hill of Forgiveness). There, we marvel over one of the most photographed landmarks on the Camino Frances; wrought iron silhouettes of life-size pilgrims, cast against earth, blue sky and fields dotted with countless *molinos* (wind turbines). Among the figures caught mid-step with *bastón* (walking stick) in hand are a handful of horses and donkeys in profile; one of whom bears an uncanny resemblance to Popeye, who I spot in a nearby meadow, chomping away on long blades of grass, which in these hills, is the closest thing to eating his spinach.

꙰

Chapter 4: Gratitudes

Otto's daily decree to Santi—*Bei fus!*—doubles as a group directive: Hit the road, pack.

I resolve to set off each morning with a ritual of my own, dedicating a given day's walk to someone who has inspired or moved me. Like the singer-activist (and Baliphile) Michael Franti, whose skin is tattooed with the words "Today I Pray for" (followed by an empty line to be filled in by Sharpie), I feel compelled to pay tribute to the people who have left an imprint on my life, by weaving gratitudes into the fabric of each day.

Over the course of the first week, I walk for my friend Lucy—whom I'd hoped had eased her way back to a balanced life in the U.K., and I walk for Shelby—who'd gone through a rough year, shifting from one illness or injury to another. I walk for my father on the very day he is scheduled to fly overseas, and for my older sister, on the day she is scheduled to undergo a medical test. On each of those days, a mental image of that person keeps me anchored to motivation, mindfulness, and meditative walking.

If nature cooperates—in other words, if I find fresh wildflowers studding the roadside—I pluck a few petals, nestle them into the crease behind my ear and intone a prayer. This mindful practice, that I adopted since living in Ubud, reminds me of how nature's gifts are woven into the fabric of Balinese Hindu culture. I need a piece of that.

In the waning light of day, our posse—minus Mani, who has forged ahead at a faster pace—pulls into the uniquely charming town of Obanos. My first impression is that of a scene frozen in time, heightened by dramatic street lighting and serenity—as if we've suddenly stumbled upon the empty stage of a Romeo and Juliet production. I half expect to see a brigade of armored knights on horseback bolting towards us through the medieval stone archways, tumbleweed chasing their hoofs. The surreal quiet of Obanos is equaled only by a total absence of litter, muted sounds of church bells, and the distant echoes of children playing soccer.

Following the crumbs of voices, we arrive at the edge of a spotless football field, rimmed by a line of recycling boxes, neatly arranged. Nearby, the local hangout buzzes with young families, beer and mindless chatter. Otto leads us inside, to an unoccupied table. While we wait to be served, a gaggle of teenage girls shuffles in to pick up a stack of pizza boxes. Four elderly women stand next to bar stools, catching up on the latest gossip; while their long-retired husbands talk sports over bottles of vino. Nobody pays attention to a TV screen hanging in the corner.

***

The girl's birthday parties were always celebrated in the garden. There were inflatable pools and paper plates and kids running around. There were friends and neighbors and grandparents and presents and a homemade chocolate cake with a greeting and numbered candles. The girl wore a crown of flowers on her head and a pretty dress, with eyelets and ribbons. Her feet were tucked into frilly white socks and sparkling black patent leather party shoes. She shared the cake and party with her older sister, because they were so close in age and birthdate: Double the fun. The sun glimmered, sprinkling speckles of joy, like fairy dust confetti all over the day. Faded photographs show her squinting into the sun, a mile-wide smile and her little fingers holding up one side of the dress, as if about to curtsey. Love was in the air.

***

Before Otto and Klara turn in for the night at a posher pension nearby, they lead me and my bag (now strapped to my carrito) a short way off, to the municipal albergue which has noticeably less glitz and more noise. Amid the clamor of pilgrims filing into the super-size dorm room, I again opt for a lower bunk, but vow the next morning: never again. The Obanos experience will convince me that top bunks rule: More light. More privacy. Less snooping and unwanted intrusions. No heavy creaking sounds from above. Plus, the invaluable proximity to fresher air; untainted by dirt, sweaty clothes, and stinky feet.

After unfurling my sleeping bag and flattening it out on the mattress, I gather a small bag of essentials for the shower: towel, toiletries, and change of clothes. I also take my Shrek-pack—with cash, cards, camera, and valuables; better slightly damp than disappeared.

As night descends on Obanos, I stand at the far edge of a square, watching locals drive away from a boisterous garden party nearby. An eerie silence soon takes over, broken only by the sound of leaves whistling from the undertow of a gentle breeze, rustling on their fall downwards. The twin doors of a solitary public phone booth swing noisily on their hinges. Street lamps bordering cobblestone paths cast a placid but haunting glow over an empty wooden bench—as if awaiting the cast of *Waiting for Godot*.

This, my second night on the Camino, proves to be a trial by fire: The initial silence of the dorm room is shattered by a chorus of competing snores—a pair of them resembling fireworks crackling mid-air. It's a well-known rite of passage in pilgrim lore; being awakened by the snoring spirits of Caminos past (and present). Those who complain about the involuntary clatter are met with disdain if not outright belligerence.

"It's not my fault!" hollers one Englishman. As if that were enough to defray debt to the sleep-deprived masses.

When a pilgrim's sleep is disturbed, pity and compassion are occasionally in short supply. Suddenly, I miss the peaceful slumber of the night before: No snores from Mani.

The next morning, I'm crouched down with Santi, in front of Otto's more luxurious lodgings, as Klara prepares to board a taxi for home. For reasons unknown (to me), she has decided to abort. Perhaps oblivious to the emotion of the moment, Santi's ears are perked and his nose on sniff alert. Sitting erect in front of me, Santi follows Otto's every move—a sure sign of their close bond. A model of composure and patience, Santi anticipates signs of movement and the clarion call: "*Bei fus!*"

With Mani and Klara gone, Otto and I are now outnumbered: Animals 3. Humans 2.

Chapter 5: The Weight of Whine

The girl picked up boxes and lugged furniture easily twice her weight. She helped carry groceries up two flights of stairs, and took the lead in deftly loading unwieldy suitcases and coolers into the car. She reveled in her body's strength.

***

As our quintet marches on, I break from the pack, gliding along at a pace only marginally faster than our donkey duo. It's a good opportunity to take stock of my provisions, sort essentials from non-essentials. My Shrek-pack typically holds some or all of the following: a small notebook and pen, digital camera, wallet, passport, mini cell phone, and piece of fruit. A collapsible, foldable plastic water bottle (eco-considerations temporarily suspended for reasons of weight), dangles to the side. I'd anticipated being able to walk a part of each day on my own, which now, barring a gravitational intervention, means slimming down my daily load to an even lighter weightlessness. If I dare drop one more gram into the pack, my sacrum will protest, then strike.

***

Battambang, Cambodia. January 25, 2009: Patient unconscious on arrival. Pain on the back. Lumbar, sacrum area, lacerations on L hand, L eyelid, L leg. Diagnosis: Coccyx #. L Calcaneus #. L Head of 5th metatarsal #. Soft tissue wounds. L eyelid, L hand, L leg. Mild head trauma.

Bangkok, Thailand. February 2, 2009: Head injury with subdural hygroma. Comminuted fracture at left-sided S1 and S2 with trans-action S3 and anterior dislocation of fracture fragment. Fracture at right and left transverse process of L5. Fracture at right 1st rib. Fracture body of left calcaneal bone. Fracture distal portion of left 5th metatarsal bone. Multiple soft tissue contusions.

***

On my return to Asia, two years post-accident, my soft-spoken Thai doctor saw me carrying a bulky backpack and firmly rebuked me: "Too heavy for you!" So I scale down, and release or repack whenever possible. If it's edible, and I'm hours away from the next meal, I feed it to the donkeys.

Packing light is not, traditionally, a hallmark of the pilgrim lifestyle—even if it is strongly recommended, ad nauseum, in all the guidebooks, websites and blogs. In fact, from the vast number of questions, shopping lists and recommendations of 'must have' items that I've seen posted on online forums, I'd say that pilgrims are notorious for over-packing. Proof being in the detritus of clothing and gear frequently dumped in albergues, bars and cafés.

Still, what strikes me most is the anxiety that sets in long before people step on Spanish soil. Like this nerve-wracked example posted in the summer of 2014: "I have been intensely researching the Camino de Santiago for a few years. I am interested in walking for about three weeks starting in Le Puy in June 2015."

Seasoned pilgrims had urged me to invest in very specific socks ("you'll never get blisters if you wear them"), a very specific brand of underwear ("they're the only kind you should taking on the Camino, they dry the fastest"), and a very specific species of thermal top ("it's the one that wicks best"). A tentative packing list appeared on a forum, with requests for input, one year ahead of departure: "I have not yet included things like a Swiss Army Knife or ablution kit, but I have pebbles, a wristwatch with built-in light, my credencial, and a basic foot repair kit. What's missing?"

I became dizzy just from seeing these panicked postings and messages, eventually deciding to ignore them altogether. The "basic foot repair kit," though, gives me pause: it sounds more like the tools of a mobile foot surgeon's clinic than a pack of Band-Aids and lotion.

Clearly, I haven't walked this Way before.

Chapter 6: Road to Wellness

By the time I reach the sleepy village of Puente de la Reina (Queen's Bridge), I've left Otto and his four-footed crew behind. Pamplona, I learn, isn't alone in permitting bulls to trample through its streets. The front gates of Puente's homes are already tightly locked and secured, in anticipation of the upcoming madness.

Walking along the nearly abandoned streets, the façades of buildings abutting the road, I hear new age music wafting out of a building. Much like Pamplona, dusty windows and shop fronts are here too covered with signs beckoning home-buyers, investors and prospectors: Al Vende—property for sale. But there's a twist to the flyers in this village: they also flog yoga classes, osteopathy training, cranio-sacral therapy, and massage sessions. Whether it's indicative of a growing global trend, recently imported into the Spanish countryside; or an ongoing and urgent need for whole-body healing during this country's implacable crisis, wellbeing is the word *del día*.

While contemplating the esprit de corps in Spain's destabilized society, I glance around for signs of Otto et al. Not a person or animal in sight. I keep on walking. On the way out of the village, I stop on the bridge for which Puente de la Reina is named, and peer over the stone parapet. Crossing bridges, with nobody within sight, still unsettles me.

***

January 25, 2009. The day before Chinese New Year. The air in Cambodia's second-largest city, Battambang, was sticky but festive.

It was afternoon and the locals were preparing offerings, handing out gifts in red envelopes, turning fake money into ash, and setting off fireworks. I was on my own, riding a bicycle heading south from the city's center, looking for a place to cross the river. From afar, I spotted an iron railway bridge; I saw pedestrians and a few others steering bicycles strolling over the river. No cars in sight. I turned and pedaled onto what I believed was safe passage. By then, it was too late to turn back. The weather-beaten planks were at once too narrow and unstable. I quickly lost my balance. Nowhere to stop. Nowhere to turn back. So I veered off the plank. I lurched forwards, my body catapulting over the handlebars. The last sensation I recall before blacking out was my body, surrendering, and as if mimicking an aerial acrobat, somersaulting through the air, headfirst. That day, I hit rock bottom. Literally.

In the emergency room, I stirred just long enough to see my clothes being scissored through, while red lights flashed and alarms sounded wildly—before promptly blacking out again. Emerging from a concussion hours later, I found myself in a large bright room, strikingly clean if not sparsely decorated. This was a hospital unit unlike any other I'd ever seen. I looked down: my body, swathed in hospital-issued checkered cotton pajamas (standard dress code in Cambodian hospitals), was tucked into clean sheets, on a simple but sturdy bed. The room and beds were all painted white. Through the large windows, slanting rays of crisp sunshine flooded in, bathing the space in calm. I smelled the scent of serenity.

The staff quietly occupied themselves with other patients—victims of landmine explosions, head injuries from fallen coconuts, sudden blindness from defective fireworks. But the staff: Asians, men, women; a few Western faces, and a solitary black-skinned doctor in their midst. *Was I hallucinating? If not, where was I?*

One week later, I was transferred by ambulance, on painfully bumpy roads, to Bangkok Hospital, for a period of intensive recovery and treatment. It was during that stay that I recalled how, just six months earlier, a Vedic astrologer in Kathmandu had strongly urged me off the traveling path, but in my pigheaded resistance I'd asked him for a 'get out of danger' card, that I followed only half-heartedly, and nowhere closely enough to avoid tumbling off a bridge. One month later, still immobilized, I was loaded onto a plane like catering or cargo, for the long overseas haul back to Canada. I lay flat, on a stretcher fastened onto a section of seats, curtains draped around me, a nurse escort seated across the aisle.

After tying my body and resources up to a two-year regimen of hands-on treatments, short stints on meds and a pain clinic support group in Montreal, I was hungering to get back on my feet. Still, chronic pain exacerbated by escalating flashback episodes, of falling, always falling, made me realize I was drowning in PTSD. For reasons of closure coupled with a need to revisit the scene, I headed back to Asia two years almost to the day, to find the bridge in Battambang that broke my body.

***

The distinct thwack-thwack sound of walking poles tapping the ground, escalates as pilgrims cross the bridge, jolting me out of reminiscence. I glance forwards and backwards; still no sign of Otto or animals. I stop under a shady tree's bough, and pull out my phone while breathing in the centuries-old scent of Spanish architecture and wildflowers.

"*Hola!*" I write to Otto, "I passed thru PR and now on my way to Maneru. Hope u r ok con los 2 burros."

I click send, pocket my phone, and guzzle down what remains of my water. Sancho and Popeye cannot be faring well in this soul-crushing heat. Their current home is a horse farm not far from the Camino's route, owned by Otto's friends. While the many horses are put through their strides and taken out on long rides, the donkeys are fed and left to their lazy ways.

"They've been spoiled," says Otto, "so it's a good idea to take them out for a long walk, and get them moving again." Maybe so, but this feels overdone. Pangs of guilt nearly derail me again. But it's Otto's project, and I depend on him—so I let trust trump my misgivings.

For the first three kilometers out of PR, I take in the unfamiliar elements; willowing dried weeds on both sides of the road thick with countless coiled-up snails, looking like bulbous leaves growing off each stalk. Chattering cicadas hide in the brush. A tempting sight, but out of reach, is a thicket of brambles, festooned with blackberries.

The clear blue sky is sliced through by white plumes of airplane effluent. Rows of cedar trees on the sides of a sloped mountain provide thick layers of green to what otherwise might be a desolate landscape. I stroll by olive groves, vineyards, corn fields, and a large communal garden teeming with produce. In fractured Spanish, using my hands more than my words, I ask the farmer about his yield.

"Enough grows in our garden to feed three families," he says while pointing to a cornucopia of plants and beds bursting with chili peppers, pumpkins and lettuce. Scanning the ground one last time before moving on, I wonder how much would remain if I let Sancho and Popeye loose on this fertile patch of earth, sprouting with weeds and donkey treats.

Chapter 7: Das (Left) Foot

By midday, the sun is baking my back. It dawns on me that the snack I packed hours ago—chocolate sandwich cookies—might have melted by now. I fiddle around in my pack, poking my fingers this way and that, until they are smeared in a puddle of sweet cream that has oozed out of its foil packaging.

Oozing happens elsewhere as well. For the first couple of days, like all good pilgrims, I lace my feet up in hiking boots. It seems like the only responsible and foot-wise choice. But these aren't just any hiking boots. They are styled and built for the European market—to better scale the Alps, apparently—and already broken in. I'd christened them back in 2008, during my season of solo *wanderlusting* around Asia. To fully test their mettle, I pushed and prodded until they boosted me up, past 5,000 meters, to the snowy summit of Thorong La Pass on Nepal's well-trodden Annapurna Circuit.

My boots may be the same, but my soles are not. In Nepal, that hiking footwear was a perfect fit; my feet safe and snug in closed shoes. But tack on a few years, an accident, one invisibly impaired foot, and a strong preference for open-toed sandals (de rigueur in the tropics), and my feet will rebel against laced-up anythings. Lingering neuropathy and muscle spasms are difficult enough; no need to subject myself to greater pain.

When I learn that the Camino path is mostly hilly rather than Himalayan, I mull over the boot prerequisite. I pack them hesitantly—but also break in the trekking sandals a mere two weeks prior to my departure.

Otto spots my change of footwear and shakes his head disapprovingly. "If you leave your toes open like that," he says, "the donkeys might step on you. Then, your feet will be kaput!"

I promise Otto to keep my feet out of hoof's way.

The donkeys are hankering for food; their snouts, a-snuffling. Otto hands me some greens, which I shake lightly in front of Sancho's mouth. Klara had a knack for it; I'm clumsier, more tentative. Sancho eyes me warily and moves backwards. These two, they sniff out newbies in a pinch. So ok, I'm no donkey whisperer. At least not yet. "Am I ever going to bond with these beasts?" I ask Otto. He ekes out a smile and feeds Popeye a long stalk. A copy of *Donkeys for Dummies* would come in handy right about now.

We stop for lunch at a sunny café, where other pilgrims have landed and sprawled out before us. Otto ties Sancho and son up to a banister. I pace around, feeling useless and out of my depth. Suddenly, Sancho begins to defecate. I offer to clean up his waste, a sizable clump of poo. Otto hands me a broom and dustpan, then heads inside to request edible remnants for his four-legged charges.

I sweep up the donkey-debris and slide it into a large organic waste bin nearby; glad that Sancho's turd will end up in a compost heap. As I brush off the last bits into the bin, I swivel around in time to see Sancho unloading for the second time. Again I sweep up his shit, and brush it into the bin. When I spin around again, out tumbles dump number three.

"*Basta, Sancho!*" I mutter as it hits the ground, trying to size up whether he is testing me, "what's your point?" Apparently, my feet do need protection—not from errant hoofs so much as their dung.

Otto emerges with a bag full of restaurant leftovers for Sancho and Popeye. Verboten. These creatures are meant to subsist on herbs, plants and flowers. But Otto likes to feast, so why not give tasty grub to the donkeys? He pulls out scraps of rice crackers, apples, and carrots. Little do I know that I'll soon up the ante, treating them to fine, albeit days-old, French baguettes—the best in rock-hard crumbs and crust.

"This is a sensitive and itchy spot," says Otto, calling me over to point out a scab on Popeye's forehead. Which explains why the donkey rubs his forehead against trees and walls—or when none are close by, he defaults to me; nuzzling in close and rubbing his head on my thigh. "He might get irritated by it, and get out of control." Thank you for the warning, Otto.

Not an hour later, Sancho grinds to a halt. "A stone must be stuck in his hoof," surmises Otto, looking for clues. A common reason for stoppage. He could also be tired. Hungry. Lazy. "Or maybe he hears the sound of sheep's bells."

"But I don't hear a thing," I say.

"Of course not," says Otto, "it's a sound that only donkeys can hear. It's not meant for humans."

Bionic burros. Noted.

As we fall forward and into step, Otto turns around.

"Do you want to lead Popeye now?" he asks. It is less a question than expectation.

"Sure, I'll give it a try," I say, unable to hide the hesitation in my voice, because what I mean to say is: "I don't think he'll be happy about that; we're not connecting very well." But I resist, because who am I to say no to my gear-schlepping, sheep-hearing hero?

Taking over the reins, I lean in closely, almost into Popeye's ear. "Thank you for bearing my load," I whisper, "but please take it easy. Don't yank me around. And for godsake, don't run away."

As Otto instructs me on rope-holding and slackening techniques, I think back to the summer I learned to water-ski, while wobbling on the surface of the lake; it took many butt-falls and belly-flops into the lake before I gauged the tipping point of tautness. Here too, I loop the rope a couple of times around my hand, and let the rest dangle. I follow Otto's lead, and try to mimic him coolly—when in fact I'm slightly terrified of getting yanked by a donkey. At least for today, Popeye and I are tightly bound together. But if he were to veer off-path, without warning, my body could easily get battered. Again. I breathe deeply, ease up, and follow his slow gait.

Following on Sancho's hoofs, Popeye moves up so his nose nearly touches his father's ass. The distance is deliberate. As Sancho bears the brunt of the stifling heat, Popeye ducks down, into the coolness of Sancho's shadow. But also: It is a no-fly zone. Popeye only needs to lift his head a smidgen for a huge swarm to gather. Not so in the fly-free pocket of air created by Sancho swinging his tail in front of Popeye's face.

As we ford highways and skirt mountains, our trail cuts through fields and hills. A shepherd nudges his flock across an arid patch of earth. It takes just one glance from an errant sheep towards Popeye and their eyes lock, both of them immovable.

Curious drivers and passengers also stop to honk and wave; occasionally, slowing down so backseat donkey-spotters have an opportunity to lean out and snap a picture. "The paparazzi are coming! The paparazzi are coming!" I call out, as Otto feeds a handful of grapes to Sancho. "They're coming for the donkeys!!"

***

It was a Kodak pocket Instamatic, her first camera. The girl was immediately enchanted, personalizing it with a sticker on top and securing her prize possession in a marbled brown faux-leather pouch. She was impatient, waiting for weeks until the lab would crank photographs out of the film cassette. Her mother, with long tresses cascading down her shoulders, posed and smiled, sending warm waves of love into the lens. The girl lovingly placed each color photograph into an album, adding names and descriptions, stacking up the albums till bursting.

***

Pilgrims on foot are likewise transfixed, whipping out the latest in imaging devices. A Polish cyclist shoves an iPad into my hand, slings an arm over a donkey's neck and directs me to the precise point from where I shall point and shoot. "No, no, not here," he stammers in broken English, "please, there, there the light much better!" A French couple sidles up to Sancho for a selfie while a young British woman asks for *permission* to photograph, as if we were celebrity agents instead of the donkey-guardians that we are—or try to be.

These starry-eyed seekers come in a range of linguistic flavors, representing the wide swath of nationalities that I will encounter along the way. Take Karol, the tall and lanky student from Lithuania, whose accent renders his speech nearly incomprehensible. Or Alexandra, from Germany, who gleefully chatters away with Otto. Elise and Sean are an unusual breed in these parts; hospitaleros, from America. Dave, from Illinois, carries a wooden bastón that he axed off a tree in his mother-in-law's garden, into which he carves mementos—shells and rabbits—from his pilgrimage. Ingrid—from Norway, Loretta—from Canada, and Linda—from Hong Kong, meet up in an albergue and become inseparable for days. There are Danes and Brits, Brazilians and Austrians and Spaniards too. A pilgrimhood of U.N.-esque proportions.

Chapter 8: Saint Santi

With copper-colored dust blowing at our feet and stuck to my stained clothes and sandals, we amble into a village that looks like a Hollywood Western movie set in a deserted ghost town—and we are the wranglers and extras. Instead of stallions, we have a pup and two wonky donkeys that poop a lot. Even if this is no *High Noon*, and Otto is no Gary Cooper, still we need a bar.

***

The girl's mother made homemade clothes and homemade cookies; drove her to piano lessons and swimming lessons and cello lessons and ballet recitals and a music class where she learned to beat on drums, play recorder and pluck on harp strings. The girl went to concerts and operas and a large museum to watch screenings of black-and-white kid-friendly films from the NFB; they were experimental but very different from another film she went to see years later with her mother, Not a Love Story: A Film About Pornography.

***

Take two. Again, we are the objects of public adoration. The clippety-clop sounds and sight of weary donkeys and a dog are enough to attract a horde of locals. A group of children drops off slides and swings, running in our direction, all of them pointing and yelling.

"*Ah burritos! Que guapo!*"

Past churches and *farmacias*, the many doorways fronting homes are draped with strips of plastic that swing gently in the breeze. We head straight for the communal wash basin—so that Sancho and Popeye get a break in the shade. I lie down to rest my aching back, while Otto scrubs Santi under the tap, after which he leaps out of his hands and rolls around in the grass to dry off.

The creatures are rested, washed, and untied from trees—only to be roped up again.

"Santi! *Bei fus!*"

Santi. Shade-seeker. Water-source magnet. Our personal Camino GPS system, navigating us down the right path. Occasionally, I mispronounce his name, calling him Shanti. Peace. No slip of the tongue, this pint-sized German pup is our compass of peace. *Om Shanti Shanti Shanti Om.*

Exuding a distinctly saintly quality, Santi may be the reincarnation of the next Dalai Lama's dog. Sleeping in Otto's room every night, his soul and paws are safe in love; a far cry from the treatment of most *perros* I see along the Camino. The cruelty towards, and abuse of, dogs is a facet of rural Spain that remains unnoticed by most passing pilgrims. But this is how I'm dishearteningly introduced to a native species; the Balcony Dogs, so named because they are bound to balcony rails or housed in filthy cages too tight for movement. These dogs, Otto tells me, are often beaten and abandoned.

His words explain why, on our approach to a village, we hear a crescendo of dogs barking ferociously. Santi shies away, distantly curious and keeping one eye on Otto. This dog is made of entirely different stuff.

❄

Chapter 9: Sit Happens

Less than one week after leaving Pamplona, we arrive, spent and hungry, in the picturesque village of Los Arcos. Otto drops my gear off at the Casa Austria albergue, and we part ways. While he heads off to herd the donkeys into a grassy paddock, I sign the register, and wait in the front yard until hauling-help comes. On a window ledge, I see one sneaker and one hiking boot, both lost or abandoned; in place of feet long gone, each one is filled with earth, sprouting buds.

After a quick shower, I meander over to the Plaza Mayor, epicenter of village life all over Spain. Stark rays of light, as if divinely sourced, stream through the surrounding stone arches. Crowds of people bask in the glaring sunshine, seated around tables piled high with pizza, empanadas, salads and mugs glistening with pints of *cerveza* (beer). A quintessential pilgrim gathering, the high point of each afternoon, when boots have been untied, backpacks unloaded, clothes changed, and faces are refreshed.

But I'm ill-prepared for this scene because this is also where a whole lot of sit happens. Every person is lazily sunk into a hard-metal chair, "savoring," as Bill Bryson writes in *A Walk in the Woods*, "the exquisite pleasure of just sitting… "

Once that pleasure was mine too: On front stoops or warming up in front of blazing fires in the Himalayas; crowding inside tiny kitchens in Laos and Siberia with villagers who did not speak a word of English; sitting on carpeted yurts in Mongolia warmed by a burning fire and yak's milk; sitting everywhere, high atop camels, water buffalos, cargo trucks, hard wooden benches on the train ride from Mandalay to Yangon—all of it, now unimaginable.

***

Despite a slight chill in the air, it was spring and the park beckoned. The mother stuffed picnic coolers with sandwiches and roasted chicken and washed lettuce and tomatoes and celery sticks and plates and napkins; and the family headed up to the mountain, where the girl made a beeline for the park hidden away behind the trees and duck pond. She hung from the monkey bars, twirled about on the carousel, then headed for the swings. Grasping for her life, the girl would lean far back and watch the world spin, upside down, so that children sprinted and baby carriages dangled as if from a sandbox-filled sky. Then the girl would vow time and again, that she would never become one of those adults, just sitting, on a park bench.

***

After a quick scan of the landscape (no padded chairs, no cushions in sight), I freeze, seized by such panic that shrapnels of thought explode, like gunfire, inside my brain. I believed I was well prepared. Before I left for Spain, I nearly splurged on a collapsible butter-fly chair at a sports equipment store, recanting at the last minute because of the added weight. I couldn't pack a pillow—too bulky. When the time came, I would deal with it. It is now time to deal. And I feel paralyzed.

There is a tall, round table with bar stools, parked at the edge of the plaza, but in the shadow of its covered walkway. On the periphery of bustling activity, I try to remain inconspicuous and order a pizza from a waitress who glances at me with a mixture of confusion and pity. That most critical phrase, the same one I can ramble off easily in a host of languages other than Spanish—I cannot sit—escapes me.

I seize up and mentally retract like an anemone on a seabed, with-drawing tentacles into itself.

The waitress arrives with my pizza. I fumble with the cutlery, though my appetite is gone. I pick at the crust, tomato slices, and mushrooms, plotting how to pay and slip out of the scene unnoticed.

From afar, a young woman in the crowd waves at me. It's Mani. My sandals feel like lead as I head over, squeezing past chairs full of raucous pilgrims. *What if they invite me to join them?* Which they do. I dread the explaining, the sight of luminous faces suddenly losing color, losing smiles. Fearing that I will drown in sorrow and self-pity, I beg off quietly, not for the first or last time recognizing that my gentle rebuff has the unintended consequence of leaving me to my-self—and perhaps causing those rebuffed to think me a snob.

There is no subtle or indirect way to explain the invisible: Broken bones. Fractured sacrum (bulging slightly, hidden under layers of clothing). Maimed leg. Crushed foot. Nerve and muscle damage. Chronic pain. My new normal. But. People. Cannot. See. And. Do. Not. Understand. (Or Do. Not. Believe.) *What do you mean, you can't SIT?*

Through the last archway beyond the Cathedral, my pending tears and I flee towards a sky streaked with shades of sun. How do I explain all that is invisible without setting myself apart, without feeling left out, without inviting pity? I have no idea. Never mind the wicking tops and thermal socks; here's where my preps have failed: I'm ill-equipped for these emotional hurdles.

Back at the albergue, my body yields effortlessly to the supple hands of a masseur. Although the Spaniard's skin-pinching ways don't hold a candle to the deep-tissue Javanese bodywork that I get in Bali, it's hard to pass up when my body is accustomed to regular sessions. Along the Camino, there are plenty of *maestro masaje*; like Manuel, a hospitalero at the municipal albergue in Azofra; and Miguel, the owner of the albergue Casa Magica in Villatuerta, who might accel-erate your spiritual seeking with mystic insights. An expat journalist recommends a talented, English-speaking *masajista* and Camino vet-eran in León. But one *noticia*, taped on a wall, catches my eye: There is an amazing man who holds a clinic under the stairs at the albergue in Santo Domingo de la Calzada. He specializes in feet. My kinda guy.

***

When school let out, scarves and boots were wrapped in moth balls while sunhats, shorts and sandals came out of storage. Summer also meant black and white saddle shoes. The girl and her sister would tag along to the shoe store, where a sales clerk with a serious shirt and pants would place a measuring device on the floor beneath their feet to measure growth spurts. It felt cold, metal tickling their soles. When the leaves turned and bathing suits were replaced by sweaters, the saddle shoes were put away. Dark navy lace-up shoes, the sturdy kind, took over. Their mother wanted to protect their precious feet.

Chapter 10: Abandonada

Despite the lustrous blue sky, I am enveloped by a palpable cloud of gloom as soon as we cross over the bridge into Logroño. We walk down a freshly repaved cobblestone path, façades of buildings painted in varying shades of pastel rising on either side, lined with micro-balconies, ornate street lamps, and potted plants. Peeling paint next to a wall of glass. On a sandwich board outside a tapas bar: Iberian ham with tomatoes. A mere seven days into my Camino, Popeye and Sancho are calling it quits. The humans and the dog will split too, heading off in different directions. In a parting gesture, Santi and friends accompany me to a tree-lined square a few steps beyond the municipal albergue. Otto detaches my backpack from Sancho, straps it onto my carrito, and turns to leave with the others, as the donkeys' tails sweep the air from side to side, flicking off unseen flies.

The glaring and sudden absence of Popeye and Mani evokes an unerring sense of abandonment. *Abandonada*. This calls for an immediate walkabout, an exploratory stroll along the winding roads of this medieval town.

The albergue doesn't open for a few hours, so I lean my backpack-on-carrito against the locked front gate, trusting that my unattended gear will be of no interest to passersby. With a glance around, I quickly determine that the square, with flagstones and neatly-trimmed trees, is presently home to a drunken foursome. Not quite the welcome I'd imagined. But this too is part of the country's current reality, dire times incarnate. Besides, in this speck of Spain, booze is easier to come by.

Logroño is the capital of Rioja province, a key wine-producing region, with vineyards dotting the city's surrounding areas. Where I expect to find charming turrets and gargoyles, bars and bakeries bustling with activity, I'm struck instead by an undercurrent of despair. The city reveals itself as a soulless place like a prized pinot noir that, once uncorked, turns out to be a sour substitute. Logroño feels like just another rural town along the Camino that the Spanish authorities have cast aside, an odor of decay permeating its walls.

Vivid examples of economic downturn are, like Pamplona, visible everywhere; shops with shuttered windows, construction projects halted midway, now covered in sheets of corrugated metal, locals looking downtrodden. Drunks and beggars congregate on stoops or roam about in broad daylight; a Roma family prepares a meal on an improvised stove top perched on a curb; the elderly and disabled are wheeled along streets by immigrant caregivers.

Walking down a quiet street behind a tall young woman, I am transfixed by the sun's rays casting elongated shadows of her figure ending at my feet. In a flash, the woman suddenly sprints to the far sidewalk, and in a feat worthy of the Olympics, leaps into the air, clutches at the railing of a first-floor balcony, catapults herself over the side, and slips without a trace into the darkness of an abandoned block of apartments. A squatter? Perhaps she is one of the many Spaniards whose financial distress has driven them deep into the shadows.

***

Even a flying leap over a bush that embedded dozens of thorns in the girl's legs, landing her in an ER, did not quash her stunts nor her spirit. She was whole again, ready to clear the next hurdles. It did nothing to temper her boundless, tomboyish ways. She was an energetic and imaginative child. Her parents called her Riot Squad, a nod to her zealousness, her lack of restraint. The girl believed: she is invincible.

***

Squinting against the bright lights of the afternoon, I spot more familiar signs of social distress: *Se Vende. Se Alquila*. A nation up for grabs. Homes, businesses, shops, cars and rooms. Empty fields, condemned buildings, restaurants and bars—all boarded up.

But even in the midst of financial panic and abandon, signs of renewal and life are everywhere—including the municipal albergue, as evidenced by the long queue formed in my absence.

The doors open shortly after I reclaim my carrito at the front of the line, trying not to interpret the glances of backpack-wielding pilgrims whose eyes are glued to my cart. When a hospitalero finally unlocks the gate, I ask him for help carrying my backpack into the building, while untangling it from the cart. Other pilgrims squeeze by, eager to register and claim a bunk. They unhook their able bodies from bulky gear, then sigh with understandable relief.

My body has lost cellular memory of that feeling.

A second hospitalero arrives to haul my heavy gear upstairs and helps me locate an empty bed. He slowly lowers my pack onto the floor and smiles. "Is there anything else I can get you?" he asks, as if he were a butler at a five-star parador instead of an unpaid volunteer in this simple pilgrim hospital.

I turn towards the two-tiered bed. The choice is clear; the decision, for now and evermore, confirmed: Upper bunk, by a window—which, in this case, affords me an unobstructed view of treetops, staggered roofs and the pastel blue sky. A light wind floats in through the open panes; ideal for drying off socks and leggings that I launder and hang in the cross breeze.

The scenes outside unfold in four quadrants—as if they comprise distinct segments of a quadriptych, a mythical story told in fragments. On the lower left, a patio still-life features a group of chocolate-nibbling pilgrims plugged into their 'smart' gadgets, framed by a rainbow of colorful clothes dangling from a line above their heads. A garden occupies the lower right side of my visual periphery, defined by its bold greenery and emptiness. At the top right, through stained glass windows, slightly ajar, I see a chorus of nuns iron, then gather for evening vespers. Finally, on the top left corner, the now-familiar drunks mumble loudly, their noisy and bottle-strewn landscape a stark contrast to the serenity of the nuns' cloister.

Long after Otto and the others have left, and as the sun arcs down into the horizon, my body shivers from chill and anxiety. Up until today, Otto has been a dependable and easygoing walking partner; conversations have been interspersed with the kind of silence that feels like a pause. His familiarity with the route, his encouragement and near fluency in Spanish also eased my immersion into pilgrimhood.

But I'm ill prepared for tomorrow's transition, when Otto will hand me over—as if I was a baton in a relay race—to a former pilgrim who has volunteered to carry my gear along with his own. Otto assures me that the man's expenses will be covered by private donations from former clients. The only other known details, about this anonymous Spanish do-gooder, is that he is of Portuguese origin, unemployed and divorced with two sons, lives in a tiny hamlet along the Camino, and once worked as a security guard and maker of leather goods. Also, he doesn't speak a word of English.

"So you have a choice," says Otto, "you make an effort to speak Spanish, or there will be a lot of silence between you."

"Ok, it'll be good practice," I say. "And what's his name, this mystery man?"

"Juan," replies Otto. Spanish for John—hands down, the most common Latin American name for men.

Who does this kind of thing, offer to carry another person's gear? Juan. He must be a saint. Say yes. Ask questions later.

Otto and I agree to meet the following morning at a prearranged spot, where he will introduce me to Juan. Strangely, butterflies take up residence in my body.

It'll be fine, I reassure myself. He's already walked the Camino, so he'll know the way. A second-time pilgrim himself, Juan must be a friendly guy. I've traveled in foreign countries long enough to take comfort in the knowledge that hand gestures work well for bridging language gaps. No problem. I've got this. It might even be fun.

Like a juggler, I'm thinking of all the languages I hold in the palm of my hand, and which one to focus on while the others follow suit. While walking with Juan, I need to file away Indonesian, Hebrew, French, even English, and pump up the volume in Spanish. If only my prefrontal cortex would fall into line.

Case in point. In Logroño, I approach the hospitalero for directions to a bakery. I know the Spanish word for where: *Dónde*. It resides deep in my brain, from where I've recalled it hundreds of times. So why does my mouth insist on uttering *dimana* instead? The Spanish word for place is inexplicably elusive, while *tempat* sits firmly on the tip of my tongue. Same happens with you (the Indonesian *anda* instead of Spain's *usted*); and he (*dia* instead of *el*). Why does *bagus* (Indonesian for good) slip out when I damn well know how to say *muy bien*?

***

Even though the girl grew up in Montreal, she was raised in a predominantly Hebrew environment; she learned English on the playground and French at school; she heard Romanian at her grandparents' home and Yiddish at the theater. Later she would enroll in Spanish class, pick up bits of Russian and Italian in her travels, and add Indonesian and a smattering of Balinese to her repertoire.

***

My neural networks go haywire. I'm mixing up words of different origins; familiar phrases are forgotten, jumbled up, falling off the linguistic radar. My languages no longer live in discrete silos. Something is lost. Abandonada.

❀

Chapter 11: Wild and Crazy

Before leaving the Logroño albergue, I track down a hospitalero. I'm in search of a walking pole that may have been left behind. "I don't need one of those hi-tech, collapsible kinds," I assure him, "a tall stick will do." As he opens the door to the office and disappears inside, I nearly trip over a paperback peering up at me from the floor. It's a well-thumbed copy of *Wild*, Cheryl Strayed's memoir about walking the rugged Pacific Coast Trail in the aftermath of personal crises. I'd heard of *Wild* just the day before, when I opened an email, in which a friend urged me to read it. I can almost hear the book begging to be rescued. Clearly, *Wild* is on the ground, waiting for me.

***

The second-floor library was a massive trove of children's books. Shelves piled high with hard-cover titles from around the world waited for a girl who read voraciously and longed to explore worlds unknown. She raced through Amelia Bedelia, Madeline and a Swedish series called Flicka, Ricka, Dicka; then discovered Pippi Longstocking. Pippi had wild pigtails, and was daring, cheeky and adventurous in almost superhuman ways. The girl decided that she would be like Pippi. For a while, and in so many ways, she was.

***

The image on the cover of *Wild* is a weathered hiking boot, its well-worn laces untied. I look down at my feet, which are again uncomfortably stuffed into socks and boots, and get a whiff of impending, final liberation. But my reverie is interrupted when the hospitalero emerges from his office, with wooden bastón in hand.

"Gracias!" I exclaim, gratefully taking it from him, and pointing to the floor. "Por favor, can I borrow that book?" I ask, even though it's unlikely I will ever return it. The hospitalero picks it up, flips it over and hands it to me.

"Sí," he says. "As long as you leave it behind at another albergue."

"Claro," I say. Of course. Which is how I end up taking *Wild* on the road. I haven't even stepped outside and the day is already full of promise.

It's still early morning when I set out with my backpack tightly strapped to the carrito, walking alone for the first time. With a slight nip in the air, I'm bundled up in layers. The streets are clean and quiet, potted plants neatly lining the façades, shops still closed—except for a bakery where I'd earlier purchased a baguette—with crumbs I can no longer feed to Popeye. The wheels of my unsteady carrito clank noisily as I drag it along the cobblestone path.

Voices approach from behind, speaking a language I know well. A young couple, enveloped in backpacks too large for their bodies, marches up alongside me, deep in conversation, their heads bent down. They expect to walk by unnoticed, unheard.

"*Boker tov*," I blurt out, in Hebrew. Good morning.

Caught off-guard, they nearly stumble, and stop in a daze.

Hebrew may be the official language of a small country perched on the edge of the Mediterranean; but it is spoken around the world, and in the unlikeliest places. I have heard it in Bali, in Nepal, and in the remotest regions of Mongolia and Laos. Even on the Trans-Siberian Railway. Why not on the streets of Logroño? Young Israeli newlyweds, Negev and Hila are trekking the Camino in lieu of a conventional honeymoon. This language, spoken far from our respective homes, binds us for a fleeting moment—before they wave and turn their attention back to the road. "*Buen Camino!*" they call out in unison, the pilgrim's phrase ever-so-slightly tinted by their Hebrew accent.

***

Visiting her mother's family and friends in Israel became an annual pilgrimage. The girl packed her clothes and books and camera and dreams. She played in the park with friends and cousins, went to camp and concerts and plays and the zoo, ate falafel and cactus pears, was spoiled by aunts, great-aunts and uncles. The girl and her family spent long hours at the saltwater pool or the beach where the Kinley orange flowed, the watermelon slices glistened, and chocolate topping drizzled off a banana-flavored popsicle, dripping onto her tanned stomach where it stuck to grains of sand.

***

The air is crisp, the sun already ascending behind the high façades of homes lining the path. A young boy on a bicycle rides by, armed with a bag full of flaky, baked dough that he cradles in one arm. Two buxom elderly women dressed all in black are seated, hands firmly clasped on their laps, in front of doorways strung with vertical ribbons made of clear plastic. I feel their eyes follow my every step as I walk by, half-expecting to be asked the same question that my Balinese neighbors pose:

"*Mau kemana?*" Where are you going?

The initial shock of being asked such a direct and personal question—"It's not your business," I'd nearly snapped back—fades once I grasp that this greeting signals a culturally sanctioned inquisitiveness and tendency towards gossip. Seen through a Western lens, "*Mau kemana?*" is an affront to our sense of privacy: we are made to feel seen; and many of us are terrified of being seen, nearly as much as not being seen. But, the seen and unseen aspects of Balinese life co-exist; distilled in the duality of *sekala* (tangible) / *niskala* (intangible), and reflected in ceremonial prayers and rituals that are conducted in the search for a balance between good and evil, light and dark, in order to attain harmony in nature and life.

In time, one learns to grin at the sound of "*Mau kemana?*" and say whatever comes to mind. Such as *jalan-jalan*. I'm going for a walk. But "*¿A dónde vas?*" It seemed altogether unlikely that I would be posed that question; not only because of cultural differences, but mostly because my outfit and backpack are dead giveaways. Claro… I'm walking the Camino.

"*Buenos días Otto*," I write, tapping a Spanish greeting into my Indonesian cell phone. A reconnaissance mission the previous night so tired me out that I asked Otto to revise his plan. "Can we please meet near the square and *fuente* on Barriocepo instead?" I add, "U can park there easily."

My backpack, and the carrito to which it is tied, wobble, swivel, and nearly topple onto the ground. I'm on the brink of exhaustion—and we haven't even left Logroño. To think that I'd initially intended to walk the entire WAY on my own. Holy Santiago! I must have been deluded. *Loca*. Crazy.

The closer I get to our meeting place, the more my self-doubt and unfounded suspicions escalate, rankle me, shifting my mind into overdrive: What's this faceless pilgrim like? Will we even like each other? Will we get along? What if he talks endlessly about himself, or complains about having to carry my bag? What if he actually IS a serial axe murderer? What if he expects me to have sex with him in exchange for his… ummm… services?

Who does this kind of thing??! Have I gone crazy?

Chapter 12: Meeting the Juan(s)

From a distance, while I wait for the light to change, I spot a van parked next to a wall. Three men stand in a cluster close by. Wide-bellied Otto, now scrubbed clean, is sandwiched in between the much leaner pair of strangers. On my final approach, Otto and another man are pulling gear out of the van, while the third stands inert. A Carrix, bundled up with ropes, slides out and is laid on the ground as if it were a stiff corpse. For the first time, I study it closely.

The Carrix, a foldable, aluminum, one-wheel trolley that resembles a lightweight stretcher, is the brainchild of a Swiss inventor. No sturdier and less personable than Sancho and Popeye, the contraption is a tribute to minimalism: metallic blue with black straps, one small wheel and a long pair of handlebars—looking like repurposed ski poles. Imagine a flattened wheelbarrow, its metal receptacle replaced by a swath of nylon material onto which you can dump up to 20 kgs worth of gear. Once you are strapped into the black harness, the handles are grasped (or you can walk hands-free!), while the angled Carrix trails behind. At first glance, it seems unfathomable that such a flimsy-looking apparatus is capable of lugging a heavy backpack, let alone TWO.

Otto looks up and introduces me to Juan. A ruggedly handsome man with a broad smile, Juan exudes effervescence, gesticulating and glancing around as if any moment he might transform into a matador, calling out "*Olé!*" Dressed in lumberjack-style shirt, faded jeans and hiking boots, he has conquistador written all over him. As Juan wraps his arms around me and plants firm kisses on both my cheeks, I feel his beard and mustache hairs graze my face. Together, Juan and I will conquer the Camino. Maybe even the world. The sun shines brighter.

I make a mental note to send Otto a text later: "*Muy bien, hombre*, you've chosen well."

As if tuned into my thoughts, Otto calls out to me. I follow his gaze as he points to the other man, a slouched figure, partly concealed by the van's shadow, as if an afterthought. Looking a few years older than Juan, and noticeably hunched over, this man's eyes are trained on the ground. He nervously clutches a wide-brimmed straw boater hat in both hands, clasped together in front. He barely lifts his head, his eyes meeting mine in the space of a blink. He could not be more of a contrast to the exceedingly affable Juan. As Otto introduces us, the man lifts his hand, almost begrudgingly, to shake mine. And I nearly faint.

"This is also Juan," chuckles Otto, brushing strands of greying hair off his forehead. It turns out that the first Juan, Señor Lumberjack, goes by Juan-*Ro*; whereas his brooding counterpart is known as Juan-*Do*.

I look at Otto quizzically, as if to ask: "Which one?" I gaze up at the sky in need of last-minute divine intervention.

"Juan-Do will walk with you," he says nonchalantly, pointing to the figure in the shadows, "he'll carry his things and yours too."

Huh? My high hopes and levitating Juan-bubble bursts.

Juan-Do twirls his boater hat nervously in his hands as his head hangs low. I size him up: brown cotton slacks folded up at the ankles school-boy style, long-sleeved checkered shirt with a hint of undershirt peeking out, a vest with enough hidden pockets to make a photojournalist proud, and ankle-height leather boots scuffed to the max, the stray end of one lace forlorn on the ground. *He's going to walk hundreds of kilometers in THOSE clothes and shoes??*

Dredging up possible escape scenarios, I wonder if it's too late to switch Juans—or go ahead with my perpetual default plan; aborting altogether.

Encasing myself in Juan-Ro's muscular arms, I am loathe to let him go. Instead, I bury my eyes into a nook in front of his warm, sun-kissed shoulder, contemplating how I might plead with him to take over. Juan-Ro extracts himself, climbs into the van, waves and drives off. The feeling of abandonment and longing is immediate, almost surreal. As if the universe has pulled the plug on hope, an alien species landing in front of me with a heavy thud.

The grizzly warmth of Juan-Ro's scented embrace dissolves into the morning mist. With every agitated fiber of my body, I turn back to the scene of instruction unfolding next to the van. As Otto gives Juan-Do a rundown of *El Carrix*, the towering walls of buildings on both sides of the pedestrian pathway seem to close in on me, casting a grey pall over this entire endeavor—which has not even begun, and is already in anti-climax mode. Looking over my shoulder towards the Calle Sagosta, I desperately want to flee.

According to Otto's plan for today, we will take the Carrix for a trial run. Otto will tag along as back-up, technician, and ostensibly, to pave the way for Juan-Do and I to get acquainted.

But my gut, as knot-prone and tied up as the Carrix, senses that something is off kilter. Even as Otto and I carry on with our usual banter, Juan-Do doesn't lift his head nor make a peep. Like a monk sunk into a silence of his own making, his eyes still avoid mine. And yet, I don't breathe a word to Otto—nor does he offer up any of his own commentary about this strange and unfriendly behavior.

In front of me, Juan-Do fidgets with the handlebars, trying to minimize wobble, find a good stride. There must be an art to nudging the Carrix along at the right tilt. But the sight of him strapped into the harness is unsettling; it must feel like a straitjacket. I can't shake off the shades of exploitation. Like a dog or errant infant on a leash. Like Popeye.

Despite my budding misgivings and remorse, I refocus my lens and size him up. From a purely physical perspective, Juan-Do is a composite of men I've known in my life. For starters, his Portuguese origins remind me of the scruffy and gravel-voiced, blue-collar workers who would congregate each weekend at a Portuguese bakery around the corner from where I once lived in Toronto. Then there is his uncanny resemblance to a dear man named Aldo. Born in Italy, Aldo immigrated to Montreal with his wife, raised a family and invited mine over for Christmas dinner. Over many decades, up to his untimely death, Aldo was my father's most trusted employee—and the surrogate brother he, an only child, never had.

Most strikingly, Juan-Do is a dead ringer for my late, Polish-born, great-uncle Yehezkel. With the same slouch and paunch, a pate of thinning hair and facial stubble, his fingers calloused—from what? Perhaps decades of manual labor—Juan-Do might be Yehezkel reincarnate.

Walking behind Juan-Do, his boater dangling behind his neck, I study his outerwear more closely. My choice of clothing, admittedly, diverges from the latest trends and standards that most contemporary pilgrims seem to live by. But if my duds are on the lower end of tech, his are decidedly old school. Juan-Do looks like he could be going to work. Which maybe he thinks he is.

By mid-afternoon, the scorching sun significantly slows down our pace. I seek coolness under the shade of an overhang—for which I'm thankful, as I must tend to my sore feet. I look over at Juan-Do, who wipes his forehead with a handkerchief that he's retrieved from one of his many pockets. He still hasn't made a peep.

Chapter 13: The Blister Brigade

A wave of inconsolable dread washes over me: *Why isn't Juan-Do talking to me? Why won't Otto intervene? Surely he must notice the lack of interaction between the Portuguese-born-Spaniard and me?* I still hesitate to express any regrets to Otto, lest he think me ungrateful and prematurely panic-ridden. What happens if I reneg on our agreement; how will I find an alternative? Dare I ask Otto to exchange Juan-Do for the other Juan? I am paralyzed with indecision.

When we arrive in the town of Navarrete, Otto leads us to the farmacia where I enter in search of tiger balm. The skin of my big left toe is heavily chafed and heading towards a blister.

"No tiger balm left," says the pharmacist, "would you like Traumeel?"

"*Sí, gracias*," I answer without further inquiry. Traumeel and I are well acquainted; the salve's anti-inflammatory properties pulled me through the first year of acute recovery and insufferable pain.

Minutes later, we reach the Albergue Buen Camino. In an empty 2nd floor room, I score a top bunk near a window with an unobstructed view of the plaza across the street. I'm standing at the window when Juan-Do walks in with my backpack.

"*¿Dondé?*" he mutters. No "*buenos*," no smile, nada. He looks past me, at the wall, much like a Balinese man might do when he wants to turn the corner on his scooter at the very moment you step off the curb onto the road, but he will not slow down, he will not allow you to pass, he may even clip your body or feet as he swerves by, ignoring you as if you do not exist.

I point to the floor near my claimed bed, where Juan-Do drops my bag with a thud. Any fragile goods be damned. He walks out of the room without another word, seemingly oblivious to my expression of thanks, leaving me in a void.

Turning back to the window, I see pilgrims gathering on the plaza. My mind reels. I churn and chew over Juan-Do's disinterest. *Do I smell of sweat or bad breath? Did I say something to offend him? Does he assume I don't (won't) speak Spanish?* I mentally try to adopt his point of view: What does he see? A middle-aged woman, fit and appropriately dressed, walking with relative ease while carrying a puny daypack, as he hauls our combined stash. To any observer's eyes, I look perfectly normal, able-bodied and dent-free. So why don't I carry my own gear? Perhaps he thinks me a prima donna, a spoiled pilgrim willing to pay for a porter. Even so. Looks are deceiving.

Maybe he still needs time to get accustomed to the Carrix. Maybe he is dealing with a loss of which he cannot yet speak. Maybe he has just learned that he is ill. But Otto has mentioned nothing of the kind, which leaves me with a deeper sense of foreboding. Then again, perhaps all the Man of Few Words needs is a day of rest, to sort himself out, freshen up, and offer up a smile.

I'm lying on the top bunk with my eyes closed when a persistent knock brings me back to myself. "It's open," I call out, "come in!" Mani's playful eyes and infectious laugh walk into the room, filling it with the breath of life; Traumeel for my soul. She drags her backpack across the floor, rests it next to mine, and we ramble off news about our respective day's events as if we were childhood friends just now reunited. She dashes out to meet Otto, leaving me to unravel my thoughts. While I wasn't looking, sparks flew. Mani, who arrived in Navarette before us, is smitten.

After a nap, I climb down to unpack all my gear on the empty bunk below mine, and take stock of my largely unmatched items, some dating back to my travels across Asia a few years earlier. Unlike other pilgrims, I'm no brand ambassador. At other albergues, I will be tutored in the language of pilgrim's gear. I will learn about de rigueur outfits that guarantee peak performance. I will learn about hi-tech hiking pants, made of stretchy fabric that minimize chafing due to their superior wicking capabilities. I will be introduced to compression socks with a price tag higher than my daily budget for food. I will meet a pilgrim whose Alpine hiking shoes were tailor-made for ascents up Kilimanjaro. I will be initiated into the world of zipped-off shorts, Camelbaks, and finally, the fabled foot repair kits:

"Don't forget to pack Compeed, Band-Aids and a sewing kit for blisters!"

Despite all attempts to mitigate stitching up sore feet and torn skin, blisters happen.

"But I wore these expensive socks!" they moan, "And I'm wearing a new pair of boots!"

"But I practiced walking for weeks and not once did I get a blister!"

"What am I going to do? I started walking last week and I have to get to Santiago by next week!"

Mani's timely return saves me from more brooding in bed. We cross over to the covered plaza, where patrons spill out from the bar at the far end, dropping their leaden bodies into chairs, dangling limbs over the backs and arms. The pilgrims are easily picked out from the crowd; a sweaty gang, in some cases borderline sunburnt or inebriated (occasionally both), and hunched over wrecked skin. They cut and slice away at pus-filled sores and blisters as if they were compulsory rites preceding a mouth-watering feast.

The plaza outside the bar pulsates with chortling, chattering in different languages, and echoes of a bell clanging. The bar's interior space reveals itself to be a pantheon of *pintxos* (aka tapas), its long countertop displaying a dazzling selection of bite-sized delights, offering up a transcendent experience. Mani and I scan the dishes, eventually settling on a platter of mixed pintxos—eggplant, red pepper, mushrooms, anchovies, and tuna served on chunks of baguette. I pay the cashier, adding a small tip to the bill, at which point a bell is rung—prompting applause and a bellowing from the barman: "*Bo-ta!*" The reason for all that clamor? A public display of gratitude for the tip.

With a bottle of chilled cerveza in hand, Mani and I carry our bounty of pintxos to a table outside—where sit happens. Again. On metal chairs; the smooth, shiny surfaces taunting me, but looking ever so uncomfortable. Pulling out an unoccupied seat that gleams in the sunlight, I turn it around. I ask a man at the next table to lend me his thick brown fleece, which I improvise into a seat cushion. I kneel on top of the fluff, pain be damned. Even if I must stand out from the crowd, my head bobbing around inches above anyone else; even if it's not comfortable and people look at me funny, I'm staying put.

Chapter 14: In Search Of…

Now freed of socks and shoes, with Traumeel rubbed into my soles and my toes tucked into Tevas, I have happy feet. While others focus on blisters, my fixation is of an entirely different species: blackberries.

As I tuck into yet another serving of pintxos, I turn to Otto, who is feeding bits of pintxo-crumbs to Santi.

"Can I get some blackberry wine in Rioja?" I ask, following up a bite of juicy mushroom with a guzzle of beer.

"I don't think so," he says, wrinkling his nose. "But I used to make banana wine and honey wine." Honey wine? Maybe. Banana wine. I would pass.

I steal inside the bar, to ask the waiter if they serve anything made with blackberries. Bemused, he shakes his head and dashes off to serve clients outside. When I return to the table empty-handed, Otto has already changed subjects, waxing philosophical to anyone within earshot.

"There are three things in life that you can't change," he says, "your family, your home—and your football team."

"Why football?" I ask, nibbling on a piece of quiche.

"It's in the blood," he replies.

With beer and wine flowing, Otto appears to be settling in for a long haul.

"You might not believe this," he says, "but I once smoked forty cigarettes a day." My eyebrows shoot up. Mani looks equally stunned.

"Then I found a book that explained the psychology behind smoking," Otto continues. "I quit the same day."

"Amazing," I say, drowned out by the ringing of the 'bota' bell, as if in tribute to Otto's achievement. "You've got willpower."

"Yes. Maybe… " he answers tentatively, biting down on a baguette. "But that's also why I gained all this weight."

I suggest another strategy.

"Maybe you could try blackberries," I say, half in jest. "You could try filling your blood with more fruit than football."

No comment. Otto wipes his brow and leans over his substantial belly, to untie laces. He sits up again with an exaggerated sigh. Turning to the bar's entryway, he waves over a loitering waiter.

"What about those blackberries on the path?" I lock eyes with Otto, trying hard to ignore the lone pilgrim at the next table, who is stitching his skin together with a needle and thread. "Did you taste them?"

"What blackberries?" Otto asks. "Where did you see blackberries?"

"What do you mean: you haven't seen blackberries?" The noise level at the plaza escalates, drowning out my words.

While Otto rhapsodizes over beer and football, and I daydream about blackberries, Mani is on an entirely different mission: She is searching for a higher power.

"I want to meet God. I want to speak to God and hear him," she says while twirling and flicking a handful of hairs away from her temple, a gesture that is also a signature habit." I am SO grateful for his presence in my life. He is with me every day."

Mani points down at her boots and breaks into a giddy smile that lights up her whole face. "I say thank you to my feet and kiss them too—even though people around me look at me like I'm crazy!"

The next morning, a Saturday, it is still early when I step down the ladder to the floor. Unfurling my yoga mat from its mesh bag, I step around quietly so as not to wake Mani. My body aches; I need a day of rest.

Outside our window, the sun peeks through slow-moving clouds, as Navarette comes back to life. Word has it that a dog festival is taking place in the plaza today. One more good reason to beg off walking today.

Before getting on the mat, I dash off a message to the football fan—in still-halting Spanish.

"*Hola Otto, hay una fiesta por los perros ahora di plaza en frente de albergue,*" I write. "*Hay mucho perros… muy bien por Santi?*" Do you want to bring Santi to a dog festival on the plaza?

I'm standing in warrior pose when Mani awakes and peeks out of her sleeping bag, looking groggy.

"I hope it didn't bother you, my moving around?" I ask.

"No," she says, fumbling for her glasses, "it reminds me to stretch and feel my body move, not just my legs."

***

The girl danced ballet, solved crossword puzzles, drew pictures and created homemade Mother's Day cards. She tried, so diligently and stubbornly, to shape a mound of clay into a mug, while her mother hunched over the potter's wheel nearby, churning out a whole counter full of symmetrical plates. She licked maple syrup off sheets of shaved snow, took up hooking rugs and knitting, started a stamp collection, and practiced her tennis serve until the net called it quits.

***

In the plaza, locals are setting up a stage and props for a day honoring the town's dogs. By midday, with dogs streaming into the plaza from every direction, the square is transformed into a Dogapalooza. Pooches leap out of cars and trucks, sniffing their way through the crowd. A van pulls up, advertising its therapeutic pet services: *Al Canino.*

Otto walks in and we line up chairs in front of the balcony that gives us a front row view of the festival. Santi is bei fus; sitting erect, his ears perk up while scoping out the scene. No sign of Juan-Do; maybe he's still not up to socializing. Or, maybe, he finds this tribute to all things caninical, objectionable.

The plaza mayor is abuzz with activity; an exhibition of dog tricks, a parade with judges, prizes, music, circle dancing, and kids frolicking about. Teens congregate and flirt at the fountain around the corner, a shooting arcade is set up by a Roma family, and gaudi-ly-clad women leave church and wobble downhill in impossibly high stilettos, teetering precipitously on ancient cobblestones. By the time dusk descends, a disco atmosphere takes over, lasting into the late hours. Somehow, I manage to fall asleep to the sounds of barking, 'bota!' and the Village People singing "YMCA."

Waking to a 7 a.m. alarm, I tiptoe out of the room still draped in dark-ness; cautiously dragging my backpack behind me. I pack quietly in the kitchen, so as not to awaken Mani, who had stayed out later than I.

When I return to the room, her sleeping bag lies untouched on the bed, and her backpack is still tied up on the floor. I text Otto.

"Yes," he replies, "I know where Mani is."

Sure he does; she's right there, beside him. Something is brewing.

As I test the weight of my Shrek-pack, my morning ritual—of paring down to the essentials: passport, money, camera, notebook, pen, banana, and orange—is interrupted by a knock on the door.

"*Sí, entre,*" I call out.

Juan-Do walks in and trudges over, not once lifting his eyes to mine. He lifts my backpack and turns to go, as if he were an inden-tured servant. Or a deaf-mute.

"*Buenas días,*" I say.

Juan-Do leaves the room without a word. Something is seriously off-kilter. How long until he warms up to me?

When I reach the ground floor, I find Juan-Do out front, ty-ing our backpacks onto the Carrix. A cloud is suspended above our heads, almost ominously. I tuck my yoga mat in between the bags and fling my diminutive daypack over my shoulder, strapping it onto my back.

With no send-off party—Otto and Mani are AWOL—and only the clanging of church bells to signal our departure, we turn the corner, and head towards the far edge of town. It will not be long before Juan-Do, who marches ahead with dogged determination, disappears over the horizon line.

Chapter 15: Go On!

We are an unlikely pair, Juan-Do and I, off to a rocky start. One hour into our walk, sans Otto, and regret gnaws at me. *What have I done? How could I have signed onto this long-term endeavor, requiring such close proximity, without an introductory Skype call?* From the looks of it, I've made a massive faux-pas.

Occasionally, Juan-Do throws crumbs my way; a smattering of words in Spanish. But even then, he grunts in one or two syllables; his few spoken words circumscribed by the weather, the Camino or the Carrix. Nothing approximating conversation. Certainly, no questions. I hunker down, close to the road, from where I can more easily study the rotating antennae and rubbery green texture of a snail lumbering by; its hard shell a mollusk's version of Sancho carrying my pack.

"*Lluvia,*" says Juan-Do. Rain.

***

Sometime before the girl turned ten; between all the birthday parties, music lessons, museum outings, picnics, television shows and heaping plates of spaghetti and garlic bread at a favorite Italian restaurant that had a fish tank with guppies and mollies; somewhere between kisses at bedtime, getting tucked in and hearing "I love you," she started hearing words that she could not understand. Beneath the girl's feet, imperceptible to the normal eye and unattuned ear, the ground began to shift and crack.

***

Somewhere on the path, Juan-Do stops the Carrix, and without warning or invitation, launches into oration. In Spanish. His monologue, about religion and spirituality, is directed towards an audience of one—me—and punctuated with unfamiliar words and phrases, like *ser de luce* and *tierra*. The sun has barely risen above the horizon line—and already this Man of Few Words is ruminating on earth, sky and spirit; stopping as abruptly as he starts.

Hours later, he stops to lecture me on universal energy and Reiki—without realizing that I too have trained in this healing practice. He then instructs me: "Don't rest or lie down on cold ground, and certainly not without a *ropa* (a piece of clothing) under your backside." I begin to understand why he calls himself Maestro.

Juan-Do then tells me how, in his youth back in Portugal, he had developed lower back pain. In mid-sentence, he suddenly stops walking.

"I was at a festival in Portugal," he says in Spanish. He stops in his tracks and continues only after I have stopped as well, my full attention trained squarely on him. "There were cows on the road. I tried to catch one by holding it down, but the cow pushed me into a wall." Ah, the origin of his back pain.

I begin to wonder whether his speech will shift into two-way dialogue. But hope is short-lived. He turns away, lifts the handlebars and resumes walking.

"Go on," he blurts out. Shorthand rules. The Man of Few Words seems pleased with himself, coercing me to walk at his beck and call—without needing to resort to actual conversation.

We approach a creek that soon widens into an impassable stream. A pilgrim is traipsing across a bridge, which Juan-Do ignores, continuing instead to walk along the stream, motioning for me to follow.

"Can we go back and cross the bridge?" I ask. He responds by growling and waving me off.

"*Hey jefa*," Juan-Do blurts out, using the Spanish word for boss. "*Hay confidencia.*" Have confidence in me, he says, a hint of derision in his voice.

"*Yo andare aqui el ano pasado,*" he assures me. He walked this way last year.

With no sign of another crossing ahead, I reluctantly follow in Juan-Do's steps because he holds my gear hostage. At the end of the gravelly path, the stream's water levels are too high for anyone to cross. I stay back, waiting for him to forge ahead and wade through knee-high water. Instead, he turns on his heel and backtracks to the bridge behind us, passing me on the way. His eyes stay glued to the ground. No apology. Nada.

The pattern is clear: his way—or no way. Perhaps silence isn't such a bad thing after all.

Hours later, Juan-Do stops in his tracks again. To adjust the harness, I think, maybe to loosen the straps binding him to the Carrix. But no. He speaks—an urgency rising in his voice. He wants to teach me Spanish vocabulary. Could this approach be his only tool to overcome chronic shyness? Fortunately, this unsolicited language session provides me with a mini-glossary that comes in handy over the coming weeks: Grapes. *Uvas*. Oil. *Aceite*. Bees. *Abejas*. Sheep. *Oveja*.

I thank him for the lesson. My expectations are low, my hope cautious, but still: Could this—and other clues—be signs of rapprochement?

Back on track next morning, Juan-Do veers off to the side of the road. He leans over a bush, flickers some leaves out of the way, and plucks off blossoms, which he turns to give me.

"Ahhh, rosemary!" I exclaim. "*Gracias.*"

"*Sí,*" says Juan-Do, "*romero. Por infusion.*"

For a herbal infusion; in other words, a tea infused with herbs. Already exceeding his daily quota of words, Juan-Do surprisingly has more to say. "A group of German pilgrims that I met last year were confused when I offered them an infusion," he says in Spanish, slowly enough for me to understand his gist. "They mistook it for an intravenous procedure—administered at a hospital, rather than served in a bar or café."

Just when I begin to hope that we can bond over laughter, I hear a shrill "Go on!", reverting Juan-Do to his state of gloom and a co-coon of one. I turn to look over my shoulder, wondering what kind of miracle it will take, for Mani to materialize.

***

A whiff in the air, something that maybe only she could smell, told the girl that something was amiss. She could not yet feel it in her body but a gnawing discomfort was growing within her nonetheless, perhaps deep in her mind. She could not put her finger on it, did not know the cause. All she knew was that, almost every time she opened her mouth, or even when she didn't, something went wrong. Pain happened. Nothing she did seemed to make it go away. And nobody else seemed to notice.

Chapter 16: In Wine Country

Ventosa is a village with one albergue and one bar. The doors of the albergue are still shut, so I leave Juan-Do with the Carrix and backtrack to the bar. Inside, I order a café con leche—the standard Spanish infusion. Every pair of pilgrim's eyes is glued to a cell phone. Weak connections. So there is silence. But too much silence is, like anything, in excess. If none of these people wants to talk, I'll go commune with Mother Nature; her lines are always open. I ditch the café.

I wander deep into the woods, in search of something vaguely defined. I find my treasure hidden under arbors or bursting from bushes; enough blackberries to whip up a few batches of jam. Or wine. Bursting with the flavors of freshly plucked fruit, I find my way back to the albergue—where the doors are still closed. The Carrix is parked in front. Juan-Do, already unshackled, sits on the ground, leaning against the wall, his wide-brimmed hat hanging in front of his face, to block out the sun. The pose of an aging *caballero* (cowboy)—minus the well-oiled boots, smokes and sexy swagger of, say, the Marlboro Man.

A South Korean couple joins our little queue. They place their luggage near Juan-Do, and walk off. With no signs of the albergue opening anytime soon, I leave the slumbering caballero to his snooze.

Like elsewhere in rural Spain, nothing much seems to happen in this sleepy village—especially in the midday hours. Locals nap. I stroll past the shuttered doors of the town hall, until I reach a sign that recounts the village's history—where I discover that locals are called *luchineros*; although most Ventosa villagers now work as vintners or beekeepers, once they were "suckling pig breeders." Those words conjure up the image of a crisply roasted suckling pig on a large tray, carried overhead by a two-man crew on a scooter, on their way to Ibu Oka's restaurant in Ubud, a place made famous by Anthony Bourdain's gushing *No Reservations* review.

As I approach the albergue, a sleek Mercedes pulls up to the front door. What a grand entrance. It must belong to the owner, José. In a village full of rusted cars and dusty jalopies, his sparkling sedan sticks out like a ruby among river stones. The villagers might feel a twinge of envy: José is not a local boy done good; he's a businessman from the big city, with what appears to be a pet pilgrim project.

We're first in line when José's assistant opens the door. She is young, beautiful—and clumsy, letting papers flutter to the ground all around her as a chair topples over. I score a top bunk near the window, in a spartan but clean room upstairs. After Juan-Do arrives and dumps my bag on the floor, I roll my eyes at nobody in particular, and get busy, giving my sleeping bag a good shake-out. I take a shower and clamber up to my perch where I settle into the next chapter of *Wild*, with not another soul around. In a strange and unexpected way, Strayed's daily battles with harrowing cliffs, bitter cold and searing loneliness, nudges me on; as if her pummeled (but ultimately triumphant) spirit was tagging along.

***

The hitch was this: the mother was beautiful. She had a warm engaging smile. She was dressed well, in pretty clothes, sparkly earrings dangling, hugging her children tightly to her bosom. She cooked and baked and helped the neighbors. She volunteered for the school, the community, did good things for her extended family. She was nice to the milkman, the postman, the man who topped her tank with gas. She was the life of a party, adored by many, a shining beacon. Her daughters, well behaved, neatly dressed, exemplary students. All the people who went to sleep in beds in houses far away, as if in another galaxy, thought she could do no harm. Except for all the times that she did, and none of them saw.

***

The stillness, so rare and sweet for reading purposes, is soon broken. A quad of middle-aged British women appears, hauling in oversized bags, sweat and bubbly banter. I slide the bookmark in to mark my page, lean on my side and wave.

"This is the first day of our Camino!" announces one of the pack. "We're walking together for a week."

Their bags have barely hit the floor when the gripes appear.

"Where's my wallet?" asks one. "Had it when I went to the shower… or did you put it in the laundry?"

"I left my towel in the last albergue," says another. "Can you ask the woman downstairs if she has a towel?"

"How many quit after the first day?" the first ponders to herself as she tears off her sweat-stained top.

"Why did that woman want a massage last night?"

Within minutes, they have rummaged through a wide array of topics; from people they know with cancer, to antibiotics, from car crashes and physiotherapy, to "let's go to Greece!"

"Should we sit out on the verandah now?" asks the one who has spoken least. Buzzing around the room, dropping items on beds, fiddling with their hair, they finally file out en masse, leaving a trail of petty grumbles echoing in the air.

***

The girl felt confused, then wracked with guilt. As if she had closely observed and taken notes from a seasoned hockey goaltender (of her hometown's beloved Habs, of course), the girl learned to expertly fend off any question that prodded too deeply; seamlessly deflecting inquiries that dared tap on her shield of self-preservation.

***

A glass of wine would come in handy, right about now—ideally, extracted from a nearby Rioja vineyard. The momentary contemplation of spirits fades once I dive back into *Wild*, where Strayed's description of Trail Angels—people along the trail who protect, guide or buoy the lost or battered souls—fills me with hope that my own angels will save me from Juan-Do… as much as myself.

Chapter 17: Camino Candy

It is 3 a.m. The dorm room is full of pilgrims. Everyone is asleep. Except for Alice. A Londoner born in the U.S., she is wide awake, packing her gear and making a ruckus. A motion detector, high above the doorframe, is triggered by her activity, besieging the room with a bright fluorescent light and droning buzz. Flummoxed and unable to switch off the light, her disturbance escalates. Long before the sun has risen, Alice leaves with her backpack. Moments later, the light switches off, encasing us once again in darkness.

Unlike the others, I'm already wide awake. *Vino, anyone?* I retreat further into my sleeping bag, where I tuck into another chapter of *Wild*. Right about now, I'm thinking that a romance novel might have been a wiser choice: Strayed is coming apart at her seams. Note to self: read *Wild* in daylight.

My ears perk up at the slightest hint of distant moans. I poke my head through the opening, and even in pitch-blackness, the sounds of chanting are unmistakable. Voices bounce around the sky as if it were a giant echo chamber. But monks? How peculiar, to stumble upon mellifluous tones of Buddhist practice, among the vineyards of Rioja in a country steeped in Catholicism? Perhaps it's a wake-up call for local workers, much as it is for rice farmers in remote Balinese hamlets or a call to prayer in Muslim neighborhoods around Indonesia.

As pilgrims wake, pack and leave, the mood feels somber. We soon follow suit. Juan-Do and I are on the path towards Najera, a couple of meters separating us, when the Man of Few Words points to a string of lights, barely visible in the distant twilight. He stops in his tracks, and waits for me to do the same.

"You see that vineyard?" Juan-Do asks, a noticeable Portuguese accent coating this morning's dose of Spanish. "A long time ago, I worked there as a night watchman." Pause. I wait for more. With nothing further to add, he picks up the Carrix poles and walks on. I lag behind, my mind reeling with possible scenarios: He got drunk on the job and was sacked. He fell asleep while thieves from a nearby village ransacked the winery, making off with a truck-ful of rosé. He did nothing while a pair of donkeys helped themselves to one row after another of ripened grapes.

At the side of the road, Alice bends over her backpack.

"Are you ok?" I ask.

"I guess so," she says. "But these open sores are a real pain in the ass." Another Camino casualty.

In sympathy, I express my regret at not having any bandaging paraphernalia on hand; my membership in the blister brigade has expired. As Alice treats her foot, I press on, trying to catch up to the morose-looking, hat-wearing caballero. Just close enough that I don't lose sight of him.

Pilgrims power on past us, many adhering to a strict walking schedule, blisters be damned. How do they accomplish this feat? Pumped up on painkillers as if they were candy.

Camino Candy. A generic, all-encompassing term for Atavans, Percocets and their ilk; and a burning topic of conversation. Pilgrims shove pained feet into boots, raising hell when 25 kilometers of ground-pounding turns their toes to mush, and their soles to sores. Infections happen with alarming regularity. Hardier pilgrims tend to disavow and soldier on, like cadets at a boot camp, rather than suc-cumb to rest or a massage. Compeed patches are taped to toes, while improvised (and rarely sterile) stitches slow the flow of blood and pus. Long rolls of bandages are unspooled, tied around battered feet, which are then reinserted, pain and all, into boots-too-tight-for-you. In no time, these borderline masochists are back on track.

***

Somewhere in the wilds of Ontario, on the edge of a lake where children learned water skiing tricks and went on canoe trips; where the menu du jour comprised pizza, peanut butter sandwiches and bug juice; where lights out meant sticky fingers from cotton candy or sneaking behind the cabin for a verboten smoke, the girl, who remembered to pack a tennis racket, Gap shorts, knee-high socks and Holly Hobby stationery, forgot to leave other, soul-wrecking things behind. So, on the cusp of puberty, while her cabin-mates whispered to each other about mascara and boys and French kissing, the girl stewed inside. By the time she would leave camp, weeks later, with linocuts, dirty laundry and autographs in hand, the 11-year old girl's biggest achievement would not have been learning to paddle a canoe or score a role in the play, but convincing herself that she was, indeed, and unlike anyone else, utterly unlovable.

***

Blister-therapy turns out to be a common (if not grotesque) rite of passage, a skin sacrifice that initiates novice pilgrims into the brigade as if they have won a coveted spot in the fraternity of self-harmers. No time or need for comfort and rest—just pack the painkillers.

I've grown leery of pharma, even though I carry my own share of pain: A few months after my accident, I'd obstinately weaned myself off all opiates, swearing them off for good. Instead, I treat both feet with kindness and kid gloves—particularly the left one, compressed from impact; the disfigurement so subtle, it is barely noticeable. I douse them with hot water and a fair bit of goop: Vaseline is my choice of Camino Candy.

Candy or no candy, the sun always rises. Its rays guide me from behind like a light beam, pointing me towards distant horizons, towards Santiago, towards the sea, towards the ends of the earth.

Under the same sun, snail walkers or fast pacers, we are all one. But what do those who rush to their next bed, or race to reach Santiago in record time, manage to see? Do they notice the brilliant sunlit grapes hanging in juicy bunches off vines? Do they spot dewdrops, like bubbles glommed onto leaves and blades of grass? Do they marvel at the buxom *abuelas* (grandmothers), in Bruegel-style peasant garb, as they hang laundry or carry baskets overflowing with produce? Do they stop to observe slugs up close or breathe in the scent of wildflowers, rosemary and deep shades of green? Do they discern the rolling crunch of gravel underfoot, examine the uneven smoothness of pebbles, cherish the sight of wet clay staining their palms a rusty red?

And the blackberries: How can they pass a thicket without plucking off a few choice gems?

What a good earth. A blessing.

I kneel by the side of the road, watching a snail clamber over a rock. A couple of pilgrims speed by, as if propelled by invisible tailwinds. The heady days of pushing my body past its limit—training for a half-marathon; playing tennis, floor hockey and softball; cycling on blistering cold mornings; competing in dragon boat races—have passed. In this new normal, my body has been forced to slow down. But old habits and dreams don't die so easily. My body is still gripped by the aches and longings for speed, for the promise and thrill of beating my opponents… and for the lean, toned muscles that once resided within. One glance at an Amazon-like apparition gliding so effortlessly past me, is all the reminder I need: Gratitude. Granditude. Greatitude. Because, hell ya, I can walk.

Chapter 18: A Thicket of Perplexities

A hint of conflict crackles in the airspace between Juan-Do and me. When I need to slow down and rest, Juan-Do ignores me and marches on, his puny metal pot, tied to the Carrix, clanging each time the cart negotiates bumps, as if it was a cowbell. But the metal pot is a godsend, an alarm that alerts me to his presence nearby, as much as its silence confirms his absence. When Juan-Do packs away the pot, all bets are off: there's no telling if I'll lose him entirely to the woods.

"Go on!" The gruff sound of his admonition nearly chars my ears. We trudge on, Juan-Do pulling ahead as if to signal his need for solitary containment.

***

Even though the girl learned four languages, none of them trained her for the jumble of harsh sounds that became the new and unstable foundation of her life, interrupted.

***

A short break and chat with a Japanese pilgrim translate into losing sight of Juan-Do. Unmotivated to catch up, I dawdle through the next village. More signs of the times. The ubiquitous Se Vende placards are plastered everywhere. New housing development projects have ground to a halt, sprouting weeds and bushes. Unused construction materials pile up, collecting cobwebs, dust and yellowed envelopes. Unfinished sections of newly-paved roads fall off into fields, leading nowhere. It's a moonscape of distress.

As the sun rises behind me, spreading its warmth, like a cream-colored ink blot into the midday sky, somewhere up ahead, Juan-Do is walking through his own orbit, schlepping our bags over sticks and stones. Words are kept to a minimum, meted out in small and unexpected doses, as if speech might rob him of walking fuel. I have no idea how to penetrate his thick veil of silence, the glaring absence of dialogue confounding. I feel lost, stranded in a thicket of perplexities; do I speak up—or leave him alone?

***

She loved the sound of words. But some words the girl would never learn to utter, while others she would banish from her vocabulary. Words became weapons. One word alone might make shut her down, freeze, withdraw deep inside of herself, like a threatened barnacle retracting. The girl backed out of life, devised her own written sign language, occasionally wondered whether she would ever encounter her doppelgänger; the stranger whose body might house the spirit of her life-in-waiting. Then, she withdrew from her own body and stopped wondering at all.

Chapter 19: SNORPS

At the albergue in Azofra, Juan-Do disappears down a hallway while I'm matched up with another woman. I'm almost guaranteed to have a quiet, snoreless sleep. But my hope is short-lived, and misplaced.

This pilgrim's snuffles are a tour de force. Her snores are like a power saw let loose on a forest of trees.

In the middle of the night, I grab my sleeping gear and Shrek-pack, and retreat to a hard bench in the corridor outside our room while heavy rains pelt the ground and stain the windows with abstract washes that look like melted silver pellets trickling down. Too uncomfortable to fall asleep, I question the wisdom of assigning rooms by gender. Perhaps there is a better way: Separate vigorous snorers from silent sleepers. Set up soundproof rooms to accommodate Snoring Pilgrims (SNORPS), so that others may rest. Remove the stigma—and prevent inevitable morning hostilities.

Still sleepless at 6 a.m., I peek out of my sleeping bag, probably looking as tattered and groggy as I feel. Well-rested pilgrims file by my post, questioning my choice of bed. I give up, get up and drag my belongings back to the room, where the nasal noises persist. If only I could call the SNORP Busters.

With my earplugs still in place, I empty all the contents of my pack on the bed, in order to re-pack. A card with a photo slips out, fluttering to the floor. I pick it up and stare at the image for a few long minutes. The robed man's softly lined face, boyish grin and sparkling eyes remind me that, even this is not so serious.

"Let go of your judgment," I can almost hear his Holiness the

Dalai Lama instructing me from within the laminated plastic sheet, "who among us is not imperfect?" I don't need his physical presence to understand that this isn't about the woman snoring inches away from me; it's as much about Juan-Do as it is about myself.

Shortly after 7:30 a.m., under heavily overcast skies, Juan-Do and I head out of Azofra.

"*Buenos días,*" I hazard a greeting. A smile. Maybe this day will be better. Maybe the ice will thaw again. Maybe he will be in a better mood. Maybe he will want to talk with me.

But as if he's not heard me, Juan-Do calls up his mantra.

"Go on."

El Carrix, our silent partner, fills the gap between us.

It is hard to determine whether chronic alienation or sleepless nights are to blame for the spiked pain. Not that it matters much; I slow down my pace, and seek my balance without stumbling.

Juan-Do seems oblivious to my physical predicament. Even if I spell it out: "*me duele.*" I'm in pain. If Otto has shared with him anything at all about my accident and chronic pain, this wordless caballero offers up no hint of this knowledge.

Juan-Do is on auto-pilot, bent over, his chin almost disappearing into the notch of his neck. The Carrix trails behind, listlessly, like a beast of burden losing strength. I want to ask if he needs a rest; and I ache to know why he so diligently, mercilessly, keeps to himself. But I balk. Anything I say could set him off; he might bark or ignore me entirely. There's nothing left to do but leave him to himself, his thoughts, maybe his misery.

***

The girl moved with her family into a large three-floor home designed by her engineer-father and architect-grandfather. Near the far end of the upstairs corridor was a bathroom perpetually bathed in sunlight and wall tiles featuring a 1970s motif that looked like a repetitive pattern of hiccups—on psychedelics. On one wall of the bathroom, which the girl shared with her two sisters, was affixed a poster with a poem: Children

*Learn What They Live. It stared her squarely in the face every time she
walked in, mocking her hopes and dreams.*

***

I turn to my surroundings. They are more responsive, pulsating with
infinitely more life than Juan-Do. Last night's downpour translated
into this morning's crop of sweet smelling grass, wet earth and pebbles that almost shimmer in the light. Further along, a garden of
kale blooms. Plucking off a few leaves to munch on, I crouch down
low, to watch snails and slugs gliding up stalks of wheat. A steaming
mound of fresh dung. A pile of leaves. Weeds. Mulch. So much shit.

Chapter 20: The Stagers

Two pilgrims steam by me at race-pace: Stagers. Hardcore followers of a man called John Brierley. Or more precisely, devotees of his *Guide to the Camino de Santiago*. A.k.a. the pilgrim's bible. More concisely referred to as Brierley, this thick handbook breaks down the Camino into stages; each day's stage circumscribed by distance, exact altitude, and availability of accommodation. I meet dozens of pilgrims who swear by this guide; leaving nothing to chance or detour. "Brierley says to go to… ", "Brierley suggests skipping… " Diehard Stagers sound like the students of an invisible guru.

Another troop of Stagers zips by; a blur of bodies, rustling nylon and Camino patches sewn onto backpacks. A thwack-thwack of poles strikes the ground as they pass. Two heavyset women, trailing behind, are much slower to overtake me. Turning my head sideways, I watch them trudge on with great effort and reddened faces. I recognize one of the women. Dear nameless pilgrim: I will walk for you today, because I want to believe that you have no idea how much your deafening snores kept me up all night.

As we reach Ciriñuela, I flag down Juan-Do, placing my hand on the small of my back—as if to indicate that I need a rest. He slows down and I crumple to the ground. Without a word, Juan-Do springs into action, yanking a foil-covered mat out from the Carrix, and unfurling it without a word.

"Lie down," he says, grumpiness forming at the edge of his voice.

"Gracias." I don't know what to make of this surprising gesture. One minute he ignores me, the next he plays the hero.

I'm sprawled out on my back, and squinting against the sun. The pain and harshness of light transports me back to an emergency room in a country far away with bright fluorescent bulbs peeling my eyelashes apart. I remember the urgent sound of voices responding to a code red. The nurses who tended to me, cutting through my shirt and pants, scurrying away mid-cut. A swell of Chinese New Year casualties required immediate triage. Young men who suffered eye injuries and skin burns; children who tumbled from palm trees, ending up with broken backs and legs.

Another burst of white light cleaves through the clouds. Sunlight also streamed into the spotless hospital ward through doors and windows, bathing the room in precious calm. Not long after I came to, a male Italian nurse with a shock of red hair and freckles cautiously shimmied me off the bed and onto a gurney. He wheeled me into a shower room at the far end. He slowly undressed me. He soaped my skin, hosed me down, toweled me dry and put me back into clothes. I had never been touched, bathed, caressed, tended to, by a man, so gently, so carefully. Seized by indescribable pain, I let go of tears. I fell asleep while he wheeled me back to bed.

***

The girl did not know that her body was keeping score, so that when ulcers ravaged the unseen linings of her stomach and soul, and when a near-death collapse and years of anaphylactic episodes transported her, with sirens turned to silence, into the ER where a battery of tests was performed, none of which would offer a conclusive diagnosis, and when nobody in the hospital or elsewhere thought to ask, "what happened to you?" she would remain lost on the trail of her life.

***

Juan-Do is standing almost directly above me, blocking out the sun. He doesn't say a word; doesn't need to. He is antsy to move on. I struggle to stand up. As soon as I re-tie the mat to the Carrix, my back goes into spasms again.

"*No possible!*" I moan.

Juan-Do keeps walking as if he hasn't heard me; unaware that each rebuff reopens wounds and hidden scars.

Abandonada.

With my eyes closed, it feels as if a wedge of forged steel is permanently lodged in my backside, its massive weight and bulk dragging my body into the ground, or deeper still, as if an anchor were plunging me into an unseen sea. I kneel to the ground, and see that Juan-Do has stopped ahead. Even from afar, I can read the weariness in his stoop. I turn away, hoping that a pilgrim will show up.

Reaching my hand down the rear of my pants, I massage the skin covering the bony zone and nerve endings at the top of my butt. It's all flesh: There was no operation, so metal bits do not reside inside. For obvious reasons, I'm reluctant to rub my rear end in public; but here, the absence of human life gives me license to knead my pain away. Nothing to do but stay put, until the spike subsides and fizzles away.

I turn around in time for a slight breeze to lift up from the road, sending specks of dust into my mouth. There is a high perimeter fence at the roadside that I haven't noticed before. Behind it, lies a gentle rolling landscape of lush, perfectly manicured grass—with not a soul in sight. An incongruous scene, compared to the unpaved road and lack of other greenery within sight. *No possible!* A golf course? Here?!

The mirage takes a back seat while I struggle to stand up. Cresting the top of the hill at killer slow speed, I see Juan-Do lean against a railing, staring into space. Waiting. I expect the worst, a tirade. But when I get closer, he suggests that I get more rest. "When you feel better," he says, "walk to Cirueña, not far away. I will wait at the rotonda."

I hobble along, bewildered by an ominous silence that envelops me. The abandoned golf course is not the only sign of desertion. Ciriñuela is a ghost town unlike any other that I will walk through. On either side of a newly paved boulevard, is an endless expanse of newly built homes and apartment buildings. All of them are empty. Dried and overgrown weeds have taken over unkempt gardens, sneaking up fences and walls. Windows are tightly shuttered, doors locked. Gaping holes and unused light fixtures decorate the walls. Cables dangle from ceilings, unconnected, leading nowhere. Parks, pool and playground are all deserted. A place of broken dreams. Posted on a fence, a placard reads: *Soliciones por el crisis.*

Walking towards wind-smeared clouds as the wasteland fades behind me, I pray that the crisis has not hit Cirueña to this extent, effacing all signs of life. I breathe a sigh of relief at the sight of locals, cars, dogs and the rotonda. But Juan-Do is nowhere to be seen. After a few minutes of waiting, I give up and walk towards a sign that beckons so insistently it might as well be neon-lit: Casa Victoria. Ahhhh, an albergue. This will do. I can finally lie down. I'll leave it to Juan-Do to find me.

Chapter 21: Pit Stop in Crueña (or How We Avoided the Plague)

The middle-aged owners of Casa Victoria, Maria and Patxi, welcome me with open arms, a cup of hot chocolate and a room of my own where four single beds, decorated in chintzy, mismatched bedcovers, nestle up close to each other. The low ceiling and lace-fringed window coverings give the 2nd-storey room a cozy feel akin to a country inn. A spacious en suite bathroom is an added bonus which I max out by luxuriating in a hot shower, scrubbing off the day's chill until it disappears into thick clouds of steam.

Toweling myself off in plush cotton, a framed print on the wall catches my eye. It is a familiar procession of costumed figures, a towering mountain in the background framing the scene. *No possible!* It's Bali. I move in closer to decode the signature: Ny Silaga, Ubud. My current hometown that once was a traditional Balinese village. I gasp, momentarily breathless, not so much because of the unlikelihood of discovering a print from Ubud hanging in a bathroom so many thousands of kilometers away; but because this moment captures the immediacy that we crave, of sharing an extraordinary sight or experience with another human being. Here and now, there are none.

Downstairs, Maria and I settle into couches in their living room, while Patxi prepares cups of tea. Their dog Toby, a shaggy little thing, flops down at my feet. Before I have a chance to ask them about the Balinese print, the front door opens, letting in a gust of wind and a bleak-looking figure, wearing a face of discontent.

"*¿Porque no attende me en el rotonda?*" he stammers. Why didn't you wait at the roundabout?

Trappings of a marital spat.

I place my tea cup into the saucer, climb the stairs, and settle onto the fluffy, flowery duvet for a nap. Moments later, Juan-Do lumbers in noisily with our bags, heaves them onto the floor and goes into the bathroom for a shower. A cloud of eucalyptus-scented steam wafts out of the bathroom behind Juan-Do as he flings open the door with a dramatic flourish. He picks up his phone, punches in a number and carries on an interminably loud conversation—as if oblivious to my presence.

After he leaves, I slide into an afternoon nap that extends to 4:30 a.m. Dragging my sore body into the bathroom, and back to bed, its message to me is clear: I'm in no shape to walk. Three hours later, I awake to the usual swooshing sounds of a pilgrim's dawn. Juan-Do, fully dressed, is stuffing away his gear.

"*No puedo caminar,*" I say, my voice sounding like a hoarse whisper.

The wordless man stops mid-pack, straightens up and leaves the room. I fall back asleep.

When I awake again, close to midday, I feel like my body has been wrestled to a pulp. The aroma of coffee and breakfast ropes me in and draws me downstairs. Patxi takes one look at me and leaves the room. Minutes later, he returns with a gel pack, which he places in the microwave. I settle onto the couch and wait for the bell. With the nuked pack warming my nether regions, Maria tutors me in Spanish and cooking, and Toby—who, true to his species, perks up at the sniff of pain—curls up on the floor beside me. I am home.

To quell my curiosity about the painting's origins, Patxi offers me a cane, then leads me upstairs and through a dusty roomful of grandfather clocks and tchotchkes. From deep behind the remnants of his antique-collecting days, Patxi fetches another Balinese print, faded, streaked and embalmed in gossamer.

When we return to the kitchen, Juan-Do is sitting at the table, dunking cookies into a cup of tea. Maria and Patxi get busy. The pup is nowhere to be seen. I feel inexplicably suffocated. Do I say something, do I not?

***

It was not easy for the girl to ask questions, even simple ones like, can I go to the mall tomorrow? Even if she thought far enough ahead, biting her nails to the quick, trying so hard to construct a question in a way that might preempt the inevitable, and even if she approached carefully and obsequiously, almost excusing her existence, still the girl would stammer and hesitate, holding back from so much terror, feeling like the world might possibly fall apart even more than it already had, until she dared to let words form through her lips, when all she heard, coming at her like a thunder clap bolting out of grey clouds, causing fear and trembling, was "Spit it out!", laden with impatience and wrath, but disguised behind a heady swirl of normalcy, high heels, a broach of coral set in gold and the sharp scent of L'Air du Temps.

***

A knock at the door is followed by a familiar lilt. "Helloooo?" The sound of salvation. The voice of light. My lifeline.

As always, Mani's arrival is perfectly timed, uncannily so: She has no clue that we are staying here. The ease with which we pick up from where we last left off, only serves to magnify the gaping distance between Juan-Do and me. No topic is too sacred or silly for us to delve into: religion, loneliness, family, relationships, death.

"When my friend Miko was young," Mani recounts, "and she misbehaved, her father would get upset. Once, he picked up a piece of wood, gave it to Miko and told her to hit him with it. When Miko asked him why, he said that he must have done something very wrong for her to act so badly."

No further explanations needed. With Mani, I am on terra firma.

While she and Juan-Do go upstairs to nap, I head out for a short walk around the neighborhood.

At one edge of the village, far from prying eyes, I bend over into downward dog and almost immediately hear sounds from a distance. An elderly couple approaches, the man seated in a wheelchair with his wife navigating from behind.

"*Buenos días,*" I offer. They ignore me as they pass.

I fold over again, my forehead almost touching the ground, when a voice calls out with a sense of urgency. I look up to see the wheelchair parked further down the street, and the man flailing his arms. His wife is gone. I hurry over to the man's perch and look over the edge. From an orchard of fig trees below, the wife waves to me. She can't clamber up the slope to the sidewalk and motions for me to help pull her up. *How did she end up down there?* I wonder. Shaking my head, I swivel and place my hand on the small of my back.

"*Perdon,*" I call out, "*no puede. Me duele.*"

As if deaf to my words, she continues to wave and shout. I walk off in search of rescue, certain that she interprets my inability for apathy. A man snipping bushes in his garden obliges and dashes off.

Retracing my steps to Casa Victoria, and the flower-bedecked bedroom, I'm startled to find Juan-Do and Mani sitting on top of the frilly floral linens, deep in conversation. A wisp of envy lands in my gut. When they pause, Juan-Do turns to me, under the watchful gaze of chintzy wallpapered birds and the light of a Balinese rural scene.

"*Tu eres la principessa del Camino,*" he says, as if reenacting the chivalry of Don Quixote, saving people from themselves, including the helpless Dulcinea. Like the mythical knight-errant himself, maybe Juan-Do too had lost parts of himself, and set out from his country refuge to conquer the Camino. "*Solo caminar.*" You're the Camino princess, he says, and all you need to do is walk.

The next morning, our sporadic threesome ties up our gear, eats breakfast, packs snacks, parts from Maria and Patxi, and heads out the door. Reaching the Camino trailhead, there is no doubt that I will walk today in honor of this lovely couple.

When we arrive at the small village of Granon, we stop in at the *oficina turismo.*

"Do you want to stay here?" asks the stern clerk behind the desk. "Sorry, you cannot. The albergue is closed!"

It's still too early in the season for an albergue to shut down.

"*¿Porque cerrado?*" I ask.

"*Epidemica de chinches.*" The dreaded curse of the Camino: bedbugs.

The cobblestoned road that passes through Granon is eerily quiet, virtually deserted, save for a handful of locals cycling by. A couple of pilgrims seek a clinic and a courtyard—to smoke out the bugs, disinfect their backpacks and burn ruined clothes. In the vicinity of the condemned albergue, more travelers huddle and talk in muffled whispers. News travels fast along the Camino; bad news even faster. When you factor in the internet and a certain social networking site, any news of bedbugs spreads like wildfire. By the time we leave the village, and see Granon receding into the distance behind us, I half-expect to see the grim reaper astride a stallion, dashing out of a thick haze, galloping wildly past us in search of a witch or medicine man.

Chapter 22: The Gift of Mani

By six o'clock the next morning, the Stager clan is up, ready to rustle and rush.

I emerge from my sleep state, look up at the ceiling, and mull over my predicament—more precisely, the enigma that is Juan-Do. Why does he ignore me? When he distances himself, when Mani is not around, nature is my panacea: *Moras* (blackberries). *Higos* (figs). *Árboles de manzana* (apple trees). And sunflowers. But the human factor is missing. Perplexedly, achingly rebuffed.

***

Fixing her gaze downward, past her dark blue school uniform and sensible saddle shoes, the girl, whose brain could not compute the damning words that flooded her ears, wondered what superhuman powers she could acquire that would let her body seep through the juice-stained carpet fibers, the floor, the concrete foundation, and, finally, into the earth's dark core.

***

Even if Mani weaves, unpredictably, in and out of my Camino, she is a constant and stabilizing presence. And even if twenty years, countries, careers, or culture separate us, we have more in common than what meets the eye. Empathy is part of our epoxy.

"I have a rare blood disease," says Mani, pulling out a compact blood testing unit. Chronic, and potentially fatal. "So I have to monitor my blood count every day." Her disorder, a blood mutation that was discovered only two decades ago, has an exotic-sounding name: Faktor

V Leiden. Every Sunday, Mani pulls a small medical kit out of her pack, tests her blood and injects herself with a dose of life-saving medication.

"I need to keep track of how long it takes my blood to… " she hesitates, "I don't know the word in English."

"Coagulate," I say.

The blood checks keep her on course—and alive. She might be in an albergue, in a tent, or in love. Blood checks do not take a holiday; and the Camino is no exception.

"I'm lucky," she continues. "I have a way to control the disease."

We veer onto the subject of pictograms that we see plastered on buses, trains and boats around the world; all those that identify the sub-set of passengers who are entitled to priority seating: Silhouettes of an elderly person carrying a cane. A wheelchair. A woman with her leg in a cast. A pregnant woman. An infant in a stroller.

"In Thailand," I say, "monks get special treatment. There's even a space on boats reserved for monks *to stand*." All of those traits, visible. "Why don't pictograms exist for invisible conditions and pain, like ours?" I ask. "Let's make one."

"Then we can tattoo it on our foreheads," Mani chimes in, "so everyone can see."

This too is part of our glue: We have both met our share of skeptics.

"I was on a train once," says Mani, sitting cross-legged on the floor between the bunk beds as she readies herself for an exam. "I wasn't feeling well, so I had to put my feet up on the seat across from me." She takes a deep breath and glances outside.

"A woman started to scold me," Mani says, shaking her head, the distress of the incident resurfacing. "She told me I was rude and had to put my feet on the ground. I tried to tell her it was for medical reasons, but she wouldn't listen."

"I wonder what kind of proof would have helped that woman believe you," I say, trying to conjure up logos that we could Sharpie-ink onto each other's forehead, "not that you owe her any."

"Maybe if I had that tattoo … " Mani says, not skipping a beat. We laugh, from a knowing that transcends all borders and beliefs.

Chapter 23: Of Crusty Bread and Peppers

On the way to Villambistia, Mani confides about her connection to a divine spirit. "I have such a deep love of God," she says, "because I feel him so strongly in my life and he is always there for me." Unlike Mani, I am steeped in skepticism, repelled by the idea of praying to a single, higher power. Growing up with two parents who immigrated to Canada from Israel, I was brought up anchored more firmly in a secular world. Even if I attended Jewish schools and camp, and my family celebrated Jewish holidays, we mostly paid lip service to religious practice.

Along with other beliefs, my own religious faith was shattered early, when I wised up to widespread hypocrisy and untenable dogma. Judaism, like Swiss cheese, was full of holes. It took a fall from a bridge to ignite my belief in the possibility of unseen spirits and guardian angels—only through which I could start to understand the unexplainable and serendipitous mysteries of my survival and life. But my faith in humanity and justice? Still largely deficient.

Before we reach Villambistia, I hear the unmistakable sound of a dog whining, yelping. He is bound to a chain fence. Another balcony dog. Struggling to free himself, he leaps in every direction, the chain yanking him back whenever he stretches the limits of his tether. There is no water bowl, no pile of food, no caretaker in sight. I make a mental note to bring him food, seek out his owner.

We reach the one and only albergue—which doubles as the village's sole café. I register with the hospitalero, climb the stairs and splay across a top bunk by a window with finely laced curtains; while Juan-Do and Mani choose lower bunks. After a nap, I wander downstairs and out to the terrace, where I join a couple of local pensioners drinking in the shade.

"In the winter season, not many residents live here," says José, nursing a beer. "Usually only about thirty. It's very empty and quiet."

The population of Villambistia increases during summer, he says, when a few hundred city dwellers—like José—escape the curdling heat in urban centers for the cooler climes and softer rhythms that a country life affords. "I live in Burgos," says José, pointing to a gated home across the road, "but I come here on weekends. It's better to leave my worries in the city, so I can come here to relax with my friends." In Villambistia, he is a man of leisure.

Later in the afternoon, down a quiet road, I follow the trail of a smell I cannot easily identify. A swarm of retirees mills about, inside an empty mechanic's garage. Some stack cardboard boxes, others sit in collapsible beach chairs, surrounded by pipes, discarded car parts, and rusted machines. Once I isolate and bypass the sharp odors of petrol, oil and grease, I realize something else is cooking. I peek into their hive of activity, and find them roasting red peppers in large batches, which I am told they will savor through the infertile winter months. "We don't make these to sell," says an elder, "it's only for us and our families." He picks out and hands me a freshly-roasted sliver, still warm and caramelizing at the edges. Which is how, despite a lack of religious faith, I get a taste of the divine.

***

A lady with a beehive on her head stood behind the display case at the bakery, from where she handed the girl a pinwheel cookie with chocolate sprinkles that delighted her each time. But even the sweetness of this treat could not erase the lingering nausea of fish congealed in aspic that had to be eaten, even if it was the following morning before school with no dog to sneak it to and even if tears streamed down her cheeks.

***

Before we leave the albergue the next morning, I ask the hospitalero for yesterday's leftover bread.

"*Por el perro,*" I explain. For the dog.

As I fling the stale pieces towards the shackled dog, I watch him devour its crust and crumbs. Only the most desperate and famished of creatures will devour these tasteless and rock-hard remnants.

Mani decides to power on ahead; she craves faster speed today. We part ways.

"Go on!" Juan-Do blurts out as he marches by, his head held high. I watch the crotchety character from behind, noticing that his shoes sink into the soft ground, leaving his sole's markings embedded in muddy patches of earth.

I pull out my phone. "*Hola! ¿Que tal?*" I write to Otto. "Can u please come and save a neglected dog? *Bitte com aqui pronto!*" If anyone can understand my tri-linguistic gibberish, Otto can. And if anyone can save one more dog, Otto can. "I saw so many dogs on the Camino that were locked up or beaten," Otto had said during our week together, "I had to rescue them." He brought them to shelters and friends' homes. "I'm sorry for the dog," Otto replies soon after. "But I can't save every dog that is treated badly on the Camino."

"Please Otto!" I am this close to writing back. "He who saves the life of one dog saves the world."

Juan-Do is a few hundred meters ahead. Mani is probably by now sipping café con leche in the next village. As for myself, I decide to walk for the love of an abandoned dog. And may a villager bring him a bowl of roasted red peppers.

Chapter 24: You Get What You Need

"Are you with him?" is a question I'm frequently asked. I get tongue-tied. Do you mean: Am I walking with him? Are we walking together? Or were we thrown together by circumstance? From all appearances, yes. There was intention. Some degree of expectation. Remote agreement. But in every other way, most definitely not.

We are still two strangers, Juan-Do and I, walking out of synch, our parallel vectors intersecting throughout the day. Even in close proximity, we mostly walk in silence. Not the silence of an extended pause in conversation, which results from unspoken mutual accord; nor a silence borne of contemplative thought. Not the instructive silence of Vipassana meditation, where a group might gather for ten days or more for an immersion into collective stillness; nor the silence of John Cage's "4'33"—where, for four minutes and thirty-three seconds, a musician sits in front of a piano, motionless, upending the audience's expectation of sonorous tunes by leading them instead through a desert of soundlessness. Nothing at all like Berlin's Raum der Stille (Room of Silence), an oasis of quiet steps away from the crowds milling about the Brandenburg Gate. Rather, ours is an invisible cone wedged in between us, demanding distance and collusion.

In the absence of dialogue, my search for blackberries—and signs from the universe—resumes.

A wooden bench on one side of the path, looks starved for company. It might have welcomed Juan-Do and I onto its seat, an ad hoc confession-chamber-without-walls, for us to breach the silence. But Juan-Do marches right past that opportunity.

Into the bench's weathered back is chiseled a familiar song title: "I Did It My Way." As if. If I had it my way: I would cover less ground every day and I would be walking with someone who opted for speech. Barring all that, doing it my way would mean telling Juan-Do to take a hike.

From Sinatra, I soon move onto The Rolling Stones, channeling Keith and Co. *You can't always get what you want.* Then, as if in answer to my angst, I see that Mani is dawdling up ahead. *You get what you need.*

"It's so frustrating!" I blurt out once we're in step again. "Sometimes, I think it would be better for me to stop walking, or to find another way to reach Santiago… I want him to go away." Which, of course, is exactly what he does, at least for part of each day; disappearing into an invisible and impenetrable cocoon of his own making. To Juan-Do, this protracted silence might be precisely the reason he signed up for sherpa-duty in the first place: An answer to his prayers. An escape from the tumult of his life. An affordable way to walk the Camino. Nothing more. But on this side of the Carrix, it's my daily dose of rejection.

After unplugging from her MP3 (*MP-drei*, in German)—a little gadget into which she ruminates, intones prayers and sings, Mani talks me down from a ledge.

"I know, he can't communicate well," she says. "But he's doing what he can." I don't have the heart to ask her to walk one kilometer in my sandals.

***

Instead of smoking pot with friends, the girl pulled weeds from the garden. Instead of hanging out at the movies, she hung laundry. Instead of making out with a boyfriend in his bedroom, she escaped into hers, alone in the darkness, where she prayed for an end.

Chapter 25: El Padre del Isabel

It is late-morning on a cloudy Saturday when we reach the municipal albergue in Villafranca Monte de Oca.

Mani and I head out in search of food. We end up at a roadside diner with grimy walls, artificial flowers, and seated patrons diving into plates piled high with mushy-looking food from the buffet stand. The total bill for our lunch comes out to 20 euros—a princely sum for a barely edible meal that leaves us both feeling leaden and nauseous. My digestive tract screams for Coke—sugar and unpronounceable preservatives be damned. Gratefully, the tienda around the corner is fully stocked.

When we return to the albergue with a stash of staples, the sun emerges. Behind the building, we find a sprawling courtyard where pilgrims hang laundry and guzzle pints of beer. Mani and I find a spot in the shade and down our Cokes lazily.

Under the hazelnut tree, we talk about God, religion, men, travel, friendship and music. "I love my people," Mani says, referring to her family. She speaks of her parents—who emigrated with Mani and her three siblings from Communist Romania to Germany, even though they did not speak the language—with genuine admiration. She tells me about the breakdown of her long-term relationship, about quitting her job and returning to live in her parents' home. She recounts the story of a close friend who recently died.

Unrelated to time and space, and despite our unlikely bond, I feel like I have known Mani forever.

While Mani followed a more conventional route, studying social work and getting a job in that field, my career path—if one could call it that—had meandered; from graphic design to law, from television production to genealogical research and public investigations. I wandered from one gig to another; from data entry at a coat manufacturing factory to clerking in an art store, where I had to retrieve change from the owner with nicotine-stained fingers and breath, who kept all the cash in his pocket. For a short time, I rendered concept ads for Honda cars while sniffing toxic-smelling markers, and edited wedding videos and documentaries in a room the size of a matchbox, for a medical doctor who never once apologized for his blatant and inexcusable dishonesty.

There were brief forays into industrial design—where I made minor and, frankly negligible, contributions to the design of a light sconce; into art gallery administration—where I would stare questioningly at a plate of orange-dyed water as it wobbled precipitously in the center of a revolving hydraulic steel base; into human rights research on xenophobia and police brutality in Europe; and into entertainment law, where early one fall morning, I gazed out the window from the upper reaches of an office high-rise, and into a cloudless sky, instinctively guessing that a secretary's comment—"a small plane just crashed into a building in New York"—did not come close to comprehending the carnage that would unfold over the day, and the extent of repercussions forever more.

In a way that I am not, Mani is intensely, unaffectedly religious. Her ruminations about religion compel me to question my preconceptions and to soften my stance. Mani's brand of religion is present and deeply personal. She neither wears a badge of faith on her sleeve, nor does she display any visible symbols of devotion to God and Jesus Christ. Her faith is rooted in an unshakable belief in the existence of a divine and sacred being. Even as she stands firm on her faith, she is not invulnerable to moments of seeking and self-doubt. "The act of knowing and believing in God isn't enough," says Mani. "He is my savior, so I need to also feel God in my heart."

There is joy in Mani's brand of religion. Joy in religious practice and prayer. Joy in speaking about God and Christ. Which stands in stark contrast to my own cynicism and alienation from religion. The Judaism that I found in private school and in Jerusalem—where I lived and studied for several years; and the Judaism that introduced me to the fouler side of my community, when an elder balked at my efforts to bring Judaism 'lite' to students at a non-denominational school; those experiences, among others, amplified the elitism and divisiveness that too often colors religious practice. I wanted little to do with any religion that preached compassion and integrity, but in reality, bred intolerance and condoned injustice. Those experiences sowed seeds of doubt inside my ever-probing soul. Which led me towards further disillusionment and dilution; plunging me into a void of belief in anything outside myself—which didn't count for much, seeing how badly my *self* had floundered.

Our friendship is midwifed not through our differences, and not even through our spoken or surface commonalities; rather through a host of intangibles. The Camino. Our heritage. Invisible impairments. A sense of humor. A curiosity and fascination with humanity. A penchant for the most basic form of communication: and, of course, the MP3, which quickly becomes a source of envy.

The coolness of dusk coaxes us inside. At the far end of the dorm room, Juan-Do is engrossed in conversation with the *hospitalera* and an older man sporting a salt-and-pepper beard, upturned pilgrim's hat and pensive look. A traditional pilgrim's cloak lies spread out on a lower bunk, a *bastón* nearby. This man—introducing himself as El Padre de Isabel—says that he uses the cloak rather than a blanket to keep himself warm at night. From his posture and soft-spoken speech, I presume that his burden is a heavy one.

Over the next hour, as the sun sets and the wind whistles, this man tells us about his daughter's murder. A law student, Isabel was kidnapped one night in 2004, then raped and killed. The news made headlines around Spain and shattered her father's life. Ever since, El Padre de Isabel keeps her memory alive by walking the Camino. He wears the same clothes; a t-shirt onto which is printed a photo of his daughter and a simple phrase: *Yo queremos Isabel*. I love you Isabel. This man will inhabit the Camino until his last dying breath.

Not surprisingly, my sleep that night is, at best, spotty and restless. The top bunk is no salve; not when I feel so gutted by the story, which surprisingly triggers memories of a man with a mustache cornering me in the mail room of my Toronto apartment building that might as well have been a meat freezer, for all the frozenness I felt before I returned to my body and fled.

A flash of fluorescence stings my eyes: an overly-keen pilgrim has switched on the lights. I squint at my watch. It's 6:15 and still dark outside. Normally, I might be plotting revenge. But this morning, I feel grateful; the floodlights put an end to the wretchedness of the night.

Eventually, I adjust to the dawn's greyness as its amorphousness filters through the window, and across the room, leaving a momentary mark on each bed. When I turn to my side, I see that Mani and Juan-Do haven't budged, unfazed by the onslaught of light. El Padre lies on the lower bunk near mine, as still as a wax figure; his face giving no indication of the pain that is his daily bread. On the pilgrim's cloak, there is a patch in the shape of a rose, with Isabel's name stitched beside it.

***

Lying on her bed at night, squeezed up against the wall, the girl stared at the tiny bumps of cream-white paint and wondered what it would take to shrink herself into an atom small enough to pass through the wall and into nothingness, where no living being would dare to tread. And when her grandfather died, she wailed at the sky, wishing only that she could have gone with him.

***

When he awakes, the look in the old man's eyes tells of agony and absence. It will haunt me for a long time, knowing that that far-off gaze might well have been my father's, had I not survived that mighty fall through a bridge in rural Cambodia.

Even before I step out into that day's generous helping of radiant warmth and sunshine, I know that I will walk today for El Padre de Isabel.

Chapter 26: The 'Strayan

When a steep slope rises ahead of me, its top sunk into the surrounding fog, I pray silently for the timely appearance of a lower-altitude detour as an insistent chill settles into my bones. The path is full of rocks and mud; a gritty juxtaposition against the incandescent pink wildflowers poking out from the weeds. As if oblivious to sallow fields and leaves of brown, the pine trees offer up a scent that tickles my nose. Acorns, *castañas* (chestnuts) and pine needles carpet the path ahead, while clouds hover only slightly above ground, as if threatening suffocation by cumulus.

Up ahead, Mani drags her heels, the usual bounce in her step replaced by a slow trudge. My guess is that she's in intimate conversation with her MP-drei; perhaps reaching out for divine guidance. "Are you there, God? It's me, Mani."

Mani finds salvation in saints, while I find mine in Mani's mere presence. Redemption enough.

The combination of a loaded Carrix and grey sky matter seems to drag the usually slumped-over Juan-Do deeper down than usual; as if weighed down by an air of resignation. He stops and steps aside. Shaking off the harness, he removes the boater and slings it over his shoulder. I stop behind him, anticipating an event.

He walks over to an immense tree, its circumference alone dwarfing him, and stands with his face within inches of the bark. With outstretched arms and a glance skyward, he grips the trunk with both arms, as if the strength of his grasp provides a bulwark against the tree's inevitable decay. He remains in that position, looking glued to the tree, for a few minutes, while I watch from afar and feel, in a way that defies reason, like a woman spurned.

Later, because Juan-Do says that trees call to him, I will ask him about the hugging.

"I pull the energy up from the tree's roots," he says. "It transfers into my body."

It is a strange and not-so-wonderful thing, his behavior. Juan-Do only speaks to me on his terms, most often to pontificate on one subject or another. But he will go to great lengths to embrace a silent chunk of bark.

I know. I KNOW. To preserve my sanity, I should leave Juan-Do to his devices and destiny. But I can't help wanting to ask: *Why do you prefer a tree to me?*

***

All one had to do was puncture through the thickly textured bark that encased the girl, chisel through layers of growth-rings, under which anyone would find not cells multiplying and muscles pumping, not blood flowing freely through arteries, but one solid mass of shame.

***

The misery of being shunned begins to lift the moment I spot a field of sunflowers, stretching off to the horizon. A bright yellow sea of textured surfaces welcomes me into its midst, as if it were a park full of children, standing neck to neck, and beaming from ear to ear. The face of every flower, sculpted into smiley faces or initials, by pilgrims who have picked off strategically placed seeds, opens towards the sun.

As Juan-Do trudges up an incline, coaxing his tired body into slow movement, his face is inches from the muddy earth. He reaches level ground, stands more erect, picks up the pace, and as if he were nothing more than a figment of my imagination, disappears into a cloud of thick fog.

En route to the village of Agés, we reach the barren plateau of

Sierra Atapuerca. Through the cloak of heavy mist, I squint hard and see a circular formation made of rocks, as if it has risen out of the earth: a labyrinth. Unlike me, Mani has never heard of labyrinths, let alone seen one.

"Historically, they were used to defend or conquer territories," I answer her searching eyes, "or they were carved into cave walls. But nowadays, they're designed for meditation and healing. I actually made one at a silent retreat center in Bali."

I ask Mani if she has any experience with meditation. "Once, I meditated about living and dying," Mani says. "I told my family that when I die, it will be okay, because it just means that I have to go somewhere else and do something else for a while." Mani moves on ahead, leaving me to chew on meditation, death and the purpose of labyrinths.

We arrive at the albergue in Agés, where the lively hospitalera offers us a soothing steaming cup of tea. Mani and I store our gear in an upstairs women's dorm room just large enough for two bunk beds. Mani conks out on the lower bunk and I head downstairs for a bite.

Long tables and benches are set out around the still-empty dining room. With no cushions in sight, I kneel on a bench at the far end, and order pasta. A young woman enters, and walks up to me.

"Do you mind if I join you?" she asks.

"Not at all," I say.

She dumps her pack, peels off layers and sits beside me. Without glancing at the menu, she orders chocolate and churros.

"What is that?" I ask.

"You'll see," she quips.

When her dish arrives, it's clear that I've been missing out on one of Spain's edible wonders. My plate of noodles looks downright dull next to her crisply fried, gooey-looking treat of fried dough filled with chocolate cream.

"Where are you from?" I ask, detecting a familiar accent.

"'Straya," she says, her inflection now familiar to me from living in Bali, which some jokingly call Australia's most northern territory, "but I lived in Toronto for a decade."

"Did you like living there?" I ask, curious to hear on which end of the love-hate-Toronto spectrum she would land.

"Do you think I would have lived in that city for ten years if I didn't like it?" she snaps back.

Ouch.

"So why did you leave?"

She flicks her hair back as if annoyed at the question.

"Because my sister had a baby," she says. "Reason enough?"

Yes, reason enough, to end the conversation, and flee. One grouch a day is all I can handle.

After lunch, I take a short nap and head out for a walk when my cell phone rings. It's my older sister—calling from the suburbs of Washington, D.C.; another metropolis that feels light years away from Agés.

***

On many nights, the girl and her older sister met in the middle of their bedroom—one elongated space, designed to be split into two rooms, at some future unspecified date, when the sisters would finally get along— playing a card game called Spit, in which each circle-shaped card was illustrated like an orange slice and featured the word "Florida" along its outer periphery. The sisters sat cross-legged on a plush blue, wall-to-wall 70s shag carpet, on either side of an invisible line that hypothetically divided the future separate bedrooms, mirror images of each other. The invisible line was bracketed at one end by two matching doors and on the other, by a full-length mirror. A gift more than a hindrance, it was there, at the borderline, a no-man's land, where they met at day's end, that the girl felt most closely connected to her sister. To the pulse of life. The only place where she truly felt seen.

***

I picture my sister eating breakfast in the sunlit kitchen of her home, sitting on a high-backed wooden chair, looking out the window onto an expansive, tree-lined backyard that doubles as a plein-air stage for a revolving cast of creatures: squirrels, robins, eagles, crows, butterflies, and the occasional errant deer. Sometimes she will point her cellphone camera at a bird on the railing or send photos of a doe nibbling at the grass. I might complain about the relentless infiltration of social media into private spheres of my life. But when you're far from the person who knows you best, who lives a life so radically different than your own, who wants to know how you're coping with your pain and silent partner, technology wins.

Long after I hang up and finish my tour of Agés, I head upstairs, where I find the churros-loving Aussie and her friend in the same room assigned to Mani and I.

Before 6:30 the next morning, the stillness is interrupted by a glass shattering on the bathroom floor. A flurry of expletives cascades from the neighboring bed—in a distinctly 'Strayan accent.

"Oh fuck!" shrieks the pilgrim with the short fuse.

And a very buenos días to you too.

By the time the accident-prone Aussie emerges from the bathroom, both women are fired up. The light is switched on, they begin to pack and talk noisily, as if blind and deaf to our presence. When they finally leave, amidst the renewed quiet of the room, the sound of uninterrupted breathing rises from below. How Mani can sleep through that entire commotion is mystifying. Bless her slumbering skills, for they are far superior to mine.

Chapter 27: Burgos Boot Camp

Most days, I manage to walk between 10-15 kilometers without too much effort or flare ups. But that is never enough for Juan-Do. If it was up to him, he would coax me past my limit. He insists on pushing on, as if waiting for me to break, or give up this charade. On this day—perhaps with Mani's presence a buffer—he marches far ahead, edging us towards a record 24 kilometers. Almost maniacally past my body's discomfort zone—as if we were bit players in the 1960s Oscar-winning drama *They Shoot Horses, Don't They?* where, in a dance marathon that turns grotesque, Juan-Do plays sleazy emcee Rocky, exploiting my weaknesses for his own ends, dragging us to our knees, if not towards our death.

I toy with the idea of stepping out of line, *à la Cirueña*, so he has no choice but backtrack with the Carrix to find me. But I don't want to crank up the heat, so I trudge on without a word.

Stopping in at a bar for lunch, Mani, Juan-Do and I order *bocadillos* (sandwiches; standard Camino fare—above all on Sundays). As resistant as I am to start up a conversation, I turn to Juan-Do, mid-bite.

"Do you have enough euros to walk the rest of the way until Santiago?" I ask, watching his battered hat cast a dark shadow across his sallow face, making him look a lot older than he probably is.

"*Sí.*" The one-word wonder.

After lunch, Juan-Do snaps himself into the Carrix harness, slumps over and goes on, his eyes pointing downwards, as if the earth were his soulmate.

For the rest of the day, while Mani dashes off ahead of us, an end-less stream of questions buzzes around my head. *Why doesn't he just quit? What keeps him tied to me? How can I lighten his load? Does he need to stop? Does he understand why I can't carry my own gear? What happened to him? Is he an alcoholic? Was he abused? Assaulted? Did he lose the love of his life? Have his children abandoned him?* But he is so unapproachable, so tightly strapped into an emotional straitjacket, that I shy away. Incommunicado, all the way.

Under sunny skies, Juan-Do and I reach the outskirts of Burgos, the capital of Castilla y León. A bridge ahead leads to the other side of the river.

"Shouldn't we cross here," I ask, "to reach the old Burgos center?"

Juan-Do assures me that the old city is on our side of the river. But I know how to read a map. Aside from which, a couple of local women confirm my hunch.

But, the Man of Few Words persists: "*¿No hay confidencia?*"

This again.

But as soon as he reaches the bridge, from where the spires of Burgos' iconic cathedral can be seen towering above the hodgepodge of medieval buildings and winding paths, he takes a sharp turn onto the span, trampling over another chance to thaw and bond, plowing towards the albergue without once turning around.

The public albergue, its entrance overlooking the Cathedral, is a gem of modern architecture and simplicity. A multi-storied shrine to min-imalist design, its interiors feature bunks tucked into wooden cubes, a shelf and nightlight nestled into the wall above each mattress, spar-kling clean bathrooms, vending machines, a spacious dining area and, most appealing of all: an elevator, a rare find in albergues.

I scout for beds with Juan-Do dawdling a few steps behind me, towing along his misshapen defiance. My bag hits the floor and he heads off to find a bottom bunk around the corner from mine. Mani, who arrived hours ago, is already unpacked. We leave Juan-Do to himself and set out for food.

The high midday sun drenches the old quarter, as much as ourselves, in warmth. Tourists and locals are lured to outdoor tables, where the cutlery and wine glasses sparkle. At a high table in front of the Café Royal, we perch on bar stools and order good food, while Mani twirls strands of hair away from her face. We pretend to be locals, rather than drab-looking pilgrims merely passing through. "Is that what WE look like?" I ask, as we dig into our salads, a mouthful of vino sputtering out of Mani's mouth.

After lunch, we split off in different directions. Mani heads to the cathedral for mass, while I seek refuge—and internet access—inside the sleek *biblioteca publica*.

Back at the albergue, I make a beeline for the elevator. As the doors are about to close, a group of Korean nuns shuffles in noisily. One of them points to the Nepali flag patch embroidered onto the back of my windbreaker.

"Oh! You go to Nepal?!" she blurts out. "Wow!"

"Yes," I say, "I trekked and taught English in a village school."

The nuns' eyes widen. "Very good, you do trekking!" Even as I walk out of the elevator, they continue to half-bow behind me—as if in tribute to my ascent.

Early the next morning, I'm jostled awake by a persistent banging that escalates in intensity as it approaches. A crazy person is whacking a stick against the side of each bunk. This is how the albergue manager introduces himself; shooing pilgrims out of bed long before checkout time.

"*Ariba, todos ariba!*" he yells. "*Salida antes las ocho!*" Get up and out before eight o'clock!

I have not been warned about the Burgos Boot Camp; where stragglers, dawdlers and sleep-inners are not welcome. So, it is a good thing after all, that I have not opted to rest up in these plush barracks.

Chapter 28: Overcoming Barriers

The spires jut up at dawn, against a steel and starry blue sky. Temperatures have plummeted overnight. When we emerge from the albergue, I am duly bundled up against the icy chill that penetrates through thick layers of fiber. I exhale a cloud of my own making.

On our way out of Burgos, morning traffic is in full swing as university students scurry by on their way to class. Along Avenida Palencia, a statue, one of many dotting the city's streets and parks, catches my eye. It's a life-size bronze casting of a young woman seated in a *silla de ruedas* (a wheelchair). Called Superando Barreras (Overcoming Barriers), this is among the first sculptures erected anywhere in Spain, that normalizes physical disability. The bronzed figure looks regal. I immediately think of Nora, an accomplished human rights advocate, urban planner and mother of two living in Brussels. Nora was one year ahead of me in law school, and while we were acquaintances more than friends, I was in awe of her boundless energy and infectious enthusiasm, but mostly her sense of purpose. Nora came sideways into her mission, appealing to lawyers, architects and authorities for a more mindful approach to city planning; easy access for the disabled, she firmly believed, should be more seamlessly woven into the fabric of urban design.

Access was more than a pressing social and political issue; for Nora it was personal. Despite her physique and wheelchair, her physical limitations have rarely prevented her from living life to its fullest; pursuing travel, a career, marriage and children. Disability is but one facet of Nora's life.

I turn back to the path. Juan-Do is up ahead, the Carrix wobbling behind him, its little back wheel bumping up against stones and pavement cracks. On this day, I will walk for those who spin through life with spokes: Nora, the bronze girl, the pilgrims on wheels (slower even than I) and a young man named Jonathan Sigworth, whose sobering account of plunging off a 70-foot cliff in India into spinal-cord quadriplegia, gave me the will to get up and walk, when I was in too much pain and wanted to do anything but.

Blowing body steam into my cupped hands, I feel myself starting to walk with a slouch, as if Juan-Do's slump was contagious. I stand erect to recalibrate my body, and nudge the Shrek-pack into a more comfortable position on my back, as I mull over the word disability. *Would the casual observer consider me disabled? Not likely: the bulge on the small of my back, the neuropathy, the crushed and shortened left foot, the throbbing pain that runs from my butt down my left leg, all of it is invisible to the eye. My impairments do not define me, but I also cannot deny their presence. In some ways, I am still completely able; in other ways, I've become unable to do certain things. So am I un-abled? Can't I just be normal, unless I need your help?*

One of the Korean nuns from the elevator brushes up against me. She waves, as if to remind me that we already met.

"Oh, you from Nepal, ya?"

Not quite, but not worth a correction. When she spots my Shrek-pack, she breaks out into laughter and points it out to her fellow nuns. "Lucky you!" she says—which comes out sounding more like Rocky You. "I envy you!"

Not for the first or last time do I hear these words.

"Lucky you," a Canadian woman will say a few nights after, as I prepare for bed in yet another albergue, "you're so lucky to have someone to carry your backpack for you."

I'm grateful. And I'm fortunate—to be alive. To walk. To use all five senses. But *lucky*?

What is the smell and taste of luck, when I can no longer pull a person up to safety or when I am asked to cradle a friend's infant in my arms, but beg off, in fear of being felled by its weight?

Am I lucky that I cannot sit with pilgrims as they laze about in the afternoons? That people stare when they see me stand or kneel on chairs in restaurants, ask for cushions, excuse myself when pain spikes?

Sure, with all that I cannot carry, it is a blessing that Juan-Do can. But in this broken endeavor, am I lucky to have him around?

I return to the matrix, alert to the call of wild blackberries. But with my hands now stuffed into woolen socks, these shriveled bulbous gems, encased in thin ice, remain beyond reach. I leave them hanging. By mid-morning, the temperature rises along with the sun. My hands, thawed and freed from socks, angle for defrosting berries.

A woman approaches us wearing sunglasses to block out the harsh light of a rising sun. She carries a backpack and a bastón, but walks against the tide: is she a pilgrim? Perhaps she gave up and decided to backtrack. Tibetan Buddhists say that walking the wrong way undoes the accumulation of positive merit, like unspooling a thread. But who's to say, which way is right—or wrong?

"Where are you going?" I ask, as if regardless of direction, we were not all tilting at windmills, all of us on the same axis, revolving around the same one sun.

"I left Santiago last week," she says, sounding quite sane. "I'm walking back to France." As if that was a thing, the reverse Camino. Then I recall that serial-pilgrim Sue had also walked backwards. "To break up the monotony," I believe she said. If you've walked the Camino Frances as many times as she has, and if you've seen the same scenery a dozen or so times, it makes sense to walk the other way. Against the grain. Into the sun. Who among us can't appreciate the value of changing direction, seeing life through another lens?

We offer the Frenchwoman a banana and she disappears behind us. A little piece of me yearns to turn around and join her, walking into the light.

***

As the girl grew into an adult—and as her brain reconfigured itself—she retreated further, into shadows and dark spaces, secreting into closets and tiny bedrooms that she painted the color of dread. She sunk into long bouts of depression, chronic unemployment, abject loneliness. Whenever the girl—who then became a woman—managed to climb out of the abyss, one word was all it took to hurl her back into the pit of despair.

***

In the pint-sized pueblo of Rabé de las Calzadas, I stand undisturbed in the middle of the only intersection. No passing cars, no pilgrims, no donkeys, nada. It may be time for siesta. Despite the micro-size of this village, we have the luxury of choosing between two albergues—within spitting distance of each other. In front of one, a jeep is parked bearing a Belgian license plate. We pick the other albergue, charming but ostensibly empty. Inside the cool and narrow hallway, with no staff in sight, we sign in ourselves, and Juan-Do wordlessly hauls both our packs upstairs. I do a load of laundry and hang it out to dry. There is nothing to do, and with only Juan-Do's hands-off aura in the house, there is nobody to speak with. I could use a dose of Mani.

By the following morning, sounds of coughing, rummaging and shuffling attest to the late-night arrival of more pilgrims. I tiptoe to the bathroom on our floor, but the door is locked. Surely there must be a second bathroom—but where? At the bottom of the stairs, I cautiously open an unmarked door, behind which I find a spacious and modern bathroom entirely retrofitted for wheelchair users, as if I was in an expensive city hotel purposefully designed with the un-abled in mind. Virtually inconceivable. In a miniscule village. Somewhere in the middle of the Camino.

After breakfast, I meet the owner, Clementera. Even though Juan-Do is eager to leave, I pull her aside.

"Does someone in your family use a wheelchair?" I ask.

"*No por nosotros familia y amigos,*" she says, "*pero para los invalides que vienen aqui...*" It's not for our friends and family, but for any disabled person that wants to stay.

Clementera. Clemency. Mercy. Today, I will walk for this exceptional human being, who thought to add an accessible bathroom to her albergue, even though she did not do so under duress or as a result of municipal regulations; and even if only a handful of wheelchair users may ever reach her doorstep.

Chapter 29: The Reverse Camino

Other than the usual yellow arrows—Camino trail markings crudely painted on rocks and poles and walls—there is no sign welcoming us into the long stretch of flatlands ahead. The *meseta*—or plateau—is, for many, the single most dreaded section of the Camino Frances. And the butt of many jokes. I've heard plenty about this lunar-like landscape by the time I reach its threshold; mostly, disparaging.

"I hear there's nothing to see on the meseta," the young Dutchman informs us.

"I've been warned. I don't want to walk across the meseta, so I'm taking the bus from Burgos to León."

"Why would I waste so many days walking through this, nothing but scrubland?"

"I can't stand the meseta," says a middle-aged American, rolling her eyes.

What is it about huge expanses of undeveloped land that people find so unappealing—or terrifying?

Landing in Thailand in January 2008, I explored Bangkok for two days, then fled. Every inch of earth was densely populated, saturated, pulsing with life. It stung all my senses at once. While other travelers scattered to points north or south, I went east. The better to find nature, clean air, smells and noises that didn't rattle me at every turn. When I heard that the bulk of backpackers typically fly on to India, I detoured to Nepal, spending months teaching English in a remote jungle village. When backpackers were jetting off to cosmopolitan Hong Kong, I booked a one-way ticket to Mongolia. I wasn't shunning people, but I did not want to lose myself among the madding crowds, the noise, and the glitter. I wanted the grit and the grime, underbrush instead of surface. I wanted to have quiet conversations. To see nuns and farmers and children playing in their bare feet. To explore the back alleys of Chinatown, the primitive hillside villages of Myanmar, the streets of Siberian towns where homes with ornately carved window shutters look as if they have crookedly sunk into the ground. I wanted to find solace on mountain tops, companionship in guesthouses and cafés, and beauty in barren landscapes that showed ever more signs of disappearing.

The landscape of this meseta is no less barren than Mongolia's virgin countryside. But its wind, somehow, seems to howl louder, and the gust at my back, feels fiercer.

An enormous field of long-expired sunflowers beckons at me with its swarm of yellow-rimmed stalks, dried-out leaves and thorns punctuating their spines. One stalk stands out from the rest, hunched over; in profile, it looks almost Christ-like, a crown of thorns on the head of an elongated Giacometti bronze figure, bending over in suffering or supplication, towards a sloping sun.

We enter a desert void. With the picturesque monastery of Arroyo San Bol lying just ahead of us on the way to Hontanas, I squint hard to bring an unexpected sight into focus; must be another pilgrim heading in the opposite direction. It turns out that walking the Camino in reverse—pilgrimming against the grain—is, as I'd previously guessed, a thing.

The distance between us shrinks as a man in wavy, jet-black hair comes into hazy view. Mani and Juan-Do, walking together far ahead of me, pass him by without exchanging a word. But we are in the middle of nowhere, traipsing further into a deeper nowhere. The man, looking younger as he approaches, carries no backpack or walking pole. He glides over the ground without hesitation or a glance backwards. He wears shoes rather than hiking boots, and drags a carrito similar to mine behind him. A heavy leather jacket is draped over an anonymously large object strapped to the carrito. Bizarre.

I'm unable to walk past this phantom-like figure without inquiry. Clearly, he has come this way before.

"*¡Hola!*" I say, stopping in front of him, "*¿Que tal? Tu hace el Camino?*" Are you walking the Camino?

He shakes his head. "No, no," he says, introducing himself as Carlos. "I am coming from Astorga."

"What are you carrying on your carrito?"

"An accordion," says Carlos, as if there was nothing unusual about hauling a bulky instrument across the sweaty Spanish plains. Meeting Carlos feels surreal; like I just stumbled onto a Fellini movie set.

I prod further. "Where are you going?"

"I just played in Astorga with my group, Il Solo," says Carlos, also known as El Solito Trovador. "But, now the summer season is finished. So now I go to Italy to play."

"From here?!" I ask the wandering troubadour.

"Yes," he says, "I walk to Burgos. From there, I will find a ride to Italy."

He waves and trudges on.

With another twinge of envy, I glance backwards at his receding figure as he walks towards the light, then hustle to catch up with Mani and Juan-Do. I excitedly tell them about Carlos and his musical journeying.

"Maybe he will find new friends and they'll set up a new band," says Mani. "Then they can walk the Camino… all the way to Russia!"

As if Mani's words have emboldened him, Juan-Do pipes up. "*L'ano pasado yo quiero escribe un libre,*" he says. "*Pero est ano estes es un pelicula!*" After walking the Camino last year, he says, I wanted to write a book. But Carlos' story has changed the script; now Juan-Do wants to make a film instead. "A silent film," I mumble under my breath.

Late into the night, on my upper bunk in the Hontanas albergue, I finish reading *Wild*. As I switch off the light, I think of Strayed's courage in plodding through the treacherous trails and camping in the dense forests of the PCT. Then I think of Carlos, fording the meseta in search of gigs and a ride. What is it that possesses us to keep on trudging, through extremes of weather, wilderness and self-doubt, across these wide expanses of land?

In the morning, my backpack is, as always, packed and ready for pick-up. Downstairs, I flip through the pile of paperback cast-offs. Books in Italian, German or Dutch won't make the cut. The only English book on the shelf sits there, mockingly; a grimy copy of Brierley's *Guide to the Camino*. I cave in. Right now, the choice seems clear: It's Brierley or bust.

Leaving Hontanas, we three fall out of step, and into jagged rhythms of our own. Mani alternates between plugging into her MP-drei, or whispering to God. Juan-Do looks up for a change, his hands today free of the firm grip on the handlebars. Mani's presence alone seems to release him from whatever weighs him down; somehow, it is also the invisible thread by which I feel we remain bound together through the days—rather than isolated.

"Do you realize," I ask Mani, "that when Juan-Do speaks to you in Spanish, you usually don't understand what he's saying? But if I hear him, I can translate for you?"

Mani looks pensive. "Really?"

"Sí, sí," I say. "And the reverse works too: when I don't understand him, you translate for me."

A peculiar linguistic anomaly; as if any attempt to converse with Juan-Do compromises comprehension.

Curious to know if Juan-Do notices this oddity, I tentatively broach my theory.

"*¿Porque?*" I ask him. "*¿Com-es possible?*"

"*Communicación.*"

Coming from the Man of Few Words, whose desire to communicate with me is, well, nil, this is no answer at all.

The Convent of San Anton is worth admiring, if only to gaze at its ornate details and imposing arches—and to get out of the sun. Taking cover in its shadow, I notice a man in a hat, his dog and a cart, ambling towards us. Mani and Juan-Do are unmoved. I walk up to the man, whose floppy hat covers a pile of ratty long-unwashed hair. His grimy clothes drape sloppily on his lean frame, and tchotchkes hang around his neck. He introduces himself as Señor Poppi. A sign dangles from his neck: Walking for Peace.

"Where are you going?" I ask the backwards traveler.

"I am from Santiago, but I walk to Rome and Jerusalem" says the eccentric-looking traveler. He is what author and outdoorsman John Muir would call a saunterer or *sainte-terre-er*, one of the medieval pilgrims who walked until the Holy Land. "I must bring peace and love to the world."

If only it were that simple. I can't even transcend the tension between Juan-Do and I long enough to negotiate a ceasefire; meanwhile, the peripatetic Señor Poppi and his scruffy dog, are boldly sauntering towards modern-day Jerusalem, carrying the key to world peace.

✼

Chapter 30: Hospital del Alma

The vast arable lands of the meseta are no different than the Camino's hillier segments when it comes to quirky characters, as well as generous ones.

From a distance, I see what looks like two moving dots further down the road. A dozen more steps under the scorching sky brings us close enough to realize the dots are, in fact, two older women, standing in the middle of an intersection, seemingly materialized out of the asphalt. A tractor rumbles by slowly.

"*Hola!*" one of them calls out.

They are dressed in autumnal wear; long-sleeved and neutral-colored clothes, their hair dyed and well-coiffed. One of the women sports a hot red pair of lips and matching eyeglass frames, neatly drawn eyebrows, a silk flower tucked into a tight bun. Her leather pouch is slung with the strap crossing her chest.

"Where are you from?" I ask. She points uphill with a grand flourish, as if to a palace.

"We're pensioners," she announces dramatically, as if she were a diva who had been pushed into early retirement. "We come down to the road every day to meet with pilgrims." I never find out if she was an actress, but if so, she must miss the stage.

The women unlatch their purses in unison. They hand out candies and, after Mani and I have taken our handful, Juan-Do accepts his portion quietly, meekly. After they wish us Buen Camino, I approach one of them for a hug—and catch a whiff of European perfume that reminds me of childhood and No. 4711, a fragrance that my grandmother used to slather on in the bathroom, leaving its scent to linger and waft into other rooms throughout the night; long after my older sister and I watched Carol Burnett tug at her ear at the close of her TV show, and fell asleep with glasses of ginger ale at our bedside. As soon as we turn to walk on, the two matronly women swivel around in time to greet the next cohort of pilgrims.

From a brief peek into Brierley, I know that the town of Castrojeriz looms ahead. An anomaly of the meseta, this village nestles up against the side of a mountain jutting up into the air, as if an iceberg out of a calm blue sea.

We round the path that leads into the center of Castrojeriz. From afar, I see a figure staggering as if drunk. But on closer observation, I realize it's yet another character of Felliniesque proportions, trying to straighten himself out on a bicycle with straw baskets affixed to the front and back of its frame. He wears a grey tunic and a peasant-like conical hat, with a pitchfork slung over one shoulder. Juan-Do and Mani walk right past him. But just one look at this lanky, heavily bearded and slightly disheveled apparition and I step on my breaks.

"Hola," I say, as he backpedals towards a full stop. "*¿Cómo te llamas?*" What's your name?

"*Yo soy Mau,*" he says, rising from his bike seat, appearing taller and more distinguished than I expect.

My brain spins into a frenzy of crossed wires. *Mau* in Indonesian means "want," as in "I want." Mau Mau. Why not? He's cute.

Mau, a native of Italy, has lived in Castrojeriz for many years. He devotes his life to service, sweeping and tidying up the convent's ruins daily. It explains why he pedals against the tide.

He invites us to drop by his home, even in his absence. "Keep walking along the main path," he advises, "then listen for the music. The doors of Hospital del Alma (hostel for the soul) are always open. It's a resting place for pilgrims. You're welcome to spend time inside, read books, relax in the garden. If you can, please make a donation."

En route to the Hospital del Alma, we stop in at a bar called La Taberna. The proprietor, Antonio, is another legend on the Camino, and the walls of his bar are plastered with souvenirs, photographs, and mementos from pilgrims, travelers and celebrities. There is a plate from Romania; a story about Hape Kerkeling, a German comic who published a book about his pilgrimage; and a clipping about the celebrated writer Paulo Coelho.

"Maybe you do not know," says Antonio, "but Coelho did not walk all of the Camino."

"No, I didn't know," I say, "So… " My thoughts trail off. I feel strangely deceived.

"He wrote *The Pilgrimage* from his notes when he visited different villages," Antonio says, "and from talking to pilgrims."

The line between truth and fiction is a blurry one, even the one running the length of the Camino. "Isn't that a bit like claiming you walked the whole way," I ask, "even if you rode a bus to skip the whole meseta?" The way that Bill Bryson allegedly claimed that he walked the PCT when he skipped over entire sections of the trail. Antonio winks at me and disappears into the kitchen.

We stand by the bar, nibbling piping hot *galletas* (biscuits) and baguette with sheep's cheese and olive oil drizzled over top, as dance tunes come over the sound system. Juan-Do turns away from the bar and walks over to a middle-aged woman (Estonian, we later learn) seated alone at a table. He reaches for her arm, gestures for her to stand and escorts her to the empty dance floor. Then, as if in a trance, he transforms before our very eyes into an agile Don Juan, holding her close and twirling her around the dance floor. I am mesmerized, as is Mani. Subtle hints of a smile spread up his face.

Who is this man, this enigma, and why does he disguise himself so?

When the tune ends, the dancers part ways. Juan-Do sees us gawking at him. He reverts immediately to his usual state of sad and sour.

"*Vamanos!*" he calls out.

✹

Chapter 31: Mani & The Maestro

As we reenter the void of the meseta, Castrojeriz fades behind us, its unusual form a rebel against the surrounding flatlands, slowly shrinking in size.

Up ahead, against a pale blue sky, another steep ascent awaits us. We reach the summit of Colina de Mostelares within the hour, all three of us feeling spent. Thankfully, Mani and Juan-Do need rest like I do. Juan-Do offers her a Reiki session and Mani accepts. She lies down on a large flat outcropping at the edge of the mountain, and Juan-Do covers her with a heavy jacket (despite the high heat). Over the next hour, the self-anointed Maestro gives Mani Reiki, while I drape my body over a low stone parapet, a short distance away, and close my eyes. When I look up momentarily from my perch, I see the Maestro's hands trembling above her head. I invert again, forcing more blood to circulate into my head.

The Reiki wraps up. Mani's face glows. She looks buoyant.

Juan-Do turns to me and offers me a session. I balk, wary of his tremors.

Reiki is also about a transfer of energy that involves touch, intimacy, and trust. All of them, patently absent—or invisible to the seeking heart.

"*No, gracias,*" I say.

We pick ourselves up and move on.

"So, how was it?" I ask Mani as we break into a stride together.

"It's like my hands are pumping blood… pulsing," she explains. "I feel a lightness in my body."

From my own Reiki practice, I know what she means. But what about the hand tremors?

"I didn't feel them," Mani says.

She rambles on, talking about spirit and light and seeing God. Basking in the afterglow of first Reiki rites, Mani sounds smitten—with Juan-Do's hands.

"Juan-Do told me that when we sleep the soul leaves the body and joins the universal spirit, where it explores the world outside of our body," she says, her rosy cheeks almost translucent, like a cherub's. "That's why, when we wake up, after our soul has traveled, we should feel more rested."

A few hours later, we arrive at the Refugio San Nicholas, where Antonio the barman had urged us to stay, to find the doors padlocked and windows shut tight. The only signs of recent human life are an ashtray with cigarette embers, and some men's underwear on the line, fluttering.

We are cranky, all three of us—but our responses, predictably, differ. Mani and I strategize; Juan-Do stews in silence, walking off to wherever. A short while later, I find him reclining against a stone wall, the hat shielding his face from the very last gasps of a setting sun, as a bush of thorns and roses blooms nearby. I call his name, then wait for him to rise, snap himself into the harness, and return to the trail.

After crossing a narrow stone bridge barely wide enough for a two-door hatchback, we lumber on towards the next village. A patch of corn stalks lines the roadside, inexplicably abutting asphalt. They are an oddity, these cornfields, incongruously located, materializing at a dead-end, or planted amidst an industrial landscape far from any other farmland.

A thick veil of gloom greets us at the entrance to Itero de la Vega—where we locate the equally soul-less concrete building that houses the *refugio* (municipal refuge). No matter how stark and dreary it might be, a bed, food and hot shower will do.

I'm tucked into bed when an obese Swedish woman enters the

women's dorm room. Limping with great effort, she collapses onto the bed next to me, setting the springs into motion. Even if we are still on the meseta flats, her breathing is strained—as if she just ran a marathon. She reaches for her bag, unzips it and pulls out a pillbox, popping a few colored capsules into her mouth. She looks at me sheepishly.

"Painkillers," she says. A Camino Candy poster child.

"Why?" I ask, nodding in empathy. "What's the pain from?"

"I have to get through all the stages by the end of the week," she says, "and I can't do it any other way."

I remember this woman from the night before, when she'd slept in the bunk below mine. Her snores were ear-splitting, bordering on mythic. I dig around inside my Shrek-pack, until I land on my earplugs.

Shortly after midnight, I'm awakened by what sounds like heifers in heat. The Swede? No. The bulldozing is from a top-heavy German woman asleep on the other side of the room. Her nasal contractions are deafening; and as if that weren't disturbance enough, her neighbor chimes in, sounding like a chainsaw on speed.

Where are the SNORPbusters? If only the powers that be would designate snoring a disability. Special 'access' would be extended to those burdened by a nasal handicap. Albergue owners would be required to meet revised building codes, retrofitting a certain number of bunks into sound-insulated rooms or individual pods. 'Camino Angels' could make the rounds of albergues in the furthest reaches from Santiago, placing a biodegradable yellow arrow patch at the foot of each snorer's bed, entitling the recipient to customized perks at subsequent lodgings—such as snoring-only spaces.

Until then, I feel as if I am bound to be eternally, infernally sleepless in Spain.

The following morning's 6 a.m. roll call startles me. But this time, in a voice I know well. "Good morning España!" Juan-Do bellows from a bed at the other end of the room, channeling Robin Williams in his breakout role. As if in response, Mani's alarm rings. Great. I'm now irreversibly awake.

Chapter 32: Tomorrow, You Carry

In the early hours of a morning splattered with dew, Juan-Do is already encased in an impenetrable bubble of solitude. I turn my attention back to the gravelly path. My toes look like Rioja grapes that have shriveled into rose-colored prunes. I look up just as a bush dripping with blackberries calls my name. A few steps on, feeling satiated from the juicy berries, I stop in my tracks. A flotilla of pedal boats, bobbing into each other like bumper cars, is tied up to the dock of a narrow river—as if we have inadvertently taken a wrong turn into Disneyworld. I lean over a railing to scan the calm surface of the water, wondering if I might spot a crocodile or mermaid.

Mani slows down, matching her pacing to mine.

"I spoke with my brother yesterday," she says. "He asked me how the Camino is going."

"What did you tell him?" I ask, while re-fastening my hair up into a bun.

"That my body is here but my soul hasn't arrived yet." One day, when I am on the brink of death, I want Mani's words embroidered into a cushion that I will press against my heart.

We stock up on provisions at a mini-market in Fromista, then head out again into the dry flat yonder. From afar, I see a pedestal placed conspicuously on the right side of the path, displaying a sign that looks blank. On closer inspection, I see that the clear slate is dotted with a flurry of tiny raised bumps: Braille. How one can translate modulations of terrain, the color of the sky, a landscape of windmills, into a tactile representation boggles the mind. The meseta, as bas-relief.

Mani and I wonder aloud how well the dots correspond to the actual landscape.

"How do you explain colors on a flat surface to someone who has never seen them?"

"Can a blind person walk the Camino, alone?"

"Has Brierley been translated into Braille?"

Behind us, Juan-Do drags the Carrix, *sin manos*—no hands. Suddenly, he grips the handles and lowers the Carrix to the ground, raising his two arms towards the sky and gestures—as if in a trance. From his repetitive hand motions, one might think he is scattering cosmic dust or communing with unseen spirits. Later on, unable to squelch my curiosity any longer, I breathe in deeply, anticipating resistance.

"What were you doing back there?" I ask.

"Pushing energy away," he says. End of conversation. It is moments like these that I will recall, months later, when a close friend suggests that Juan-Do might have been too shy to admit that he had a crush on me.

***

On the cusp of teenage-hood, the girl ejected the word 'love' from her vocabulary, as if it were a compressed ball of unsweetened cocoa disguised as a Christmas ornament, all glittery on the outside, but so bitter on the inside that it made her nauseous. Years later, when a boy unexpectedly wrote that four-letter word in a funny card that he penned especially for her, the girl—with all the elation and disbelief that confusingly braided itself together and coursed through her body—panicked and fled. She would not, could not, dare not let him love her.

***

Hours later, back on track, Mani decides to pick up her pace—and I sulk. Juan-Do and I revert into our respective cones of silence.

Moments later, Juan-Do stops in front of a sculpture in the shape of an oversized ant. A monstrosity forged of metal, taller than either of us, its spindly legs pierce the ground. Juan-Do motions for me to climb up and straddle the massive insect.

"I can't sit." I say, looking at him inquisitively. "Don't you listen?"

"I don't believe you," he says. Right now, I could find good use for my bastón.

"In Navarette, you said that you can't walk," he says, sounding insolent. "But I see you walk far every day."

"I never said that I can't walk."

"You say that you can't sit," he continues, "but last night you sat on a chair."

Sitting. Squatting. Kneeling. Crouching. Reclining. To Juan-Do, it's all the same. I turn to face him as I crouch. "Is this sitting?" I ask, pointing to my feet. He nods. As far as he's concerned, I sit. I can't tell if he is serious or goading. Hard to argue with someone who refuses to recognize the difference between crouching, kneeling (uncomfortably) and sitting.

My combative side, the fiery element within that has always railed against injustice, lies and small-headedness, is coming apart at the seams. You don't believe me? Would you like to see my battle scars?!

I feel a blood-red cloud of combustible exasperation gathering force, swirling between earth and sky, much like Edvard Munch's *The Scream*. I am this close to unzipping my pants in full view, turning my back to him and pulling down my underwear. As if the bony protrusion on my lower back, the scar tissue that still tingles, my left leg shortened by sudden impact from a hard landing, and my bundle of nerves still vulnerable to stabs of electric shock could ever be evidence enough to convince him, beyond a reasonable doubt, that I was legit.

Thankfully, the prosecution rests. There is nowhere to go but on, and right back into silence.

When we reach the municipal albergue in Poblacion de Campos, it is quiet, empty, without a hospitalero in sight. We pile into the dorm room at the far end; nothing but bare walls and bunk beds. Mani and Juan-Do dump their gear onto lower bunks, while I stake out an upper.

Mani and I churn out a hearty feast for dinner: canned lentil soup with chorizo, a big salad with beets, tomatoes and pasta. Over dinner, mindful of the gentle buffer that is Mani, I try again to explain to Juan-Do the reason for my in-abilities. But he remains skeptical.

"Why can't you carry?" he asks. As if he hasn't heard a word.

"I'm sorry," I try again to clarify, in shaky Spanish and on the verge of a stutter. "I broke many bones so I'm not allowed to carry." It's so simple, but he still doesn't get it. Or want to. It's infuriating.

Any moment, I expect him to utter the very words I've grown accustomed to hearing—from complete strangers: "But you look so normal!" I expect him to say "I don't believe you." Above all, I expect him to say: "Tomorrow, you carry." Which he does.

I lose my appetite, resignation crumbling to my plate.

Chapter 33: Trail Angels

As the dawn's blue light seeps into the room, glittering webs of frost reach across the panes. I slip out of my mattress in the steel grey darkness and unfurl my yoga mat in front of a window. I barely recognize the face that looks back at me, so encumbered is it by rage and rejection. I try warrior pose. I try tree pose. I try *trikonasana*. My body resists, topples, seizes. I give up on finding tranquility, and slip back into bed.

Juan-Do stirs and, without so much as a whisper, shuffles to the kitchen, boils water and prepares an infusion. The moment Mani and I arrive for breakfast, Juan-Do rises from the table and goes off to pack. What would happen if I leaned in, asked him for a hug? Would he welcome the gesture or recoil in disgust?

We sip quietly from our mugs. Mani gazes outside until her thoughts coagulate into words.

"I'm so confused," she says. "When I left home, I was sure that I want to walk alone. After breaking up with my boyfriend, I needed to know that I can survive on my own. I wanted to find out if I can live without a relationship. And still be happy."

"And now," I ask, "how do you feel about that?"

"I also like to walk with other people," she says. "I don't want to feel guilty about it, even if… even if I made the plan to walk alone. It's ok, no? To change plans… without feeling confused?"

Mani is distraught. Deeply connected to her parents and siblings, she has always lived up to their expectations. Stepping off the conveyor belt of conformity means shaking up her family and faith.

"They don't understand me." Deeply anguished, she worries about disappointing her parents. "My people, they don't know why I have to do this," she says. "But I want to live differently, I want to travel … I want to have new experiences."

***

When they sat, en famille, on matching Marcel Breuer chairs around the kitchen table on Sunday mornings, breaking bagels, lox, cream cheese, eggs and vegetables, chugging it all down with freshly squeezed orange juice, before everyone went their separate ways; or around the coffee table in the family room, playing rounds of Boggle or Scrabble, until that evening's quota of nonsensical words was wrung as dry as the day's news playing out on the muted TV; or around the extendable dining room table, during festivals such as Passover, when the relatives (and assorted others who had nowhere else to go) came in and the doilies came out, and after the chicken soup and gefilte fish, when the singing and mingling happened, it was the grandmother's turn to read with her heavily-accented Yiddish twang, so that even after decades of the same shpiel and schmooze, pearls of laughter wafted out the room and up through the chimney, enveloping the solid brick exterior with an invisible dusting of joy and normalcy.

***

As soon as Juan-Do returns to the table, Mani changes gears, veering from sacred to safe.

"I have to tell you," she says, her mood transformed in an instant, "what I dreamed about last night."

She leads us through the walls, doors, trees and wind gusts of her dream; in great detail.

"There was also a man's face," she says.

"Whose face?" we ask.

"I don't know," she says.

On the path later that day, Juan-Do pipes up. "*No miedo,*" he says to Mani. "Don't be afraid, of seeing a face in your dream. It is a good sign." They carry on, speaking about love and fear and light and movement and communication and the afterlife. I slow down, falling far behind them.

After a lunchbreak, Mani and I fall into step. She offers me one of her MP-drei earbuds, and presses play. As if we were called to replenish the barren landscape, we cut our voices loose—belting out the lyrics to Lindsey Sterling's "We Found Love," and dancing up a dust storm. Ignoring our dervish-like swirls and playful antics, Juan-Do marches steadily ahead. Ominous storm clouds gather.

"Remember that very long dream you wanted to share with me?" I turn to Mani, who fumbles with the MP-drei as the song comes to an end. She nods vigorously. "Do you want to tell me about it now?"

"Sure," she says. "But do you have time?"

We stop and stare down the path that lies ahead of us, extending hundreds of kilometers past the horizon line.

"Time?" I ask, once our giggles die down. "Yes, I think I have a little time today."

We gradually acclimatize to the monotonous rhythms and sights of this griddle-flat section of the Camino. But even on the meseta, we are assured of being upstaged by Stagers; they sneak up on us from behind so stealthily, that their breathless "*Buen Camino*!" startles me. As suddenly as they materialize, the Brierley groupies are gone with the wind.

Not long after Mani wraps up her story, we encounter an elderly Spanish gentleman standing at the close edge of a town. He leans on a car parked perpendicular to the path and waves off two young women. Perched on the car's front hood is a large handwoven basket. Guillermo is armed with a stamp, eager to ink it into our credencial. He offers us pre-packaged sweets out of the basket. Camino Candy. The real deal.

"Are you here every day?" I ask the candy man.

"*Si, claro*," he says. "Every day, for twelve years."

Like the female sentinels before him, Guillermo too is a 'trail angel.' These Spaniards live and breathe the Camino each day, transforming the pilgrim's walk into a human experience of connection, even if transient. Those fleeting moments of contact act as a buffer against full-blown solitude—Guillermo, the countrywomen, Mani. Each of them, a godsend.

Guillermo also shares stories about the Camino. "The path through this village was the original route of the Camino," he says. "Then the politicians got involved." Ostensibly intending to improve the economic prosperity of shops and restaurants along the main highways, the better-paved SENDA lured pilgrims away from many villages and local businesses. After a sobering lesson about the Camino's less attractive aspects, we go on.

Downhill, on the near side of a stream shaded by trees, we spot our friend Pippa packing up a tent after camping overnight. Solo. The ever intrepid, sea-faring, British-born Pippa, whom we met at an albergue, is in many ways, the quintessential global nomad. While she walks the Camino, her boat is moored off the coast of northern Sweden.

Muscular and burnished from the sun, Pippa towers over all of us, as if she were the tallest flower in the field. Her height is matched only by her long stride. Dressed always in a tank top and shorts, a wide-brimmed straw hat covers her long tresses. Pippa seems rugged and adventurous, tilting at nothing. But it doesn't take me long to tune into her softer edges; she is attentive, thoughtful, compassionate, funny, very kind. A born pilgrim and perpetual seeker, Pippa is drawn to the simple life.

Pippa and I walk on together, discussing serendipity, the surreal beauty of Castrojeriz and an American pilgrim named Ken who, even in mid-life, is as adventurous as if he were thirty years younger.

Juan-Do leads our growing posse, hauling the Carrix, while Mani rambles loudly—in German—into her MP-drei. Again I'm overcome with a twinge of MP3-envy. It is a better option for recording my sightings and stories; much of them fade from memory long be- ♦ fore I can scribble notes at evening's end. I simply must find one of these gadgets for myself.

Pippa pipes up, distracting me with tales from her teaching gigs in London's inner-city schools.

"I worked in the library of a school," she recalls, "and was nearly sacked from that job."

"Why, what happened?" Mani and I ask almost in unison.

"I refused to put books about Tibet in the China section," says Pippa. "And that pissed them off."

Pippa is a repository of impressive adventures and anecdotes; a latter-day female Robinson Crusoe, she has plenty of tales from the high seas, acts of daring and defiance.

"One day, on a whim, I sold everything I owned," says Pippa. "The very next day, I invested all the money in a sailboat. Even though I know how to sail in all kinds of weather, my boat was hammered by very rough storms. It felt like being in the middle of a hurricane." Her sailboat was rammed by a ship and nearly sank.

"Another time, I was moving through these straits on my own," she says, "when I was held up by pirates. I wasn't completely surprised, but it was a little scary at first because I needed to keep my wits about me. Eventually, the pirates and I… we became friends."

Chapter 34: Lights. Brierley. Action.

The following day, Pippa packs up and moves on; she has pilgrims to meet, places to go, a tent to pitch. Juan-Do is unusually cheerful, whistling like a fairy tale dwarf, while he schleps the Carrix down the path. Mani and I are equally stunned. She tugs at my sleeve.

"I have a lover," she blurts out, winkling and chuckling loudly.

"What?!" I ask. "Who?" I'm expecting to hear more about Otto.

"My MP-drei," she laughs. "And I love him so much!"

"I want one just like yours!" I say. "Except that I want one that speaks English." The hitch is: where to find one along this barren stretch of savanna?

We stop in at a café. Juan-Do orders water for himself, wine for Mani and me; much the same way he stirs in a spoonful of ginger powder into each of our morning infusions—as if each of us perfunctorily knew the other's culinary preferences, after years of friendship. When Mani and I stock up on staples, we know that Juan-Do steers away from alcohol, milk, coffee and eggs. So, in addition to the baguettes, bananas, patatas, dried fruit, chocolate and rare vegetable that he helps himself to, we pick up a pack of sliced ham.

Back on the path, Juan-Do finds an apple and places it on a stump at the side of the road; turning to me and gesturing, as if to indicate that it is a gift for me. Perhaps in return for the small bunch of wildflowers that I had plucked the other day, handing them to him. Who knows; maybe that is the extent of his willingness or ability to make contact with me. Always, an enigma. *What secrets lie buried deep his pockets, the linings of his soul? Is he gay? Bisexual? Both? Undecided? Who cares? Why does he alienate me so?*

Mani catches on. She snips a handful of lavender and gives them to me, half-bowing and flicking away strands of hair that cover her face. She dashes on ahead, her backpack strapped tightly to her narrow back and hips. Juan-Do is a few steps ahead of me, when I almost step onto a pair of reading glasses. I pick them up and show them to Juan-Do. Plucking them out of my hand, he takes ownership—regardless of whether the prescription fits, and even if the frames are, like those of the abuela-angel at the intersection, a shocking shade of red.

We are en route to the village of Carrion de los Condes, when Mani doubles back towards us—as if she were a town crier, bearing news of what lies ahead; or a loyal puppy, who disappears for hours at a time, sniffing his way into adventure, only to return to his home base when he is need of company, food and hugs.

The skies are aglow in pink and purple by the time we arrive at the Santa Maria albergue, also a convent. We are assigned the last three available beds in the upstairs dorm. The room is one massive farm of bunk beds, and I claim the last top spot in a corner by the window. I hear the thud of my backpack being dropped behind me, and think to myself: Go ZEN….

Mani and I head back down to the foyer, where a crowd is forming into a circle; the daily gathering is about to begin. Two Peruvian sisters in habit and veil, sit on benches and conduct us in a sing-along, after which pilgrims are invited to share songs from their native countries. Mani and Juan-Do then join the other pilgrims for evening prayers at the church nearby, while I seek enlightenment via a sunset stroll.

The rituals surrounding bedtime, most easily observed in these larger dorm rooms, is a constant source of fascination. The young Korean guy on the top bunk next to me, for example, energetically crams many items into the bottomless pit of his sleeping bag: a jacket, book, bag and oversized smartphone. (It's a wonder he can sleep, with his feet so tangled up in pilgrim paraphernalia.)

Lights out. The scent of wood and sweat mixes with the sounds of sniffles and coughs to create a camp-like atmosphere. But it doesn't take long for the silence to be shattered with snore-song (Snorp-alooza!). Earplugs prove ineffective. In the absence of SNORP-busters, I mentally conjure a letter I might post on the door in the middle of the night.

Dear SNORPS: If you insist on subjecting us to your rattles and snores, please forgive us for suggesting that you be housed, collectively, in airport-style glass enclosures—much like smoking lounges in airports. We mean no harm and we promise not to castigate you further. But we are helpless and in agony. Please have mercy and free us from your nasal knocks.

I am sleepless in Spain, awakened by the faintest sounds of breathing and scraping at the far end of the dorm; sounds that have been in my ears all of my life. I flick on my watch. It lights up: 4:52 a.m. I am gripped by the thought that I may have left some gear at a bar in the last village. The hat and socks are replaceable, but the plaid scarf less so. It is a keepsake from my return visit to Battambang; remnants of my life, woven into its threads.

***

Her body, ever vigilant, stiffened at sounds barely audible to the unattuned ear but like a clap of thunder to hers; the key turning and opening the front door, or the rhythmic squeaking of the garage door opener, aging rollers skipping along its track. At the first thump of feet climbing stairs, then approaching her room, a place of never safety, the girl would disembalm herself from the darkness of her closet, switch on the light, and sit at her desk as if she had spent the last few hours buried in her studies, not kneeled and concealed, behind blue button-down shirts, Levi's jeans, a bulky sheep's wool Cowichan sweater knitted by her mother and a velveteen dress that she wore only once.

***

To quell my racing mind, I step down the ladder, feel around for my yoga mat and tiptoe to the landing outside the dorm. I unfurl the mat, and step back into downward dog. When I sneak back into the dorm, it's not yet 6 a.m.. I climb the ladder, and shimmy down my bag. The lights are switched on. Pilgrims mill about noisily, dashing off to the bathroom, loudly discussing stages and comparing blisters. Another marathon is underway; if not to the finish line, then to a free bed.

Lights. Brierley. Action.

I peek out of my sleeping bag, and glance down at my backpack, across the top of which is spread my checkered scarf. On the far side of the room, sitting up in her lower bunk, Mani yawns, and swipes her hand across her cheek. Bleary-eyed, she squints up in my direction and waves, then reaches for her glasses. Her eyes and mine shift in unison towards Juan-Do. He lies spread-eagled on his stomach, fast asleep, deaf to the escalating commotion. This morning we are not going anywhere fast.

The orgy of morning ritual escalates around me. A Spaniard on a lower bunk dives into his first-aid kit, pulling out bandaging tape, scissors, cotton. The lanky Korean teenager beside me empties his sleeping bag, tightly rolls it up, jumps down to the floor and packs his gear. He lets out a shriek—while clutching his left wrist—as if he had touched burnt coal. He frantically unpacks and pulls every item out of his bag, then scampers up the ladder and throws off every last bit of bed. His watch resurfaces and, as suddenly as it started, the panic stops.

As a steady stream of pilgrims flows towards the exit door, a trace of music rises, ever so faintly, from a distance; a serenade for those departing. It is Simon and Garfunkel—"A Bridge Over Troubled Water." I glance over and see Juan-Do look up at me, then look away. Our waters are troubled.

When we reach the Cafetería Los Condes, Pippa is at the bar. The owner looks thrilled to see our small bunch of customers.

"How is the economy doing in this village?" I ask, sidling up to the bar near Pippa, and ordering the usual.

"It is terrible," he says, toweling off a glass. "Six million Spanish people are unemployed. Salaries are being cut."

He thinks that younger people should take to the streets. "Where are the protesters?" he asks, placing the cup and saucer in front of me, and serving drinks to Mani and Juan-Do.

While I nurse my café con leche, the owner tells me about a friend who quit law to train as a manual laborer. "Better pay," he says, while wiping off the counter. "Then he started his own business, and now he is earning much more than he did as a lawyer."

By the time Juan-Do stands up—signal for us to move—the owner has conceded that he is not as badly off as others; his family is heading to the Canary Islands the following day for a vacation.

With Pippa tagging along, we leave the restaurant. This little quartet of ours, loosely cobbled together for purposes of the Camino, is like a mobile UN unit, with fluency in more than a few languages; Spanish, Portuguese, German, Italian, French, Romanian, English, Hebrew and Indonesian. Pippa may even have some ancient Norse tucked up her sleeve.

After stocking up on staples at a nearby supermarket called Lupa (Indonesian for 'forget'), Pippa, Mani, Juan-Do and I trudge off towards the far edge of town. Even bundled up in layers, and my feet sandaled in wool socks, the precipitous dip in temperature catches me off guard. Like a Montreal winter, the sky is smeared with a shade of grey that precedes blizzard. My hands shiver inside a wool sock (replacing the gloves that went astray), while clouds of hot breath escape from my mouth. Passing the last gas station in town, I plead with Juan-Do.

"Please, let's stay another day," I say, lowering my scarf to let my words escape. "*Muy muy frio*. We can get back on the road *mañana*. *Sí?*"

Signs of Irritable Juan-Do Syndrome appear. There is fury in his eyes, wrath on the tip of his tongue.

I glance backwards. Mani and Pippa, seemingly immune to the chill, stroll cheerfully far behind us; unaware of the frostiness that continues to spread between Juan-Do and myself. I want out. Or bed. But this?

The Maestro digs in his heels on the matter.

"Go on!" he barks.

With the scarf wrapped tightly around my hat, I lower my head against the chill, vowing to keep my distance from the dictator. It doesn't help to recall that the next albergue is still 18 kilometers away.

Chapter 35: The Cool Camino

Over the weeks of traveling with Juan-Do, I develop a sixth sense for retreating from his foul moods. As we trudge along the SENDA, I retreat into self-preservation mode, in extremis. By focusing my attention on the solid white line that stretches out ad infinitum, I can slip into a meditative state. With every step, I study the line's changing characteristics; spots, stains, cracks, bumps, wheel marks. Here it's straight, there a little crooked, here a smudge, there a newly painted patch.

Fortunately, I'm saved by a familiar pilgrim. When Ken rejoins us for a few hours, he sweeps me away with kind words, comical anecdotes and plans for traveling to distant lands. I find my bearings and sanity again.

A young man whizzes by us at bad-ass speed. Is this a pilgrim—or a marathoner? A patch with a Canadian flag is sewn onto his backpack.

"Hey there," I ask, "where are you from?"

He stumbles, then turns around.

"Ottawa," he replies.

Oh, Ottawa. Tulips in the summer, ByWard Market, a skating-rink-river in winter. So pretty. But also: The Capital. Government. Lawyers. Politicians. Pin-striped suits. Yawn. My guess is he's a public servant. Indeed; this pilgrim beefs up online security for the government.

"Do you like your job?" I ask, taking long strides to keep up.

"Sure," he says, almost breathlessly, as Ken steps out of pace to join the others. "It's a great way to see the country for free!"

"How long have you been at your job?" I ask, while adjusting my Shrek-pack.

"Fifteen years," he says, his voice brimming with excitement. "Only nineteen left to go until I retire with a full pension—at 55."

Recalling the two years that I worked as a public servant, I could never appreciate the allure of working at the same job for one's entire career. In fact, I fled from that possibility as soon as I could; taking a leave of absence to travel around Asia for six months. Which extended to one year. And which ended for good when I plunged through a bridge and could no longer sit in front of a grey computer in a grey cubicle in a grey office. I had found color—and light.

"Why are you walking the Camino?" I ask, even though the Ottawa native seems eager to push on.

"Cool, it's very cool," he says. "Never been to the continent, so I thought it would be a cool way to do Spain."

The Cool Camino. Never thought of it that way. Coolness was not on the radar of another Canadian pilgrim I'd met a few days earlier. "I've just gone through a year of hell," he had said. "A rough divorce, my own battle with cancer; and, as if that wasn't enough, my sister died in the middle of it all."

"So," I ask, my curiosity getting the better of me, "what do you think about Spain so far—or at least the Camino?"

"Cool," he says, "but sometimes it's very flat, like Saskatchewan."

As a teenager, my parents, younger sister and I took a road trip across Canada, which included passing through the prairies of Saskatchewan. More rural and uninhabited than anywhere else I had ever been until then, it was all flatland, farms, silos, fields, cows, mailboxes and highways, like softly undulating ribbons of grey asphalt halved by dotted white lines, perpetually stretching into the next field or province. There isn't much to see or do in Saskatchewan. But, for peace and stillness, other than, say, Mongolia or Siberia, there are few places like it.

"How many days have you been walking?" I ask, picturing him at a desk, dressed in a tie and suit.

"Day 17 now," he says. "I started on the 27th. Then I took two days off in Burgos, so I got off track. But now that I'm back on Brierley's schedule… "

He pulls out the Stagers' sacred text, flips through the pages and stashes it away. A servant of the people; no wonder he goes by the book. No detours for this dude. It's Brierley all the way.

"It's also preparation for me to hike the Appalachian Trail from Georgia to Quebec," he adds. "Not in one go, of course, but I'll go for a month next year and then I'll do another segment the following year… "

The conversation becomes stilted. I miss my people. Where is Ken? Pippa? Mani? With kilometers of flatlands ahead of us, it is no easy matter to seek leave. A small grove of trees nearby offers salvation; nature's safety net.

"I guess this is it," I say, pointing to the grove, "I need to pee."

With that, I lose him to the dust.

While Juan-Do stumbles along up ahead, Pippa, Mani and I walk together for a couple of hours. We cover more ground in our conversation than we do in kilometers, weaving between a lifetime's worth of subjects: school, education, Montessori, religion, self-fulfillment, travel, mysticism, spirituality, love, regret, fear, radical thinking and how to live one's truth. By the time we come full-circle, back to the Camino, Pippa is struck by a flash of inventiveness.

"I'm going to make a personal-use gas stove," she says. "I'll collect a few tin cans, then cobble them together and add fuel to make a flame. I don't like staying in the albergues, even when it's cold. I'm going to keep camping out."

"Then what?" I ask.

"Then I think I'll turn around," she says, "and head back to the UK and Sweden. I'll probably walk the Camino del Norte."

I don't know about the Camino, but in my books, Pippa is cool. I picture her wearing shorts, a tank top, backpack and hiking boots, sailing solo across the English Channel, high winds and all. Pirates be damned.

Chapter 36: Tomates

As sweat-soaked pilgrims flock into the Refugio Camino Real—a stark, single-storey facility—a mutt leaps out from behind the corner towards us. I know that dog. Santi. A hair-breadth later, Otto.

Mani squeals, throws her arms in the air and runs towards him, after which she is promptly swept away for an impromptu romantic interlude. Love is in the air—and her MP-drei is put on indefinite pause.

Mani's sudden absence upsets my equanimity—translating into more solitude, with Juan-Do at my side. Our dysfunctional duo falters without Mani; without her, the fragile balance is upended, and my days are weighed down by obligatory silence.

Juan-Do carries our backpacks into the barracks-style dorm room, and waits impatiently for my signal. He dumps my backpack on the ground, as rays of glorious afternoon sun stream through the window, baking warmth into the mattress.

Temporarily released from his duties, The Man of Few Words hulks off towards the far wall. He drops his hat and jacket on the lower bunk, then burrows himself into the corner. What does he seek or find there, in the shadows? Does the darkness ease his sleep?

That evening, a crowd of foreigners gathers for dinner at the neighboring hotel. Otto and Mani (who are by now an item), Pippa and Ken, Federico and Tatiana (an Italian couple I have not yet met). Because Juan-Do and I arrive last, we are relegated to the last two chairs at the far end of the table, where we must face each other. Juan-Do's eyes are glued to his placemat, as if it is an object of great fascination.

As I peel off my fleece jacket, Federico calls to me, gestures wildly and rushes over.

"Emergency!" he exclaims, pointing to the bold, tomato-red logo printed on my t-shirt. "How you know Emergency?"

The logo is instantly recognizable to Italians the world over. But Federico is the first to swoon.

"They saved my life," I say, tempted to move to the other side of the table, where pilgrims speak.

Until our dinner plates arrive, Federico peppers me with questions.

"I ended up in Emergency because of a Khmer couple who live close to the bridge," I say. "The husband speaks some English because he trained as a medic on the Thai border. He and his friends found me underneath the bridge. They carried me up to the road and drove me to the hospital."

"How did he know about Emergency?" Federico, a longtime and avid supporter, asks.

"Everyone in Battambang knows about Emergency," I say. "But his wife also works there."

The hospital where I had been driven to—The Ilaria Alpi Surgical Centre for War Victims—had been established by an Italian humanitarian NGO called Emergency. In war-torn countries and areas riven by conflict and dire poverty; in danger zones such as Iraq, Afghanistan, Sierra Leone and Sudan, Emergency sets up highly specialized trauma and surgical centers (as well as cardiac and pediatric hospitals), where the costs of urgent medical services and life-saving treatments are covered by contributions from around the world. In Cambodia, trauma care is extended to impoverished Khmer citizens and hapless foreigners alike. The staff is a mix of locals in training under the watchful eye of highly skilled surgeons, nurses, and other medical professionals from Western, English-speaking countries.

The trauma center in Battambang was strategically established in the country's northwestern province, to train and guide a new generation of qualified medical staff after the Pol Pot regime wreaked havoc in the region, torturing and killing off a high percentage of its medical professionals. In that corner of Cambodia, where travelers rarely stop; in a city populated by citizens still traumatized by decades of Khmer Rouge rule; in a sterile and well-designed hospital, its scattered treatment pavilions and wards situated amidst an oasis of lush, well-manicured greenery, I was x-rayed and treated, like everyone else, for free.

Federico shakes his head in disbelief. "You are so lucky," he says. Damn right. This Emergency facility, the only one established in all of Southeast Asia, was located a short drive from the bridge through which I fell. It was the highest form of luck; the life-saving kind.

The next morning, Otto and Mani are nowhere in sight. Understandably. Juan-Do and I leave together. Rather than dwell on the impasse between us, I turn my attention to the date. October 14th, auspicious: my eldest niece's 14th birthday. Today's walk has her name all over it. I pick a bunch of tiny purple wildflowers—her favorite color—and place them atop a cairn.

I pick up my pace until I reach Juan-Do's side.

"*¿Quieres a Ledigos?*" I ask. Do you want to go to Ledigos?

"*Qual que tu quieres.*" Whatever you want.

On the way to Ledigos, a fox scampers across the brown earth and green fields. A flash of color appears in the distance. A vintage Citroën 2CV, painted bright yellow, is parked by the front edge of a sunflower field, the colors almost dissolving into each other. Edging closer, I hear someone calling out. An older balding man waves at me, furiously trying to catch my attention.

"*No entiendo!*" I call back, looking down to see a fuzzy caterpillar slither by, inches from my feet. I don't understand!

The breeze lifts a single word from his mouth.

"*Tomates!*"

No translation necessary.

"*¡Sí, sí!*"

Juan-Do is too far ahead for me to alert him about my detour. I also don't bother sending a text message; he rarely checks, and rarer that he replies. Excited to find a gardener with a love for tomatoes, I veer onto the garden path, treading carefully through pumpkin, lettuce, cucumber and sweet pepper patches.

"*Soy Eugenio*," he says, motioning for me to follow him through the garden, past bushels of pears and pumpkins. He plucks a handful of ripe tomatoes off their vines, placing them into a plastic bag. He ducks into a plastic-covered hothouse that drips with humidity and a wide assortment of plants. I'm ecstatic. *Mucho tomates y concombres!* Eugenio places a handful of plump ripened cherry tomatoes into the bag.

With an armful of organic produce, Eugenio leads me back to the road and hands me the stash. He is heading home to join his wife for lunch. I offer to pay for the goodies, but he refuses, feigning disgust.

"I don't take money from friends," he says.

Eugenio drives off, waving at me from his car window. I dive into the bag and pull out a plump tomato, breathing in the scent of earth. One bite is all I need of this Camino Candy.

Chapter 37: King of The Castle

Somewhere in the region of Palencia lies a tiny hamlet called Moratinos. Since most pilgrims barely lift their heads from the trail while walking through, they don't see the quirky, hobbit-sized doorways skirting the hillside; nor do they see the white-haired man standing on its peak, surveying the landscape—for arriving pilgrims, errant dogs or (who knows?) an invading army. The metal chair at his side lets him rest on his watch.

I have explicit reasons for stepping off the trail in Moratinos: the promise of excellent Italian fare; a break from my pain, and a visit to the Peaceable Kingdom.

The pasta at the Hospital San Bruno does not disappoint. Nor do Rebekah and Patrick, former journalists and keepers of the Peaceable Kingdom. In the months leading up to my Camino, I had contacted Rebekah for advice. She had tried to dissuade me from picking a walking partner at random. "Finding a companion willing to help you along is another challenge I am not sure I can address," she had written. "I know some people who might do it in exchange for room/board along the way, but mutual compatibility is another question." Touché.

At their home—which doubles as an occasional pilgrim refuge—I join them for tea, and a few tales about retiring to a remote village with a foreign language and expat population of two, plus their sizable menagerie of dogs. While Rebekah shares local lore, I remember Eugenio's tomatoes, and offer her a handful. She recounts dramas between neighbors, the kinds of feuds and sagas, characteristic of village life, that might last for years if not decades. "Like anywhere else," she says, laying down a platter of biscuits and grapes, "the locals hold grudges and grievances. But with such slim pickings, people are at least civil towards each other."

When I ask Rebekah about the old man on the hill, she is unfazed. "It's a common practice in Moratinos," she says, "because once upon a time, wine-making used to be the village's chief source of income. The wares stored in cellars around the hillside were so valuable that the owners of each bodega would take turns watching the surrounding fields and paths to keep prospective thieves at bay." Little surprise that the hill is called El Castillo.

Each of those curious-looking entryways leads into a cavernous wine cellar, or bodega—primarily used to store wine bottles and barrels that hold crushed grapes as they ferment. The bodegas are now cool caverns where vintners gather to dine on seafood or sausages, while drinking large quantities of mosto—the not-yet-fermented booze that results from the first crushing of grapes. Even though most bodegas have been abandoned, village elders still stand watch on El Castillo. Like the white-haired man I'd seen, a King of the Castle.

The next morning, my body insists on a rest day, and Juan-Do relents.

After the pain subsides, I head out to explore the hamlet; no big task, given its tiny size. The wind is at my back and the clouds lie low like thick foam on a cappuccino. I spot a round building in the middle of a barren field. By the time I reach the dilapidated structure, my sandals are thick with mud and the bottoms of my pants are full of prickly burrs. I poke my head inside and walk around. Empty cubbies, at varying heights, line the thick but broken brick walls of the circular *palomar*; a nesting place for pigeons. A pair of pigeons cooing on the other side, catches sight of me and flies away, a few feathers fluttering to the ground.

Ready for a rest, I return to the albergue, where I find Juan-Do giving Reiki to a young bearded man. When the session wraps up,

I ask Marko, of mixed British-Serbian descent, how it went. "It was really good," he says, "I feel so relaxed now." El Maestro extends his offer to me, again. This time I accept, with trepidation; Marko hasn't breathed a word about it, but I'm still wary of his hand tremors.

Juan-Do places two blankets, in layers, across a long bench. I lie down and he covers me with a third blanket. I wait for him to ask standard questions and reassurances, Reiki etiquette: "Where is the pain? Do you want me to touch your body or not? If you feel uncomfortable, please let me know." Nada. Instead, without warning, he places his hands directly on my head—and I quiver. His hands are shaking. I bite my lip. I want to ask him to hover his hands above my body, as effective but less intimate than direct touch. But I hold back. *Am I afraid to hurt his feelings? Am I wary about a backlash that might escalate his antagonism?* My mind races. How do I stop this awkward session, this act of intimacy with a person who appears to want nothing to do with me?

From the other side of the room, my cellphone rings shrilly. The sound rattles the placid Juan-Do. Saved by the bell. In an instant, he yanks his hands off my head.

"*Perdon*," I say, while lifting myself off the bench, bringing our session to a sudden close. "*Y gracias.*"

Outside the window, rain clouds taunt us with their low-lying threats. I climb up to my upper bunk perch, from where I get a front-row view of hamlet-life. A few rusty jalopies and tractors trundle by. Then a produce van, its driver honking. A dog that I find out later is called Rocky saunters down the middle of the road, likely in search of another dog or food. Five male pensioners in blue coveralls lumber by, each carrying an unidentifiable object. Then Juan-Do enters and exits the frame, shuffling by in slippers, hands clasped behind his back, searching for who-knows-what on the ground below.

I can't understand why he seems repelled by me. *Have I insulted him? Does he even care?* Mani seems to have cracked his code. She accepts Juan-Do's silence, comments and antics with an equanimity that eludes me—which might be explained by the fact that she is not in his presence every day nor does she rely on him. Only when we are alone together, Juan-Do and I, the others far from sight, will he stop without warning, lower the Carrix, unhitch himself, wrap both arms around a tree, close his eyes and squeeze tight. How is it that he prefers the company of a tree to me?

Tucked into my sleeping bag, with eyes closed and my mind a whirling mush of meditative mantras and affirmations, I hear a faint but familiar accent. When the door opens, I lift my head—and spirits. Mani stands in the doorway. "*Holaaaaa!*" she yells out, laughing and shaking her arms above her head, her face beaming and radiating its warmth towards me.

I slide down to the floor, we hug and drop into catch-up mode, rat-a-tat, until the dinner bell clangs. The pasta is creamy, the wine tart; but best of all is Bruno's tiramisu. Simply irresistible.

Before I leave the albergue in the morning, I take a last look at a framed poster hanging on the wall, with a Latin phrase that I jot down for future reference: *No Habere Timoris / De Audeo Habere.* Bruno translates the words of Pope Paul II: Don't be afraid to have courage.

✼

Chapter 38: The Plague

As Juan-Do, Mani and I wade into the next village—either sunk deeply into siesta mode or a state of abandonada, its shuttered windows and beaded curtains hanging undisturbed in front of doors, no cars in sight—a priest cycles towards us. He smiles and directs us to the albergue Santa Clara, where Rosa the hospitalera greets us warmly.

Rosa leads us through a courtyard to our room, and Juan surprises us with an announcement that he will sleep at another albergue with a friend. He dumps my backpack at the foot of a bed, turns away and leaves without another word.

My attention returns to an itch that has been pestering me for a few hours. I ask Rosa to look at my back. "*Ayy… chinches,*" she says. I feel instantly awful, guilty for hauling the plague into their courtyard.

***

Using a dull HB pencil, the girl wrote her address on the back of an unused Hilroy school notebook and then "Grade 4." She was not yet 10. This pale mustard notebook, similar to the others, would not be suspect. Opening to a clean page, she wrote words that did not belong in a child's vocabulary but ended up there because they were spoken and she could not understand. Phrases that did not sync up with the weltanschauung *of a girl who, until then, would stop at nothing until she stopped at everything. And, because she so loved to paint and draw, the girl made a crude illustration in pen, of a forefinger touching a thumb, a gesture that she could not compute because she only knew it as the universally accepted hand signal for zero.*

***

Without another word, Rosa and her husband leap into action, un-perturbed, as if they were seasoned medics tending to a wounded child. They instruct me on: spraying, burning, washing, drying, cleansing and fumigating. Rosa sends me to the shower, with a change of clothes from her closet. Here too lives an angel.

Mani checks herself and her gear thoroughly. But I need to let Juan-Do know too. I fire off a text to the minimalist speaker. " …*hay chinches…* " I write. "*Es possible que tu laves tu mochila y tu ropas y vestidos hoy?*" You might want to wash your backpack and clothes today.

No reply. Naturally.

With my clothes and skin nearly singed and dried by the next morning, crisis is averted. Even though Mani and I are packed and ready to leave once Juan-Do arrives, Rosa insists that we first nourish our bodies. Following Rosa into her kitchen, we gawk at the extraordinary spread laid out in front of us; far surpassing any other albergue breakfast: cereal, yogurt, fruit, juice, whole grain bread, jams and other treats. While we devour our meal, the hospitalera shares her story.

The owner of a successful holistic center in Barcelona, Rosa was diagnosed with cancer a few years earlier. Despite treatments, her health deteriorated and she was given months to live. Barely able to put one foot in front of the other, Rosa's last resort was to walk the Camino. At the Iron Cross memorial, she met two Italians. She told them of her diagnosis. They urged her to seek treatment in Italy. Which she did—promising herself that, if she survived, she would devote the rest of her life to the Camino. When her cancer fell into remission, she moved to this remote village, where her albergue remains open the entire year—except for one month each summer when she visits family in Barcelona and returns to Italy for medical checkups.

Claro, I know for whom to walk today.

❊

Chapter 39: Lovers

We arrive in León, a city of high buildings, streetlamps, ethnic restaurants, supermarkets, baby carriages and drooping clouds. On a cobblestoned road in León's old quarter, I spot Ken. He's light on his feet.

"Hey Ken," I call out, "what are you up to?"

"I'm done with my Camino," he replies, pulling me in for a hug, "need a change of direction."

This is not the first time I hear a pilgrim say that they are "done" with the Camino—as if the timer has rung, and the chicken is cooked.

"It's too long."

"It's too hot."

"It's too boring."

"I don't get it… "

With Ken's inclination for flitting from one adventure to the next, it's no surprise that he's aborting.

"So, where are you heading to next?" I ask, feeling a little tug from my travel bug as it whispers: go with him.

"First off, an overnight train to Barcelona," he says. "Then, I'm taking a boat to Italy. I'll travel around a bit and head overland to Asia." A true hippie and explorer, giving up the Camino, boots and all. I wonder if our paths will ever cross again. On our way to the albergue, I also wonder what else lies beneath his upbeat exterior.

While Mani attends mass at church that evening, I take off to El Corte Ingles, the iconic Spanish department store. I'm on a mission—of love, to quash the envy. Within five minutes of reaching the electronics counter, a red, near-weightless MP3 that fits into the palm of my hand, is paid for and clipped to my jacket: my *MP-tiga* (in Indonesian). When I see Mani later, her eyes widen at the sight of buds in my ear. "You found your lover too!" Yes, I want to say, but it doesn't have a beating heart, like yours does.

On the way back to the convent, we talk about lovers—mainly Mani's. Then she turns the lens on me. Here, growing uneasy, I hedge. I have never found a suitable way to explain that my relationships would barely have registered on a Richter scale of human connection, so detached was I from emotion; and that my handful of boyfriends were—but were not. A Canadian soldier in Israel. An Israeli student in Montreal. A Russian lawyer in France. A struggling artist in Montreal. Conflated memories and images of men warehoused in my shadow, like concealed mementos from previous incarnations. (And then, an unexpected blip, showing signs of life: a Balinese healer.)

We reach Villar de Mazarife the next day. After dinner, Mani and I layer up and head out for an evening stroll. The moon is full, dousing the village in bright light. A plume of smoke rises from a nearby building. Classical music drifts out of an open window. An aproned woman stands outside her building, tying up window shades for the night.

"I'm done," says Mani. Like Ken, Mani is also signing off early—but for other reasons: "I'm going to walk with you tomorrow until the albergue," she says. "But then I need to go and meet my man."

I'm no match for the man who stole her heart.

As gutted as I feel, I know that Mani's Camino is not mine, nor is mine hers. Our paths have intersected, revealing friendship. Her imminent departure is merely a reminder that each of us is bound to walk the single highway line of life on our own.

Chapter 40: A Thin Place

When our trio arrives in Hospital de Orbigo, we head straight for Albergue Verde, at the far side of town. The business card with a logo of a green snail that I found at Rosa's albergue said it all: *otro mundo possible* (another world is possible). Good enough; but there were other reasons to stay: Cosy atmosphere—garden and prairie—beautiful sunset view—yoga—breakfast & dinner with vegetables naturally cultivated from our own garden—fireplace—hydromassage showers—adapted for handicapped people. If it met my expectations, Juan-Do could not lure me away.

Mincho and Sara lead us up and into the rustic living area of their 2-storey home and pilgrim's sanctuary. Mani parks her backpack outside the door, and joins us inside for a cup of tea. As the afternoon sun begins its descent into the fields beyond, she hoists her pack onto her back and leaves. From the upper floor balcony, I watch her walk off, until her solitary figure, silhouetted by the setting sun, disappears among the fields. (We do not know then that five more years will pass before our paths cross again.)

I find refuge in the cozy dorm room, with its terrazzo floor, hardwood bunk beds, ornate light fixtures and rays of sun streaming through the windows. The space is quiet and empty, heavy blankets placed on each bunk. Juan-Do drops my backpack onto the floor, skulks to a bed far away, removes his hat and jacket, and flings himself into the lower bunk.

After a short rest, and in the absence of willing company, I head out

for a walk. Which, in Galicia, I quickly learn, often entails the possibility of bumping up against corn. This town is no different. On
the road near the albergue, asphalt meets corn; towering stalks, more
commonly seen growing in wide expanses of countryside, weirdly
sprout and shoot up across the street from a row of townhouses.
Perhaps these are free pickings for the neighbors, a farmer's barter.

Back at the albergue, I pick figs from the tree in the yard, and
David the Baker shows me how to fold them into nut bread. In the
early evening, the sweet aroma of baking drifts downstairs, where
Monchi and I meditate and practice yoga. At dinner afterwards,
Juan-Do is there—as are slices of piping hot fig-nut bread.

Early the next morning, after a cup of tea and warm breakfast, we
get going. When we reach the village of El Ganso, Juan-Do leads us
directly to the Cowboy Bar—a popular pilgrim's hangout. The bar's
décor is a surprise find in these parts; funky Wild-West trinkets and
posters, wall hangings and other knick-knacks. A place you would
more likely find on U.S. Route 66, or maybe Bangkok. Even if Juan-
Do shuns alcohol, I suspect I may lose him to the joint for a few
hours. Except for one thing: since we've arrived between meals, the
place is empty, the kitchen is closed, and the cook is on a siesta break.

With a shrug, Juan-Do swivels the Carrix around and we go on
until we reach an albergue tucked in among a dusty stretch of road
crowded tightly with one-floor dwellings. The young hospitalero—
Señor Grino, who is also the owner—greets us effusively and leads us
upstairs, to a large and high-ceilinged space, with a circular formation of beds set along the outer walls—as if it were a yurt. Juan-Do
dumps my bag in front of a bed of his choosing, and heads outside
in search of food.

After a warm shower, I hang my freshly-washed clothing on a
railing to dry out. A Spanish-speaking pilgrim lumbers upstairs and
we introduce ourselves. Jakome, a separatist-leaning Basque, is from
the outskirts of Pamplona. He takes umbrage when I naïvely call him
a Spaniard.

"*No soy Espagnol!*" he exclaims.

While Jakome and I are talking about the country's crises, Juan-Do returns and sits down close to the Basque, greeting him, and as if I wasn't there, brashly interrupting our conversation.

At 7 a.m., I wake with a start and an itch. Damn this curse of the chinches! With great difficulty and loud knocking, I finally manage to rouse Señor Grino. He responds to my announcement with expletives, then stomps around the albergue, spewing his anger into the washing machine along with all my gear. He might learn a thing or two from Rosa.

On our way out, feeling unimpressed with Señor Grino's performance, I help myself to compensation: a wooden bastón that leans against the wall by the front door. Perfectly tailored to my height, with a grip that fits like a glove, it is the perfect replacement for the stick I received in Logroño and ditched the day before. It is also 100% compostable. A find, perfectly timed: A steep ascent awaits. But food is a necessary preamble to hitting the slopes. Fortunately, the albergue in Rabanal del Camino is on our way. By mutual but silent assent we stop in front of its entrance, where Juan-Do unhinges himself from the Carrix and we enter the courtyard. We walk up to the bar and, almost immediately, the Man of Few Words begins to flirt with the waitress. She glances over at me, then looks at him dubiously, a question forming in her eyes.

"*¿No es ella tu novia?*" she asks. Isn't she your girlfriend?

Visibly alarmed by her question, Juan-Do points to me.

"*No tenemos nada!*" he blurts out, quickly alleviating the waitress' concerns. There is nothing between us!

I order a sandwich and move to the far end of the bar. How can he say that there is nothing between us? Till Santiago does us part, for better or worse, we are conjoined. I am alone with myself, and together with him. Lost with him, and lost without.

Our climb lands us, late in the afternoon, in the hilly but tiny hamlet of Foncebadon. The mist seems to touch the ground, with a nip in the air so sharp that it coaxes us inside. With few lodging choices, I opt for the Albergue Monte Irago—with its distinctly bohemian aura, farm animals, homegrown produce, and granola bars. Like a modern-day Woodstock or Burning Man outpost. Two charming, post-modern hippies—Manuel and Felipe—run the joint with a crew of hospitaleros. It's a place for nourishment and company; I'm in dire need of both.

After a hot shower, I help myself to a snack of hot chocolate, with a side of organic muesli cake. I settle down in front of the fireplace, rubbing its sizzling warmth into my hands, toes and ears. When the fire's heat fills me with enough fatigue, I seek refuge upstairs on my chosen top bunk, while pilgrims down below feast noisily on Felipe's paella and red wine. It will be a long night. Eventually, I fall asleep to the gently clanging sound of cow bells.

It is still too dark and too early, when I feel around for my headlamp, slide to the floor and tiptoe down the stairs—in leggings, a fleece top, scarf and sandals. Opening the back door, frost sticks to my face as I pass sniffing bunnies and cows in repose. Mist rises from the pastures beyond, casting a ghostly pall over distant mountains. Beyond the farm, the yoga studio is also steeped in darkness. I enter and unroll a mat, then try unfurling my body into a few *asanas*.

Buckling under the weight of chill and my thoughts, I scramble upstairs and slide back into the depths of a mini-doze.

Dawn ushers in the usual ruckus: crackling plastic and paper, zippers in motion, flashlights roaming around the dark room, boots plodding heavily on the floor. Perhaps the word whisper does not appear too frequently in Brierley.

After a filling breakfast of muesli, peanut butter, jam and chai tea, Juan-Do straps himself into the harness and we hike up and out of Foncebadon. I spot Jakome and point him out to Juan-Do, who shakes the cows and birds out of their early morning reverie with the unexpected rumble of his voice. "Aaaaaaaaa, Jakome!" To Juan-Do's dismay, Jakome does not react.

With the sun lying still low at my back, my shadow stretches far ahead of me, elongating as if I were a piece of rubber. The occasional cloud puff shifts place overhead, casting opaque shadows over cowhides before moving on. In the middle of a green meadow that cascades into a valley below, I see a cracked and rusted porcelain bathtub, its clawed feet still intact. An orphaned fixture. Inexplicable. Abandonada. The ejected remnant waiting to be rescued from tall blades of grass.

A few steps ahead of me, Juan-Do is stopped in his tracks. He drops his hands from the Carrix and swerves around to face the rising sun. Clouds sidle up to hillsides, landing lightly upon silky pastures. As if in trance, Juan-Do raises both hands towards his face, with the palms facing each other. And then, he starts to... clap—which is his way of capturing the sun's energy. I get it. I've practiced Reiki, and I've lived in Bali long enough—where I've had my share of experiences with healers and bodywork and ceremony and sound healing and meditation and kirtan and kundalini—to know a thing or two about unseen spirits and energy fields. The truth and the pretense. Juan-Do lowers his hands, and stays glued to the ground, unmoving, as if in silent prayer.

Fluffy, dew-covered cobwebs are pulled taut between branches and chain link fences. Stout bushes, punctuated with yellow and purple wildflowers. Birds of prey soar overhead. Cow bells clang to their own rhythm. Dried leaves and castañas crunch underfoot. A bucolic expanse of virgin land. Where heaven and earth fuse. Truly, a thin place.

❧

Chapter 41: Barter

Compared to the meseta, our ascent up to Alto de Cerezales, at 1,508 meters, is nothing short of grueling. Juan-Do hauls the Carrix up a mountain, steering it over jutting rocks, slippery stones, battling bone-chilling temperatures—and all without a protest. Even if miles of understanding separate us, he is a hero. Only he doesn't know it, and doesn't appear too interested in hearing of it. The desire to take a load off of him, unburden him of my gear barrels down on me. Some days, the strain of helplessness guts me, wears me down, sends me spiraling into a pit of self-pity and despair. Thankfully, on the way down, Jakome shows up and takes off at breakneck speed with Juan-Do.

The descent is eerily similar to that of Annapurna. By the time we reach the scenic hillside village of El Acebo, the three of us are ravenous. We order and Jakome says he thinks he has chinches. I scan his skin, covered in red blotches. He decides to stay on until his skin clears up. Damn. Like Mani, Jakome too is a balm and buffer. I feel despondent at the prospect of more long days alone with, and even if imperceptibly, bound to, Juan-Do.

Leaving Jakome behind, Juan-Do and I push on, eventually crossing a bridge that leads into Molinaseca's warren of meandering cobblestone alleys and low brick medieval buildings seemingly sunk into the ground. Close to the far end of the village, from where we will continue on to the albergue, I duck into a shop on a corner, in search of bananas. José, the shop owner, refuses money. "Please take them as a gift," he says.

The next morning, while Juan-Do ties up the Carrix, I look around for my bastón. Gone.

"*Quieres caminar hasta hacienda*," I tell Juan-Do. I want to return to the shop, hoping that retracing my steps will be fruitful—and won't create further friction between us.

José is an early bird among the shopkeepers. When I arrive, he is rearranging boards and baskets of produce in front of the windows. José sees me approach and waves excitedly, rushing into the store and returning moments later with my bastón in hand. I know he will not accept a gift, so I stock up on enough inessential provisions leaving him no choice but to accept payment. Still, he does not let me get away without one more token of generosity—an extraordinarily gaudy bracelet made of polyester thread, with a faux-gold heart dangling from its green and white fibers. Proudly, he says that he made it himself.

If only I could barter one Juan-Do for this José.

With the bracelet on my wrist, and my bastón safely in hand, I beat my way back to the albergue. Perched on a bench in the sun is a sour-looking Juan-Do. Except for producing a treat from José's store, I don't know what more to do, to penetrate his armor, to lighten his mood. So, I beat him to the punch.

"Go on."

Chapter 42: Sir Pepe

The Man of Progressively Fewer Words takes off ahead of me, the Carrix teetering behind him on its single back wheel, forever threatening to topple. Occasionally I get a burst of energy and stride past him—taking quiet note of his stamina; and glancing sideways just long enough to gauge if he might be amenable to exchanging a word or two. But Juan-Do does no such thing. Instead, he develops a curious habit of speeding up just before he plows by me, blowing me off as if to say: Don't talk to me, I'm just passing through.

Which is why, when we arrive at Ponferrada's Albergue San Nicholas de Flue, I'm relieved to learn that men and women sleep in separate quarters. Juan-Do trails behind me long enough to drop my bag and disappear without a word.

When I enter the city's center—Plaza Mayor—my pocket rings; my younger sister in Toronto has corralled up her two kids for a quick catch-up. As I squat against a town hall wall, my niece rambles off stories about school, friends, gymnastics—a stark contrast to the scenes that unfold before me: tricycles and balloons; pilgrims and beggars; a handful of seniors lounging on a bench, clasping folded newspapers above their heads to ward off harsh rays of late afternoon light. My nephew, older and more pensive, stays mum.

Strolling down a winding path, I round the corner on an imposing medieval structure; the Castle of the Knights Templar. I walk up the path to its stony ramparts, and a local on the road below calls out, waving at me.

"*Hoy, cerrado.*" The castle is closed today.

When I turn around, I notice a yellow ball on a low stone parapet that lines the walkway. As I approach, I see that the ball is actually a parakeet, and it doesn't budge. I crouch down, to look at it from up close. Still no flutter or hop. The little fuzz-ball of a bird eyes me keenly, and quivers. A drop of liquid appears on the stone beneath its body. I place a twig in front of the bird; it pecks away, still watching me closely. Helpless, I appeal to a couple that stops nearby.

"*¿Ayudarme, por favor?*" I ask. Can you help me, please?

All offices are closed on Sundays, they tell me. There is nothing to do but wait until tomorrow. But that won't do because this parakeet won't survive out here until tomorrow. I can't imagine that the albergue will take in a bird. Reaching out slowly, I pick up the quaking creature and tuck it into my palm, patting its feathered back. A passing pilgrim points to a café across the street. "Take it in there," she says. "You might have some luck."

There are no customers inside the Godivah Café when I walk inside. The owner mills about behind the counter. A business card on the counter reads: "*espacio gourmet, charcuteria, chocolateria, pasteleria, cafeteria, heladeria, panaderia.*" This gourmet space is not your typical Camino-style café; Godivah serves meat, chocolate, sweets, coffee, ice cream, breads. Among croissants and tchotchkes for sale, are cards printed with heartfelt messages; "Be Happy." Sanctuary for an injured parakeet.

The owner steps out from behind the counter, introduces herself and, seeing the bird in my hand, asks if she can help.

"*¿Que eso?*" Mirtha asks. "*¿Porque tienes … ?*" Why are you holding the bird?

"It's broken," I say, unfamiliar with the Spanish word for injured.

Mirtha springs into action and rushes back and behind the counter. Improvising, Mirtha turns a bell-shaped container into an ad hoc birdcage, covers it with a piece of crocheted material, and places it into a cardboard box. She carefully lifts the parakeet from between my hands and slips it under the bell and onto the plate.

She glances up at me and asks: "*¿Cómo se llame?*"

"I don't know the bird's name," I tell her, "it's not mine."

"*No importe,*" says Mirtha, shaking her head, "you found the bird. You're like its parent so you need to give it a name."

"How about Pepe?"

"*Muy bien,*" says Mirtha, "*Pepe, yo quieres es nombre.*" She agrees, likes the name.

Which is how an injured parakeet gets saved by Señora Mirtha, the latest in a string of trail angels, and initiated into the outer circle of Knights Templar. So, if you should ever encounter a yellow-breasted, brown-feathered parakeet in Ponferrada that fits into the palm of your hand, please address him as Sir Pepe.

When I part from Mirtha and the injured bird, the beggars of Ponferrada are waiting for me, extending their palms and pleading for coins. One panhandler among them looks incongruous; out of place, dressed in leather loafers and a suit, once well-tailored now tattered. His hair is neatly trimmed if not a little greasy. This man, perhaps an unemployed victim of the economic downturn, looks to inhabit a world that once was alien to him. He fiddles with his jacket as if it's a size too big.

Inside a pizza shop, I wait for a slice, intending to offer it to a beggar who sits on the sidewalk looking to the sky. Glancing out the window, Juan-Do crosses my line of vision. Shuffling by in his slippers, shirt sleeves and vest, his eyes are glued hard to the ground, his hands clasped behind his back. Deep in thought. Without a jacket as camouflage, his misshapen back is even more pronounced. I could mistake him for a beggar. No matter how many weeks we have spent together, and despite our physical proximity, he remains altogether elusive.

On the edge of a modern residential quarter, I cross a rotary to enter a large public park called Parque Gil Y Carrasco, which features well-manicured gardens typical of large European cities. There are fountains and grassy knolls. Ball-players. Children running and playing. Couples of all ages ambling along a boardwalk, their silhouettes framed against the glow of a setting sun. I half-expect to see Juan-Do with a young woman, strolling arm-in-arm, whispering in her ear, a wide but unfamiliar smile on his face.

In the early morning cacophony, I'm lying on the top bunk contemplating the wisdom of hiding out for the day, when Juan-Do's bellowing voice cuts through my reverie. Burgos Boot Camp redux.

On the way out of town, as clouds threaten to wipe away the blue sky, we reach the Godivah café. The tables are empty and the box where Mirtha placed the parakeet is gone. My heart sinks. Mirtha comes out from the back and waves at me. She senses my disappointment and points to the back of the café, where I find Sir Pepe snuggled into a dainty, filigree-covered contraption, with a small container of water at his claws. He hops about, flapping his wings and nipping at seeds. A bird of joy.

Today, I walk for Mirtha and a rehabilitated bird.

Chapter 43: The Witnesses

With the Man of Few Words trudging on ahead, and my new, bright red MP3 in hand, I blather on, unburdening myself of stories, questions, observations. Two exceptionally well-dressed women approach and stop in front of me, together breaking into extraordinarily wide smiles. They wear almost identical long coats, leather boots and skirts down to their knees, and their faces are similarly caked with thick layers of make-up. One of the pair opens her purse and pulls out a brochure; I don't need to see the cover to know their spiel.

"What language do you speak?" she asks, in Spanish.

"I'm not from here," I say, "*yo hablo ingles.*"

"*Nosotros somos videncias,*" she continues. We are witnesses.

I stop her mid-sentence, keenly aware of their M.O.

"*No, gracias,*" I say, shaking my head, offering a weak smile.

"*¿Conosos nosotros?*" she asks. Do you know who we are?

Indeed, I do. I'm all too familiar with the proselytizing pitch of bible-totin' Jehovah's Witnesses around the world. The men travel in pairs; dress in matching black slacks, white shirts, a name tag and shoulder bags out of which they pull evangelical goodies. From Toronto to Ulaanbaatar, I spot Witnesses a mile away. But the Witness women-folk are harder to pin down. Which is why I'm slow to catch on today, because these women are not dressed in trademark black-and-white garb; they are decked out in colorful tops.

"*Sí, sí, claro,*" I say.

I walk on and glance back for a moment. From behind, they are both dressed, top to bottom, in Witness black.

Minutes later, the skies open, showering us with a sudden and generous downpour. Juan-Do and I duck under an awning, where we quickly unfurl and don our wet-gear. I imagine the Witness-Women are unfazed; evangelization happens, rain or shine.

Chapter 44: A Message for Frank

Like a scaled-down model of a Rioja vineyard, the bucolic landscape in this part of Galicia is lush and fertile. Mainly in this fall season, when clouds congregate above with greater frequency. Stubby trees grow in the vineyard, sculpturally unique and unusual. Leaves crunch underfoot, their colors a spectrum of bright green, golden yellow, to brown. Grapes hang off branches, heavy bunches drooping to inches from the ground. A long-tailed kingfisher swoops down and lands on a tree. It pecks at a worm, scoops it up, and flies off to feast in private.

The bird's catch reminds me of my own search for blackberries. But with the onset of another downpour, my hunt is on hold. By the time the rain tapers down, my berry obsession falls away. In its place, I feel flush with the dizzying scents of rain-kissed grass and earth. How do I bottle up those fragrances for posterity? I bend down to sniff nature up close.

Juan-Do comes up behind me. "Go on," he mumbles, yanking me out of my all-too fleeting fantasy. I cringe. He marches past, as if driven by ambitious dreams of his own. Of which he does not speak. I let the gap widen.

A wall of graffiti catches my eye. *Open your Heart, Frank.* If I could only catch up with Juan-Do, I would ask him if he read the sign. But I stop myself because we are all a little bit Frank. Me too.

***

You will look upon the girl as you do upon a Fabergé egg. She will look glazed, refined. But you will not know how fragile and hollow she feels

inside. You will not be privy to her belief, invisible to all, of not belong-
ing. You will not guess that she is nothing but a shell of her former self,
that her eyes see far too much and her heart intuits more than it should.
She is, after all, only ten years old. Only twelve. Only twenty-four. Only
thirty-seven. Only fifty.

***

Walking through the outlying fields of Cacabelos, my ruminations
are sidelined by a rising chorus of voices. I follow its trail until I reach
a non-descript building that borders a field. Peeking inside, a smattering of locals and pilgrims stand in a circle, feasting and laughing.
There is a distinctly festive air. One pilgrim sits at a table, writing in
a book. Among the strangers, two of whom wave me inside, I spot a
familiar face: Jakome.

"*Hola peregrina!*" a stout older man greets me. "*Entrada por favor.
¿Quieres vino?*" Would you like some wine?

"*Claro que sí!*" I reply. "*Yo vengo!*" Of course, I'm coming!

Yes to Tomates! Yes to Vino! Always say yes.

A garage transformed into a food-testing lab, this is where local
retirees and wine-lovers concoct delicacies using mushrooms for-
aged from the forest, then paired with wines. Amadoro, the robust
and jolly owner of this covert bodega, is also its ringleader and chief
sommelier. He pours a glass of white wine and introduces me to
his friend, "Professor" Pepe, who brings over a hefty guidebook to
mushrooms. Pepe is a diehard mushroomist; this, his bible.

"Have you made any mushroom-based wine?" I ask the professor,
only half-joking, while slurping on a spoonful of mushroom and
herb sauce.

"Not yet!" says the professor, winking. He flips through the mushroom guide, pointing to various species that grow in Galicia. "The
more beautiful they are," he says, "the more they are poisonous."

Out of the corner of my eye, amid the commotion of pilgrims
coming and going, I see Juan-Do standing at the entrance. He peers
in and looks around, his eyes intensely focused. They land on me, and

he quickly glances elsewhere. I can't read his face. So, with half my attention trained on Amodoro, I wait for Juan-Do's next move. *Please do not rain on my parade.* All at once, his brow relaxes. He loosens his burden, disentangles himself from the harness and steps inside. He shakes his head when offered wine, but digs into the plates of mushrooms with gusto. I wonder why wine is taboo; perhaps he once drank too much. But this too, I cannot know, and dare not broach.

When Juan-Do gears up to leave, his gaze narrows, gluing itself to mine.

I make my rounds, thanking the hosts. Then I sign my name in the visitors' journal, which is when I contemplate penning a letter of Few Words. Open your heart, Juan-Do.

Before I know it, regardless of the actual distance covered, we are back to square one—on a trail of dogged silence.

"Go on," I announce, and fall far behind.

❧

Chapter 45: Figs

On our way to Meson Tio Pepe—a favorite of locals in the village of Cacabelos, we bump into Señor Amadoro, the mushroom maven, who points us in the right direction.

While Juan-Do unfastens himself from the Carrix, I choose a table by the wall—better to lean against while we order and wait for food. Entering Tio Pepe's feels like stepping into a classroom of Asian students at recess. A dozen or so Korean teens, the only customers besides us, sit around a long table, waiting to be served. Silence; every pair of eyes is either fixated on a TV screen hanging from the ceiling, or on a smartphone. When Juan-Do arrives and sits down, he stares at the table. I am infuriated. Puzzled. Hurt. Insulted. Annoyed. I don't know what to say. What to ask. There is fear. There is panic. There is sadness and broken faith in humanity. *Why won't he talk with me?* I roll my eyes and, in resignation, look up at the television. *The Simpsons*. Marge in dubbed Spanish doesn't even remotely sound like Marge in English. Regardless, canned comedy is the only distraction that gets me through a meal glazed in silence.

After lunch, Juan-Do ties himself into the Carrix and we walk on.

"I don't want to stay in Cacabelos," I say, certain that my sudden change of heart sits well with him. We will walk longer, further, ever closer to Santiago. Even if it only adds 2 more kilometers to today's quota.

El Serbal y La Luna is the only albergue in Pieros. It advertises itself as ecological and vegetarian; reason enough to stay. The lodge-like dorm is small and cozy, the Bulgarian hospitalera, a fount of warmth and cheer. While settling in, we see that Jakome too is in the house. He has conquered the chinches. I clamber up to an upper perch in a corner directly across the room from Jakome—far enough away to shield myself against another possible bedbug incursion.

When my siesta ends, I head out to explore Pieros—which seems less a hamlet than a pilgrim's pit-stop. There isn't far to go. Walking down a small path from the albergue, I see a fat, apron-wearing abuela waving me down. In a shady garden behind her, a leafy fig tree dangles its plentiful crop.

"*¿Quieres higos?*" she asks, in apparent response to my unreserved ogling. Do you like figs? Eugenio gave me tomatoes; Amadoro, his mushrooms and wine; now this grandmother wants to share her bounty of figs.

"*¡Sí, claro!*" I reply, enthusiastically, while I process the sight of ripe purple bulbs, everywhere.

The abuela invites me into her yard, carpeted in fallen figs; some still hang from limbs. Over the next fifteen minutes, we bend over to collect as many as will fit into two bags—one of which she offers me. I carry it back to the albergue and dump the figs into a bowl. When I place them on the dining table, three women engrossed in Camino-talk fall silent.

"What are those?" the youngest woman asks, pointing to the bowl, and reminding me of my early days in Bali, when I would visit Ubud's morning market, scan the fruit stands and ask an expat friend about all the strange-looking fruit.

"What is this?" I would ask. Rambutan. Mangosteen. Dragon fruit. Durian.

One of the older pilgrims helps her out. "I think they're figs. Right?"

The following morning, the figs are still in the bowl, untouched. I dig into a hearty breakfast—of toast and homemade apple jam, and indulge in a few figs, while savoring a cup of herbal tea.

***

One day in the future, when the girl-now-a-woman finds herself living on an island drenched in light, she will revel in the newfound taste of coconut water on her palate—so transparent and refreshing—and in the certainty of its power to cleanse and heal.

***

I am on the main road, waiting for Juan-Do to tie up the Carrix and join me, when I am startled by unfamiliar snorts and thundering hooves touching ground. Clop clop clop. I crane my neck to listen more closely and speculate on the creature that will soon appear from around the bend: Two stunning horses, their manes perfectly manicured and aglow, saunter over like well-trained stallions in a royal parade. With the early-morning sun rising behind them, the steeds are quick to respond to command. A couple of Italian travelers, one astride each saddle, is crossing Spain on horseback. "Our horses are from Rimini," the man says, tipping his leather hat backwards, exposing his forehead. "This one is Pipo and that one, Melkor."

"How far are you riding?" I ask as I gaze longingly at the horses and wonder if this might be my chance to split from Juan-Do.

"We will go as far as they take us—even if we don't arrive in Santiago."

Because I am facing into the sun, I don't see (or hear) Juan-Do leave the albergue, turn onto the path and walk ahead. The Italian woman, however, has spotted him. I follow her gaze until I land on Juan-Do, who is standing a short distance away, facing us, his eyes closed. He is brushing himself off, pushing away energy, greeting the sun, communing with invisible spirits, the universe. He gestures with his arms, in all directions. I look up at the Italian couple and shrug. They grasp their reins and nudge their mares into forward motion, walking slowly past the Man of Few Words.

Chapter 46: Magic Mushroom

A crescent moon still lurks in the sky and the cool autumn air feels refreshing. Water glistens in a river rushing by on the other side, the sun streaming down, shining through the trees and leaves, small yellow golden leaves falling off trees, swirling around as they tumble to the ground. I, unfortunately, discover that we must walk a large chunk of today next to the *carretera* (highway)—one arm's length from speeding cars, rumbling trucks and swirling fumes. Which explains why leaves that looked shimmering green from a distance are, up close, thickly layered with dust.

From afar, I see a magnificent solitary house perched on a hill, graced with two old trees, a large lawn and vineyards as far as the eye can see—a scene evoking the graceful estates that pepper Jane Austen's novels. A long winding gravel road leads to a gate, through which one would reach the imposing residence, a pastoral paradise. El Castillo Magnifico. I could retreat there for a while.

Chestnut trees, with fallen castañas spread everywhere, create a carpet of baubly fuzz, along an obstacle course of fig trees and blackberry brambles. The relative stillness of nature quietens my mind as I walk. For long stretches of time, I almost believe that Juan-Do might be a figment of my imagination.

I search for locals as I arrive in the sleepy village of Trabadelo. None in sight. I pick up a few snacks at Carmen's *supermercado*—though I fail to appreciate what is so 'super' about a miniscule, airless store that carries little in the way of staples and produce.

After registering at the still-empty municipal albergue, I do a load of laundry and hang clothes out back to dry. I'm unloading food in the kitchen when the front door opens. In walks a strikingly handsome Italian man, holding two massive mushrooms; the top of one as bulbous as a meditation cushion. He waves them in front of me.

"*¿Quieres bolletas?*" Do you want mushrooms?

"Yes, thanks. But how do I cook them?"

The Italian guy shrugs, grins and turns on his heels to leave. My heart opens—and promptly melts.

"*Mille grazie!*" I call out after him.

Great. I have two gargantuan mushrooms. Now what? One thing is certain: they will feature in tonight's dinner. If only I could call on Jakome's spirit to manifest in this kitchen; he knows his mushrooms. Laying aside my concerns about dinner, I curl up with a book in front of the fireplace. Graham Greene's *A Burnt Out Case*. I've barely cracked the spine when I hear the front door open. Jakome walks in. *No possible!* He takes one look at the bolletas, and his eyes light up. I willingly don the role of sous-chef.

Following his instructions, I return to Carmen's for garlic and eggs. Jakome whips up a Basque-style mushroom specialty called Revuelto de Hongos, which despite its name (nothing revolting about it) ends up looking like a magical mishmash of mushrooms, scrambled egg, parsley and garlic—which it proves to be. Two young women, one French and the other Korean, join us. Juan-Do is invited as well, but he opts to chew on a ham bocadillo, his second of the day.

After dinner, the fire still crackles in the corner hearth. I wipe up crumbs from our four-star pilgrim dinner, while Jakome grumbles about his battle with bedbugs.

"*Cada día, muchos chinches,*" he wails, "*basta!*" Every day, so many bedbugs! Then, Jakome and Juan-Do start to bicker, the Spaniard telling the Basque how to combat the plague. Jakome looks more annoyed than grateful. I am done, excusing myself for the night.

When I wake up the next morning, Juan-Do is not in the lower bunk. I come down for breakfast, and find him fully clothed, asleep in front of the fireplace.

✤

Chapter 47: (Un)Bound, Together

After a quick breakfast, passing through a valley covered in heavy grey mist, we hoof it out of Trabadelo. The mist crystallizes, hardening into frost. Carved into window glass, the rime fuses dew drops onto hardened leaves, and snowflakes leave their dainty imprints on rocks. The temperatures plummet, as days tilt ever more towards winter. The unexpected rush of cold seeps through my body, leeching into all extremities. My finger-tips are chilled to the bone. My feet, clad in warm wool socks, resist and insist on the sandals.

I'm bent over, picking through a bunch of castañas, when I hear Juan-Do calling out at me.

"*Mira!*" Look here. He waits for my undivided attention, then launches into the most pressing monologue of the moment.

"The Camino is hard work," says The Man of Few Words. "For everyone, it must be hard work."

"What do you mean?" I ask, stuffing castañas into a bag of groceries. "Do you mean hard on the body?"

"In every way."

"Please elaborate," I think of adding—but don't, because just then, as if to unravel the mystery, the lyrics to James Taylor's "Shed a Little Light" rise to the fore; reminding me how intricately bound up we still are in each other's journeys.

And so it is. Until we reach the end of this road, Juan-Do and I are bound—inadvertently, confusingly, unspeakably—to each other. Bound, and (un)bound, in the hard work of the heart, and in silence.

And yet. Another filament of hope: He will hand me a fig. A

purple fig. But Juan-Do doesn't eat purple. Only green figs. Green figs and ham.

Over the next few hours, I shed layers, flex my Spanish muscles with locals, and crouch down low to photograph the cracked beauty of castañas.

Straggling behind Juan-Do, I look up in time to catch him responding to a call of the wild. He is like Marcel Marceau, the great mime, spreading cosmic dust around his aura.

Chapter 48: Castañas y León

A concrete divider on the way to Vega de Valcarce features a familiar flourish of graffiti. *Open Your Heart Wider*. Frank, are you paying attention? Who is this elusive Frank anyway, and where is he? Ahead of us? Trailing behind us? Is he a real pilgrim or does he exist inside each of us?

Stop judging him. Give him a break. Maybe he needs his solitude as much as you need connection. Don't take it so personally. Keep your heart open.

I'm keeping a safe distance behind Juan-Do, when I arrive in a valley dotted with apple trees, flirting butterflies, cud-chewing cows and a wall-to-wall panorama of nuts hidden among leaves. Shells, whole and opened, are scattered across the ground like an enormous game of marbles, some half-broken, in play. Like a game of hopscotch, I crush nuts with every second step. Beyond a clearing, I spot Jakome in a grove, gathering fallen walnuts. I crumple over the stone parapet edging the grove, for a short rest before joining Jakome in gathering up handfuls of nuts.

After Juan-Do passes by without a word, Jakome and I walk the path together, with conversation wandering—from bedbugs to mushrooms, from the struggle for Basque independence to the scruffy growth of his beard. We pass through villages, many sheathed in an almost sinister silence. Ghost towns of the Camino. No dogs barking. No cars passing through. No cow bells. Only in gardens do we find the occasional signs of life; vegetable patches recently seeded, crows picking at cornfields, CDs dangling from the eaves to ward off birds. Not long ago, humans have been here.

Other signs of life are on the horizon. Juan-Do slumbers in the shade, his weathered boater pulled down over his face, looking every bit like a silver-screen cowboy at rest—minus the horse and a dried weed dangling out the side of his mouth. When he hears us approach, Juan Wayne rises stiffly and buckles himself into the harness. He plows ahead, past the last houses in the village and into a forest of castañas, barely acknowledging our presence.

When we emerge out of another chestnut-filled canopy, I pull out a shell from my pants pocket—one of the few I've carried from places far away; Florida, Israel, Indonesia. I place it on a way marker, nestling it among a pile of stones. These are the stones of pilgrims, who carry them on the Camino and leave them behind, on markers, memorials, the Iron Cross. But the combined weight of a handful of stones in my pocket would tip the scales—so I carry lightweight shells instead. The difference doesn't elude me: Stones are smooth and solid. Each of the shells I carry is fragile, vulnerable to cracks.

As I round a curve, I spot a bramble bursting with blackberries. At their peak of ripeness, and despite the ice coating their skin, these berries glimmer in the light. After the past few days of berry-drought, I am thrilled at the sight of these juicy jewels. The bastón reaches out for the dangling berries, as if it had a mind of its own. With the stick hooked over branches deep inside the bush, I spear a handful of berries, and gorge until sated. Winter's frost be damned.

The small front patio of the La Faba refugio is decorated with prayer flags, statues of Buddha and Ganesha, handmade jewelry and a collection of spiritualized tchotchkes. I help myself to a cup of tea and settle onto a cushioned chair that wobbles with each movement. A middle-aged woman trudges in, drops her pack and sits close by. Without introducing herself or commenting on the mounds of chestnuts we have passed, she dives right into an inquiry about my plans for All Saints Day, her accent unmistakably French.

"I don't have a saint," I reply in French.

"But yes, of course you do!" she exclaims, with a level of disdain that might be better reserved for her partner.

"I'm pretty sure I don't have a saint," I try to clarify, reverting to English from my rusty French. "I think I would know if I had one. Anyway, I'm not Christian."

"But you must have a saint," the French pilgrim persists. "*Everyone* has a saint."

Not Jews, I want to say. *I don't need a saint*, I also want to say, because I have angels. But instead, I shake my head and take a slow sip of herbal tea.

"What's your name?" she forges on; insistent.

"Amit."

"In what language is that?"

"Hebrew and Hindi," I say. Take your pick, I think of tacking on; you won't find most Hindus revering Christian saints either.

"Oh then," she says, "then no, I don't think that you have a saint."

Duh.

I stand up and carry my now-emptied cup of tea inside.

On the rocky and circuitous path towards O Cebreiro, I see a sign marking a border. It reads "Castilla y León." Contiguous regional borders along the Camino are only symbolic, permitting nature's wildness to freely straddle invisible boundaries. Mushrooms flourish on both sides, as do wildflowers. Moss and lichen, valleys and forests, are oblivious to borders. But, this region is so flush with chestnut trees and fallen nuts, perhaps a more fitting name would be *Castañas y León*.

During this excruciatingly long and physically demanding stage, the pain—in my back, my foot, along my left leg—aches with each step; that I deliberately count, as if it could help or distract me from the remaining distance to the peak. The pained regions of my body contain invisible boundaries, blurred and overlapping. I am *this* close to tears, and falling. Laboring upward, I remember the words of a former colleague, spoken years earlier, when I shared news around the office about my plans to hike up Annapurna. Most wished me well. But Nadya, a young Slavic woman with a long mane of dirty-blond hair, known to keep a stash of voodoo dolls in her cubicle, had other ideas; she stopped me in the corridor, stared hard and murmured: "I hope you don't fall off the Himalayas." She was off by roughly nine months and 4,000 kilometers. But dammit, she'd jinxed me.

A lone figure emerges out of the haze up ahead. A sherpa in shining armor? Not quite. The Man of Few Words stands taller than before, striking a command-pose, both hands fixed on his hips. The Carrix is out of sight. He might be mad, possibly irate. But the sight of Juan-Do fills me with an unfamiliar feeling of relief and gratitude; even as I've summited one of Galicia's highest peaks, he still hasn't abandoned me. With my last vestiges of energy, I clamber up to reach level ground—where, on a different day, with other people, I would not even need to ask for hugs because they would be given freely, woven into a tapestry of triumph, with the crisp sounds of revelry echoing off the mountains.

And so ends a momentous day; a milestone in my Camino—and not just because of this day's steep ascent: It's been forty days and forty nights since I last stepped out of a motorized vehicle, and began walking through the wilderness—of nature and man alike.

Chapter 49: Sun Salutation

The dawn brings with it a fresh layer of powdery snow on the ground and icicles hanging from eaves outside the window. If I thought of opting for a rest day, this chill is so off-putting that I would prefer to barrel through in one shot. After getting dressed inside my sleeping bag, I pack up and leave my bag behind for Juan-Do, taking refuge in the only open place at that hour, a bar/café that is dimly lit, as if in deference to the hungover. Dried garlic bulbs, antiques, posters, knick-knacks and a picture of a matador hang on a wall. Last night's revelry (pilgrims are known to party here) is replaced this morning with pilgrims hunched over cups, wordlessly rousing themselves with a shot of café con leche.

I glance around for Juan-Do. Nowhere to be seen. Mug in hand, I peek out the window, catching sight of a rising orb already spreading its rays in all directions, inviting locals and pilgrims alike to emerge and shake off last night's deep chill. Juan-Do is out there too, standing in the middle of the road, facing the sun, his arms clasping the energy in front of his body. Indifferent to passing vehicles, cyclists, pilgrims and cows, he greets the sun. A sun salutation, minus the sweat and incense.

In that quiet moment, perhaps because of the window that separates us, I see him in a new light. He is shrouded in peace, welcoming whatever may arise in this day. I think I know what it is he seeks in these precious moments of sun worship. Grace. Understanding. Forgiveness. Acceptance. I know because I seek the same, though he knows not.

I step outside and stand waiting by the side of the road, watching his movements.

The warmth of the sun entices pilgrims out from bed and bar. Even cyclists, known to careen past slower walking pilgrims, hit the brake pads and pull over to the roadside, overcome by the sumptuousness. Struck by its magic and majesty, few other phenomena can bring humanity to a standstill, bring them closer to a sense of peace. As the day makes its grand entrance, the audience is enthralled.

A young and extraordinarily handsome pilgrim, his tanned face punctuated by salt-and-pepper stubble as if he had rubbed it with frost, approaches me.

"Do you know what that guy's doing?" he asks, gesturing towards Juan-Do.

"I know it looks like he is playing an invisible accordion," I say, "but he is actually connecting to the sun's energy." I suddenly feel compelled to protect Juan-Do's sacred space.

The man looks at me strangely, and walks away.

Juan-Do lowers his arms and opens his eyes. He turns around to the crowd of sun-gazers, catches me observing him and turns away.

After Foncebadon, O Cebreiro was supposed to be the second highest—and last—peak. I had been told: It's all downhill afterwards. But when I another mountain range juts out ahead, I feel dejected, deceived and close to giving up.

Fortunately, nature softens the blow and boosts my morale. Dew-tipped grass stalks glisten like ribbons studded with diamonds. Hardy trees of pine and holly send their scent into the path. Layers of ground frost cover tiny yellow wildflowers that crumple from the grey wind and chill. Large patches of browned and wilted ferns twinkle in the sunlight, last night's rain now crystallized into ice-drops. The silence of frost is entrancing; as if the entirety of nature has been stopped in its tracks, numbed into stillness, reluctant to rustle leaves or budge an inch for fear that one slip-up will trigger a hiss, crackle and pop.

***

Whenever the woman lost herself into a void of darkness, she would peel off layers of fragmented existence, scrub off all traces of intent or despair, and envision opening a door into the final exit of relief. Through days and nights of interminable silence, the phone might ring until the answering machine clicked on and recorded what the woman could not bear to hear in real time, which was the sound of her older sister, calling from miles away and across the border, pleading with her to pick up, please just pick up or send me an e-mail, please let me know that you are okay, or at least alive.

***

I nestle three shells into a pile of frosted leaves and petals, struck by the incongruity of embedding them into a cold and wintry landscape, so far from their native tropical climate. Who will break first, the shells or me?

❧

Chapter 50: The Empty Tank

The powder-packed trail from O Cebreiro leads us through the village of Linares, where we stock up on snacks. Just in time: Another uphill hike, another sizeable ascent awaits. Juan-Do walks by me hauling the Carrix. If I squint my eyes just so, there is something Jesus-like in his stoop—as if he were burdened with a wooden cross on his way to crucifixion.

With his hat almost touching the ground, so low that it could very nearly scrape off the ice, this I see and know: Even if he avoids me, Juan-Do is exerting as much strength as someone half his age might. He's on a quest I recognize well; he is emptying his tank.

***

Summer 2007. It was the last season I'd trained and competed with my dragon-boat league in Toronto. Back when I could still sit and paddle. My dragon boat practice and racing career, though short-lived, brought out my competitive side. My teammates and I dug deep, pushing ourselves to the farthest reaches of muscle power and stamina. Pockets of stored energy, lying dormant in the recesses of my body's physical abilities, materialized. Invisible became visible. Our coach challenged us to tap into a reserve of hidden power. From his bench at the back of the boat, his voice would crackle like a lightning bolt, driving us towards the finish line, pain and exhaustion be damned: *"Empty the tank!"*

***

The Stagers who power past us, fueled on adrenaline and Camino Candy, empty their tank frequently; Juan-Do empties his intermittently. With a sudden spurt of energy, he rushes by, the Carrix trailing behind him, its wobbly wheels groaning against gravel. As if the cart itself could transmit the message: Go on, speed up!

We reach Hospital de la Condesa, where I ask a sun-wrinkled elder, sitting on a stone in the shade, for directions to the hospital. "*No abierto*," she says, her ill-fitting false teeth clacking with every word she utters. "*A las doce*." It's closed until noon.

"*Caminar más rápido*," she says. "*Si quieres llegar a Santiago*." You'd better walk more quickly, if you want to reach Santiago. This granny would also like for us to empty our tanks. Trouble is, she can't tell that I've already emptied mine.

Juan-Do approaches and intervenes: "*No puede*." She can't. I let his words sink in. Maybe he has understood something after all.

***

As soon as the suitcases were packed into the back of the station wagon, the front door locked and the garage door closed, the girl was buffered by her sisters—which meant she could (usually) exhale. New York meant Broadway plays, the Met, delis and shopping sprees. The Caribbean islands meant tennis, beaches and club sandwiches by the pool. Books were read, games played, skin tanned. In Spain, there was flamenco; in London, pigeons at Piccadilly; in British Columbia, plucking cherries; and in Vermont, watching Nixon lie. Adventure and possibility lay everywhere. On the go, in the air, under the sea, all else seemed suspended, almost inconceivable, as if fallen into abeyance.

***

I cross the road and, responding to the call of my back, I collapse over a stone parapet. I turn and lie down, grateful for the leafy canopy above that blocks out the blazing sun, without which, my face would shortly be baked into a crispy caramel flan-like tan. A flock of chickens crosses into a field of greens nearby, pecking away at scattered food morsels, and zigzagging between a maze of stalks laid out as if it were an obstacle course.

Across the road, two young men, too young for beards, are seated at a table in front of a bar. A guitar leans against the wall. Juan-Do pulls up a seat next to them, reaches over for the guitar and starts to strum—and sing. The genie escapes again. In Castrojeriz he found pleasure and laughter in the dance; here, there is joy and sweetness in his voice. Why he refuses to share those moments with me remains a mystery.

Even after my pain subsides I stay put. I don't want to be a killjoy. As I turn my gaze upwards again, I see clouds morph into billowy patterns against a baby blue sky, every so often sliced through by a vapor trail. Yellowed leaves hang precipitously off a tree's limbs, and a pair of twittering kingfishers swoops down to the field below, landing on the backs of cows. All the while, Juan-Do regales the bearded ones by plucking away; the young pair seemingly unbothered by the fact that his humming is unmistakably off-tune.

For the first time in a long while, and perhaps because there is music in the air, and a garden shooting greens up into the sky, and nobody going anywhere fast, my tank is empty and I am content to be right where I am.

Chapter 51: Fonfria

We are closing in on three o'clock, when I spot a sign that reads Fonfria. My relief is so raw that I nearly step into a pile of donkey poop. With its handful of buildings set back from the road, Fonfria might be just a blip on the Camino map. But its rolling meadows and valleys, grazing cows, wildflowers, and sun rays elbowing their way through clouds, conjure up images worthy of IMAX.

As I step into the Refugio Privado Reboleira it feels like I've walked into a friend's country cottage. Welcoming smells waft towards me from somewhere deep inside; the scent of home cooking rising from pots on the stove seeping into the hallway, embracing me into the warmth of a home. Ángela, the owner, hugs tight; while Lola, the receptionist, glances at my Canadian passport and exclaims, "I loved Niagara Falls!"

We're led past a dining room and lounging area full of books and games, to the large, wood-paneled dorm room at the back. Juan-Do drops my pack without fanfare. By now, my bed-prep is on auto-pilot, completed in seconds flat. On top of a thick mattress in a small alcove with two parallel bunk beds by a window, I unfurl my sleeping bag for the umpteenth time. Sunlight streams in as I clamber up the ladder and lie down for a long rest. Another day, another bed.

A load of laundry washed and hung later, I head out to explore the micro-hamlet. From the middle of the main road that intersects the village, I can see both ends of the village. Cows moo in the distance, but otherwise, Fonfria is so quiet that I could lie down on the road undeterred, unbothered.

Higher up in the village, I investigate the minutiae of small village life: a farmer's compound, with cows, dogs and hard-working country folk—women in aprons, boots and headscarves; the men are in standard-issue lumberjack wear. They scoop up cow manure, haul bales of hay into sheds, stock up on logs. I wonder what the villagers do on their down time. If they take vacation. If they have ever been to Santiago, if they have ever seen the sea.

A sandwich board, set up at the top landing of a staircase, reads: *Queseria*. With just a trickle of pilgrims now passing through, it's a curious marketing strategy—for a cheese shop. But how else would I have discovered its culinary treasures? I step inside the small, brightly-lit room, which houses a squeaky-clean cheese production 'facility,' with a one-woman 'assembly-line.' She is carving smaller chunks off a block of cheese, squeezing them into plastic tubs that she arranges on a table nearby.

"*Hola. ¿Di-me?*" the cheesemaker asks, in abridged form. What would you like?

"*¿Hace queso vaca, uveja,o cabra?*" I inquire. Do you make cow, sheep or goat cheese?

"*Vaca,*" she says. Just cow. Most likely, the cow down the lane. About as farm-to-table as it gets.

I buy a small container with one round patty, intending to save it for tomorrow's breakfast—but with my weakness for freshly made anything, my willpower wilts quickly. In the fading afternoon light, I stand among my jungle of nearly-dry laundry that hangs off lines in the back yard, talking to my older sister an ocean away, while picking away at half the mound, in geometrically-considered slices.

My tour of Fonfria and its cheese industry concludes just in time—for dinner. Juan-Do and I are first to arrive at a round table large enough to seat ten. He waits for me to sit, then pulls out a chair for himself—diametrically across from me, the furthest point away. For some time, we're alone a table. I look across and see him staring down at his hands. He still wants nothing to do with me.

***

In her first year of high school, when she stood at her parents' bathroom window and watched through the glass and now-denuded tree branches, as her classmates gathered in front of a boy's house for the first bar mitzvah of the year, to which she was not invited (nor would she be invited to any of the others, save, for reasons unknown, to the very last one), and when her unholy sadness masqueraded as feigned disinterest, with nobody to wrap her up in concern or strip her of calcifying shame, the girl folded so deeply into herself that she would not, not ever, never never—as her paternal grandmother used to say with a smile and a kiss in other circumstances—be revealed.

***

We are still alone, almost comically seated opposite each other, when Ángela serves us bowls of piping hot *caldo gallego* (Galician traditional soup), with potatoes and *grelos* (collard greens). While I take a close-up whiff of herbs in the soup, two French pilgrims walk in. Laure is petite; I hear she will be my bunk neighbor that night. Beni, an older man, is also slight in build—but robust in opinion. They spread themselves out, sitting in between Juan-Do and me, unwittingly creating a buffer zone.

"I can't stand the people who snore," says Beni. "Especially the women." Ouch. I scoop up another spoonful of soup instead and chew slowly.

When Laure, Beni and I start talking in French, I become acutely aware that Juan-Do is left out. I wonder whether he minds, but he seems cast off into another world, perfectly content to be slurping the soup, his nose sunk halfway into the bowl, then into a dish of lamb and sweet peppers. Married to his meal. Food might be his meditation, as it is in Bali, where locals are expected to eat in silence.

In spitfire French, Beni runs through a checklist of his Camino highlights. "I already reached Muxia on the coast—in record time," he says. "I'm on my way back home now."

At meal's end, and as if we weren't already well-fed, we find sufficient stomach-space to dig into slices of Tarta de Santiago, the traditional Galician cake that satiates a pilgrim's sweet tooth cravings. Almond-based, this moist, marzipan-tasting pie, is dusted with icing sugar forming the stenciled emblem of Saint James (Santiago). While nibbling away at the pie, I ask Laure and Beni about their reasons for walking.

Beni pipes up first: "*Pas pour les raisons tres gais.*" Not for very happy reasons.

Nothing more. I turn to Laure.

"*Et toi?*" I ask.

"I was very sick," says Laure. "I walked the Camino a few years ago. Then I became sick again last year."

Like Rosa, she too is on Camino Redux, hoping to stave off her recurrent illness. Laure's belief in the power of walking towards healing resonates deeply. But when she says that she committed to walk as the original pilgrims did, centuries ago, I'm all ears.

"I sleep in simple accommodations," she says. "I wash my laundry by hand and I don't use a cellphone or public transport like other pilgrims. I walk and live in a *primitive* way."

I'm in awe of Laure's vow of simplicity. I wonder what it feels like, such an immersion in tech-less simplicity for weeks on end, while all those around her digitize their entire experience, in word and image. I'm reminded of Simone Weil, the French Jewish-Catholic writer, who for most of her thirty-four years, had sought to live no better than the peasants and factory workers in her midst.

After dinner, I lie in bed reading by the light of my cellphone. Falling towards the cusp of sleep, I switch off my phone, zip myself into the sleeping bag and peek over to say good night to Laure—who is at that moment reading from a Kindle. The *primitive* kind.

The next day is November 1st, All Saints Day. *Oh dios!* The village is draped in a cold and dreary darkness—which was preceded by a howling and violent wind overnight. Although the winds have died down, the gloom persists.

Slinking stealthily down the ladder, I draw open the window's curtain and peek outside. Through heavy fog and threatening clouds, I see leaves quivering, pummeled by the wind. Here is Mother Nature, at her wicked worst, paralyzed by ice. My fleece sweater is no match for this chill.

It appears all the saints are marching in on this day, heralding their arrival with the full force of a divinely-guided climactic intervention.

Lola turns the corner, sees me shivering. "I'm sorry," she says, almost apologetic in tone. "But today we must close. You will have to leave the albergue." Right about now, I would be grateful for a saint of my own.

I dress in thick layers, pack, pull up socks, strap on my sandals and step outside. By then, the blistery winds and downpour have tapered down to a light drizzle. I dig into breakfast by Ángela: *Cola Cao* (chocolate milk), a leftover piece of Tarta de Santiago, and a delicious but slightly congealed slice of Fonfria's finest cow's cheese.

A sign at the reception desk proclaims the official end of pilgrim season: CERRADO. Closed. What a blessing, that we arrived at the edge of time. On our way out, I thank Ángela for her hospitality. She embraces me as if I was the first pilgrim of the season, not the last.

"*Yo siento como en mi casa*," I say. Here, I felt at home.

Chapter 52: A Young Buck (or Gratitude for Juan-Do)

On the way out of Fonfria, now shrouded in heavy mist, there isn't a single dog, cow or chicken to be heard or seen anywhere. My guess is that farmers keep their animals out of sight on All Saints Day. Either that, or those creatures have refused to go outside. Smart beasts, on strike.

While I blow hot air onto my sock-covered hands, I wonder about the saints. In the book I've been reading, *The Burnt Out Case*, Graham Greene writes that our definition of a saint should not be limited to those anointed by the church, but should include common folk, regular people in the world. People on the Camino. People like Ángela and Rosa and Eugenio. Who knows, maybe Juan-Do is a saint in disguise?

Since the church-saints have ensured that all commercial activity today grinds to a halt, I decide to rely more on nature's offerings. On this trail strewn with rocks, fallen leaves and shards of chestnuts, there are slim pickings. But my patience and hunger are soon rewarded, when I spy a few blackberries dotting bushes, their purplish-black juicy bulbs camouflaged by darkened, spiky shrubs. Well done. Thank you, saints.

As the strong overnight rains taper down, they leave strong scents in their wake. Nature's freshest fragrances come alive as if they were on a scratch-and-sniff greeting card. I pluck and nibble away, walking among the holly trees whose gem-like reddish berries stand out against deep green foliage. Kingfishers glide by, homing in on a target in a nearby field. The path, ahead of us and behind, is muddy, caking my sandals so that brown goop spreads up to the heels of my socks.

We stop for hot drinks and snacks at a café. A few locals, mostly elderly men, huddle inside. I order a slice of cheesecake and hot chocolate. Juan-Do orders a bocadillo, then asks for hot water, with which he prepares an infusion of herbs and ginger powder. I chat with the lady behind the bar while the Man of Few Words chews in slow motion, as if transfixed on every bite.

When the waitress leaves to prepare food for another pilgrim, Juan-Do dons an unfamiliar pair of glasses. The frames are purple. Purple?! No purple figs, but purple-framed glasses get the green light.

"*¿Dónde… ?*" The word for glasses escapes me, so I motion with my fingers, drawing circles in the air around my eyes.

"*En el Camino.*" Enough said. But my gut curdles with a longing. What would it take to stretch these micro-exchanges into a semblance of genuine, heartfelt conversation? Dialogue. Connection. All of it, so elusive. Weeks later, we are strangers still.

"*¿Entonces, dónde es el otro?*" So, where is the other pair?

Juan-Do retrieves the red-framed pair out of his shirt pocket. For someone whose wardrobe consists almost entirely of neutral colors—beige, brown, blue, black—he certainly has an eclectic taste in accessories. Or maybe he likes—or can only afford—other peoples' castoffs.

Satiated and warmed up, we head further downhill, treading carefully on slippery, chestnut-laden paths. On our way into the next village, passing huge rolls of hay and mushrooms growing on the roadside, and ducking under towers that emit a constant buzz of electricity, the smell of fresh cow dung has an almost spellbinding scent.

Behind me, the sounds of creaky wheels and plodding soles come to a stop. I turn around. Juan-Do is hugging trees again. Except this time, his back is glued to bark.

"*¿Porque quieres tu dar abrazo a los arboles?*" I ask, cutting through the silence. Why do you like to hug trees?

"*¿Porque no?*" he says. "*Porque yo quiero.*" Why not? Because I like to.

Long pause.

"*Y tu,*" he pipes up. "*¿No dar abrazo a los arboles?*" Don't you hug trees? As if doing so was the norm.

"*Normalmente no,*" I answer. "*Pero a veces.*" Usually not, but once in a while.

That's it. Conversation over. I don't know how to tell him that, as much as I love trees, I prefer to hug people.

Until we reach the doors of the next municipal albergue, we are caught in a web of silence. Triacastela. Three castles. Far from being a castle, this one—in stark contrast to Ángela's homey lodge—is devoid of soul and color. Each room is accessed through an open doorway with saloon-like swinging doors, effectively ensuring that sounds will circulate through all rooms, at all hours of the day.

By evening, it becomes apparent that there is no chance of blocking out sounds of pilgrims who like to revel into the wee hours. I glance at my watch; 22:22 p.m. Long past pilgrim bedtime. I traipse down the hallway, intending to plead for quiet. An all-black ensemble is seated at the far end. Most of them, with tattoos covering large swaths of skin. Tattoos are common enough, but this group emits an ominous aura. They are either black-hooded pilgrims or members of a Goth-themed, wine-guzzling, motorbike brigade who have taken a wrong turn. Either way, I slink back to my corner of the saloon, and into my upper berth, acutely aware of their vocals, carrying on into the late-night hours.

The All-Weather Saints are still with us the following morning: Overcast skies. Rain. Chill. Wind. A stalking greyness. If I were anywhere but here, expressly in Canada on an early winter Saturday morning, I'd be curled up under a duvet, cup of tea in hand, reading a book—and waiting for the next day's *New York Times*. Instead, I wake up feeling smothered by Triacastela's brooding dampness, and feeling tired from a sleepless night—attributed partly to the presence of those loud-mouthed, black-garbed, pilgrim-entities in the next room. To make matters worse, a young Australian cowboy-wrangler-type lies spread-eagled in the bunk below mine, snoring up a storm.

After a little café con leche, banana and yogurt, we're on our way. Most pilgrims leave this village bound for Sarria or beyond. But the weather does funny things to my body; it wears it down, ups the ante on pain and slows me down. Much to Juan-Do's dismay, today's destination is Samos, on the way to—but nowhere near enough to—Sarria.

The wind picks up, the chill sinks in deeper. I slip my sandals off to pull on socks. Rendering me a true fashion icon. Camino-style.

A slippery slug moseys across the road in front of me, aiming for grassy cover. Juan-Do, up ahead, searches for I know not what. He leans forward, hauling with great effort the load that now looks astonishingly larger than when we began. For all his lumbering, through mud and rain, his figure, in profile, now looks strikingly similar to the character of Tevye the Dairyman in *Fiddler on the Roof*, who is forced to leave his farm with all his belongings stashed on a wagon. Sometimes I wonder if, from age, effort, or illness, Juan-Do might completely break down.

I also wonder what mysterious forces came into play when they paired us up.

Why can't I be blessed with a young buck, instead of someone on the far side of mid-life; someone who could lift 'n carry easily, whose health and wellbeing don't hover as potential challenges? Like that boisterous wrangler type from Oz, who'd bounced into the room late last night, belching and hollering.

"Ya," he roared. "That was a great night walk!"

"Did you have a night lamp with you?" I asked, recalling the night of an empty moon.

"Naaah," he said.

Conversation then switched to the Camino.

"Where did you start off from this morning?" the Aussie asked.

"Fonfria," I said.

His eyes grew wide, as if he were duly impressed.

"That's awesome!" he raved. "Wow, you did 50k. Really amazing!"

No chance, buddy; not this body, not in this condition. Not yet. I thought it best to clear up any misunderstanding.

"No, not Ponferrada," I corrected him. "We left from Fonfria."

At which point, he made a quick mental calculation, realizing that I'd walked a fraction of the distance he'd calculated, thereby significantly lowering his esteem of me. Our exchange came to a halt, at which point he headed out to drink with new buddies, a swagger in his step.

As he bolted out the squeaky swinging doors, it occurred to me that I might have been spared the short end of the stick. Would I really have fared better if I'd been accompanied by a strong, but burly, overly talkative and testosterone-driven guy such as this? Could I have handled a young buck's penchant for partying and, most likely, hangovers? In the absence of a bona fide boyfriend, life partner or lover at my side, perhaps I could be thankful for what (or who) I had to deal with—regardless of the downsides and possibility of desertion. Given such a choice, I might have opted for the one who has been with me until now.

Chapter 53: The Rains and Pains of Spain

Today, there is much mud on the Camino. The walking paths are grimy, soaked, full of puddles. Even though we only have nine kilometers to cover, the path feels extraordinarily long and treacherous. Full of pain and unrelenting rain. At some point, water glides up my legs from below, coating the skin inside my supposedly impermeable pants with glistening droplets. But my footwear is gold, treading through mud and soupy water. Sandals of Steel.

The rain accompanies us as we reach the quaint village of Samos. Though chilled and drenched from top to bottom, I join a group of locals at their annual *magosto* festival—celebrating the harvest of castañas—taking refuge with the others, under the covered terrace of the local council hall.

The acrid smell of flames rises from below. Chestnuts roast on an open fire—in a garage, where a group of men tend to them inside a discarded metal washing machine basket that roasts while it rotates. The villagers offer us empanadas, red wine and castaña-filled paper cones. Music plays and small children scramble between the legs of adults. While I chomp on the warm chestnuts, a sculptor confides he has lost much of his livelihood because of the depressed economy. Spaniards must be hardier than my sandals; their celebrations eclipse their sufferings. In this remote pocket of the country, like elsewhere, Spaniards may as well be living off the grid.

The wind and rain continue unabated, pelting us as soon as we walk out from under the covered terrace. Juan-Do would prefer to stay at the picturesque Benedictine monastery; but, when I hear there is no hot water, I nix the idea without further thought.

"*Hay confidencia,*" Juan-Do says, less energetically than he has previously.

A sign for Albergue Albaroque appears, like a beacon out of a grim sky. Not only does it feature an open bar / café; but a functioning laundry machine and a rarity on the Camino—a bathtub.

While Juan-Do unbundles the Carrix, I follow the hospitalero upstairs, to our assigned room. It is miniscule: Our beds are less than one meter apart. Once Juan-Do walks in and unloads my gear, I start rummaging furiously through my backpack, partly to distract us both from feeling panicked at the proximity. I get busy; doing laundry, showering, nibbling on fruit and snacks stashed in a soaked plastic bag. When Juan-Do heads downstairs for a meal, I slip into bed and snuggle up close to the wall. Despite my anguish over the prospect of unavoidable, but unearned, intimacy, I will myself into sleep.

***

Her father agreed to try out acupuncture. She hadn't even been at the family home for 48 hours when she found herself clear across the city, having accompanied him to that session, and his cell phone rang. He was on a table, supine, so the girl-who-was-now-a-woman answered. She was still jetlagged, so she had to listen carefully. The quiet and steady voice on the other end gave no hint of a body in the throes of unbearable pain. The woman's mother shrunk into her usual stoic self, keeping illness and distress under wraps. But today and for the next many days, as the woman's sisters worried from afar while juggling children, work and lives, and her father felt panicked and helpless, her mother lay writhing in a hospital bed while the woman herself, the middle daughter, wheeled, washed, wiped, fed, folded, tossed, tied, and, come hell or high fever, slept by her side.

***

By the following morning, the clouds have parted, revealing a fresh coat of paint in the color of sky. But traces of nature's tumult are everywhere: Water still rumbles downstream with unimaginable force, weaving its forceful way through every nook, ditch and pipe. Rivulets form on dry matter. A family of spotted salamanders has turned to roadkill overnight.

Wading through the doused outskirts of Samos, I spot yet another misplaced cornfield bordering the path. I still wait to hear a local, in the style of Eugenio and Amodoro, calling out to me, a couple of ears of corn in the palms of his hand.

If corn is abundant on the road, chestnuts still pad my pockets. As we walk towards Sarria, I chew on a handful of nuts, leftovers from the previous day's fiesta. With every crunch and step, the sun rises higher at my back. I stop to admire a fig tree—though it is denuded of all fruit. Same thing at the next tree, and the next series of bramble bushes; no figs, no blackberries. Or, no edible ones. Frost has cracked down on these fruit, they are in deep slumber.

The dire cold triggers my need to pee. But, with no toilets in sight, I climb instead over a low stone wall, and into a field, where I unzip and squat. Suddenly a farmer materializes a few steps away, as if he had fallen from the sky. I freeze. He walks right by me with a pail and shovel in hand, ignoring my presence in order to preserve my dignity. By now, he probably knows better than to gawk at unsuspecting pilgrims who are contributing to the world's much-needed compost pile. But it is also a cringeworthy scene that I hope never to replay.

Eventually, I return to my senses and catch up with Juan-Do. A meandering vertical path, bisecting the lower town with zigzagging roads and staircases, leads us into the upper reaches of Sarria; for many, a pilgrim's paradise, riddled with cafés, albergues, restaurants, internet outlets and shops hawking Camino collectibles and souvenirs. Even during off-season, Sarria is abuzz. It's a major destination and rest stop for *aficionados* of Brierley. Juan-Do and I have slogged through too many weeks' worth of villages, to be waylaid by the fanfare. The patina is wearing off, the combined weight of our walk taking its toll. We are merely passersby.

As we crest the top of the hill leading out of Sarria, a young wide-bellied man, dressed nothing like a pilgrim, waves us down.

"Do you speak English?" he asks.

"Yes, why?" I say. "Do you need help?"

"Can you give me money please?" he says. "I finished my money and don't have enough to stay at an albergue." I detect a Slavic accent. And a scam.

"Why don't you go back into town," I suggest "and withdraw money from an ATM machine?"

"I don't have a bank card," he says, unwilling to meet my eyes.

"I'm sure you can find a municipal albergue," I say, "where they'll let you stay for free—at least, until you sort out your money." The Slav on the hill glances past us and down to the next wave of pilgrims. He is hopeful that alms are on their way.

"No," he says, "I don't want to do that."

A whiff of entitlement catches me off-guard.

"How were you planning to get to Santiago?"

"With the kindness of pilgrims."

"Well, I'm sorry that I can't help you."

"It's ok," he says with a snub, "I will find good pilgrims who will help me."

Good pilgrims. Are we not all good pilgrims, good people? Even those who have gone astray or who insist on silence?

I continue to climb. Past Juan-Do, next to Juan-Do, behind Juan-Do. At the top of a steep incline, we pass through a chestnut-carpeted valley. The road is strewn with dead salamanders. Moss cascades off jagged rocks. Apple trees emptied of apples. Meadows with a smattering of cows. I find Juan-Do at the top of the hill. He doesn't move, as if in wait.

"¿*Vamos?*" I ask him. Are we going on?

"*Casi…*" he says. Almost. Enigmatic, as usual. He won't say what for. Not then, not later.

I glance over at the vista that has brought him to a standstill. He gazes out, speechless. I see why. This particular landscape is breathtaking; a panoramic view of an elevated highway, straddling across the valley below, while perched on top of magnificent carved columns like an ancient viaduct. It's a stunning piece of architecture that only lightly touches the earth; as if engineers intentionally sought to minimize the ecological impact of metal, asphalt and petrol. It is the kind of transformative experience that would prompt you to reach for your partner's hand in silent contemplation and shared appreciation. If you had such a partner. Which, unmistakably, I have not. Not even close. Not now. Not today. But one day, I will. And he, that man-of-my-imagination, will envelop my hand with so much love, desire and understanding, that I will have no choice but to let the memory of this strikingly tense moment, perched on a majestic cliff high above the clouds, turn to dust.

"Casi!" he roars, sounding like an animal in distress. Which, in this particular instance, I interpret as a minimalist, one-word alternative to "Go on!"

❧

Chapter 54: The Sarria Effect
(And Other Mysteries)

By the time we reach Barbadelo, I hear that the public albergue is filled to capacity with younger, partying pilgrims; a blessing, since our reservation at Casa Carmen, a private lodge, entitles us to skip the frat house-like ambience. From afar, the grounds at the top of the hill look promising. A grove of old-growth chestnut trees borders a well-tended lawn, a freshly washed crop of laundry billowing in the breeze. Horses are corralled inside an enclosure, chomping away at grass. Their heads jerk up as we approach, the chewing momentarily suspended. A path to the front door winds past stone buildings and a fountain.

Leaving Juan-Do to his routine of unhooking from the Carrix and unloading our gear, I duck into the hallway, where a woman named Consuelo greets me. We are in luck: Like the albergue in Fonfria before it, this *habitación privado* closes tomorrow. It feels as if we are grasping at wolves' tails on the eve of hibernation. Consuelo tells me that we are also being upgraded to a private room; the only one available.

She leads me up a small set of stairs into a quaint hallway with low ceilings. It is filled with wall hangings, embroidered stitching, heirlooms and ornately chiseled pieces of wooden furniture. Consuelo opens the door to a room, warmly bathed in soft yellow light. I expect to find a roomy suite, but it is tiny, Lilliputian almost; with flowery wallpaper, European antiques, a carpet, drapes drawn across the windows—and one double bed. I gasp.

Consuela sees the look on my face.

"*¿Hay una problema?*" she asks.

"*No puedo…* " I say, shaking my head and trying to sound less frantic than I feel.

She smiles and assures me that the double bed is actually comprised of two singles. I urge her to quickly separate the beds with me, moving them as far apart as possible. I don't even want to hazard a guess as to Juan-Do's possible reaction were he to see the same set-up—but I would wager on horror over humor. Consuela and I leap into action, shifting around pieces of furniture—night tables, recliner, stool, lamps—until the beds are placed as far away from each other as humanly possible. Perfectly timed for Juan-Do's entrance. Consuela and I trade knowing glances, and she slips out.

On the way to dinner, I meet Carmen, the owner who is also the brains behind most of the cooking. I ask her about the albergue further downhill.

"Why is it so packed with pilgrims?" I ask. A curious anomaly so late in the season. Which is how I learn about the Sarria Effect.

According to Camino lore and regulation, pilgrims who seek to obtain the church's highly-coveted *compostela*—certificate of completion—must begin their pilgrimage to Santiago no less than 100 kilometers from Santiago. Which makes Sarria the ideal jumping-off spot. Which explains much else as well, as I will soon find out. All accommodations, now leading to Santiago will necessarily, and to the perpetual consternation of pilgrims starting off further afield, be filled with the thousands of souls who launch from Sarria. Even during the lowest of seasons, there is a fair chance that all beds will be claimed. Thanks to Casa Carmen, we are rescued from a night of bedlessness.

Instead, we are treated to this season's last supper. In the dining room, I pull out a chair at the table where 3 Italians are gathered. Vicenzo, Pierantonio and Michaela.

Consuela arrives from the kitchen and reads out the set dinner menu: *sopa Gallegos* and *pollo con patatas*, followed by a *tarta de queso*

or *tarta de chocolate*. After we call out our choices, Vicenzo throws a
question into the ring.

"Do you know how to tell the difference," he asks, "between
people who walk for spiritual reasons and those who do so for
other reasons?"

"No," I say. "How?"

"You see the *luz*," he says, "the light in their eyes." If I looked hard
enough, I wonder if I'd find any light in Juan-Do's eyes.

"Look for it when you reach Santiago," Vicenzo adds.

In the late morning, we leave Barbadelo under a cover of clouds
and falling chestnuts. As we pass yet another bizarrely located
cornfield, a gust of wind drizzles water onto us at a slanted angle. It
tapers down long enough for me to pick out the sound of Stagers at
our heels. Harried pilgrims, dashing by. Brierley disciples? Sarria
launchers? Hard to distinguish by sound only.

Visual clues come in handy: their gear is spotless, their hiking
boots showing no trace of dried mud; their still-creased rain ponchos
draped over bodies and backpacks—resembling a flock of multi-col-
ored Bactrian camels crossing a wet desert. Clearly novices, Sarria
starters. They stride across an inflatable cloud, visible to everyone
but themselves. A sudden burst of wind sends their plastic coverings
flying off in all directions, flailing above them in the destabilized air,
shrinking from sight as they push ahead, heads hanging low. Their
clothes don't get as muddy, and they rarely get a taste of the blistered
life. Some have been known to call it: Camino Lite.

The flock passes and my mind veers off into thoughts of blackberries. *Muros.* The brambles are plentiful, but each berry looks more
withered than the one before. A long-feathered kingfisher settles into
an apple orchard nearby, its wings shedding the wind. A pack of un-
leashed dogs takes cover nearby, under cars or inside entryways. One
sniffs at the Carrix, then, feigning disinterest in our snacks, dashes
off to join the others. The winds and rain finally begin to die down.

We reach a stream that is virtually impassable. If only Juan-Do had
the power to part the waters like Moses, I might regain confidencia.

But in the absence of miracles, Juan-Do's cosmic connections and other forms of divine intervention, I wade through muddy waters. In my socks-and-sandals.

Further on the path, with no sight of a village, town or local, I turn to Juan-Do.

"*¿Dieciséis kilometros hasta el albergue?*" I ask. Sixteen kilometers to go till we reach the albergue?

"*Ahora*," he says, "*no se a dónde estamos*." At this moment, I have no idea where we are.

The Man of Few Words pulls out his little guide and flips through the pages. We don't know where we are, and we don't know where we're going. Which doesn't mean that we are lost; we are not. With highly visible way markers posted all along the way, it is virtually impossible to get lost on the Camino. As long as we go the 'right' way, rather than the contrary way. Juan-Do tries to reassure me. "*Hay confidencia!*" But I am not entirely reassured. It's pouring again. I'm chilled, and in pain.

Chapter 55: Un Poco Mas

A way marker, piled high with stones, ribbons, photographs and crumpled notes, reads 100 kms. A milestone that calls for a shell, which I add to the mound.

"*Vamos,*" says Juan-Do. "*Un poco mas.*" Let's go. Just a bit further. No hay confidencia.

"*¿Dónde?*" I ask.

"*Camas,*" he replies. "*Aquí, aquí.*" There are rooms here, Juan-Do believes. But no, we still have a long way to go.

By the time we reach Morgade, well into the afternoon, I'm exhausted, wet and fed up.

When I find myself in times of trouble,
Mani's voice sings out to me,
He's just trying to help you
Let him be...

At the stone-walled *casa rural*, I'm led to a room with three single beds lined up next to each other. I head for the one at the wall, featuring the room's sole window and radiator. I undress quickly, lay my drenched clothes on the radiator, and slipping into long-johns and a dry fleece jacket, I fall onto the bed.

Juan-Do barges in, wielding my backpack on his shoulder, like a latter-day Atlas. He trudges over and drops my pack at the foot of my bed, as if it were a freshly bundled corpse in need of forensic autopsy. He turns away from me in silence.

"*Me duele,*" I had pleaded to him earlier. I'm in pain. We should have stopped a long time ago.

"*No me preocupado con eso*," he had said. "*Un poco mas.*" I don't care, he had said. A little further. Poor man, so deeply buried inside his bubble. Seemingly so desperate to disentangle himself from me. Weeks later, and I'm still mystified. Dejection courses through my veins, amplifying the pain.

Love cannot breathe inside our orbit. It cannot sustain itself when choked too long by silence. I must search for it where it dwells freely. At least for today, maybe it breathes downstairs.

In the rustic living room, flames dance in a fireplace, breathing warmth into the space. I flip through a basket full of magazines and books, landing on a short story collection by Miranda July. Its title: *No One Belongs Here More Than You.*

A jovial-looking pilgrim in a beard and baseball cap settles into a divan nearby, shuffling through the basket's remains as I had. Alan, an Australian native, one of the few I meet on the Camino, squints at me, looking puzzled.

"Hey!" a startled Alan cries out, as the flames light up his already rosy cheeks. "Aren't you the woman walking with that big blue cart on wheels?"

"Yup, but not just me," I nod. "And it's called a Carrix."

"Everyone is talking about it on the Camino," says Alan, removing his cap and tussling his hair.

He dives into the basket again and pulls out an unblemished English magazine.

"Would you like to read this?" Alan asks, flipping it over to show me the cover.

"*The New Yorker*?!" I blurt out, stunned. Finding a recent issue in these parts seems about as likely as finding a bramble bush of ripened blackberries on the moon.

After a nap, I head down for dinner, where I join Alan and two other pilgrims. When Juan-Do enters the dining room, I gesture towards him, suggesting that he pull up a chair. He looks away, sits at another table and eats his meal. Alone.

Fortunately, I am instantly distracted by a story Alan is recounting, about a tourism professor studying the feasibility of establishing a pilgrimage route in South Korea; followed by a story of a Finnish octogenarian, who is walking the Camino with an assistant, neither of whom can speak a word of English or Spanish.

"Did you hear about the group of people walking thirty-six hours at a time?" asks Alan, drawing out more stories, as if from a bottomless backpack of tricks.

"Why would they do that?" I wonder aloud.

"I'm not sure," he says. "Possibly because they want to finish the Camino quickly, in 2 or 3 weeks."

"What about Doreen," Alan continues. "Did you meet her yet?"

We all shake our heads.

"She carries a bunch of plastic bags," he says, rubbing floating ash from his eyes, "but won't tell anyone what is in them."

Doreen is walking with a Frenchman named Frank. "They walk at the oddest hours, arriving at albergues very late at night," Alan says, with a chuckle. "They sleep in, and leave much later than the others."

I wonder to myself, if this is the same Frank who is being summoned to open heart procedure.

"I was sitting outside the albergue in Hontanas, drinking beer with a friend," Alan leans in, indicating that the next story might be even more worthy of our attention. "Two vans pulled up. A small group of men stepped out of the van and walked into that pricier albergue down the road. From their appearance—no backpacks, no hiking gear—we thought they were wealthy tourists. But they weren't. We found out later that they were prisoners, participating in a release program that involves walking part of the Camino under supervision."

Rehabilitation by Camino. Innovative idea. I make a mental note to relay the story to Mani.

The following morning, after my usual guzzle of café con leche, I bundle up and wait for Juan-Do's signal.

The next way marker indicates that we are 99.5 kilometers away from Santiago. That .5 makes all the difference. No shrine here, just a solitary stone, unadorned. The marker pilgrims forgot. Today, it could use a shell and a trudge in its honor.

I inadvertently step into a deep puddle, thoroughly drenching my feet. I stop in my tracks, close my eyes, search for a pocket of stillness, and inhale a few deep breaths. It's not even 10 a.m., my body is beat and my heart beats even faster. Is this the day I must walk for Frank?

***

It was a sun-drenched weekend afternoon in 2007 when an unseen hand, a divine intervention perhaps, coaxed the girl (now a woman) away from the blistering heat of a Toronto summer and into a bookstore. A bookstore she had walked by many times but never paid much attention to. And in there, guided by that same invisible compass towards a wall, the woman was reeled in by a book on a shelf. It opened itself to an English word that she had never heard before, but its definition almost made her lose her balance and glance around to make sure nobody noticed what she had found. It was as if she was sneaking a peek at a centerfold in a XXX-rated magazine in a store down a rat-infested alley, when it was nothing of the kind. Though it might have been, for the startling effect it had on her, causing everyone else in the bookstore and the world itself to darken and fall away in an instant and dissolve into a void. The only thing that mattered in that flash of recognition, was that she might begin to find a way back to herself. She had been found by a book, by a single word, as if it was the only word in the entire universe that could tell her what she was about, even when she had no words for it herself—This, this is how you have lived and coped. Dissociation. That, that word, the one word that brought the thick red ruby velvet curtain separating her from the world, tumbling down, made all the difference.

***

As I descend along the trail's downward curve towards Portomarin, a hillock of green earth rises to my right, behind a fence. Something catches my attention. An ostrich. *Avestruz.*

Juan-Do stops behind me. "*Hay mucho*," he says. There are many. "*¿Sí?!*" I ask. "*En Camino?*"

"*Sí, sí,*" he continues, "*el hombre come eso.*" People eat them.

I cringe, suspecting that Juan-Do is teasing me—until I return to Madrid weeks later and see a sandwich board advertising its weekly special: Afrikaan Burger. *Hamburguesa de avestruz, queso gouda, tomate, lechuga, cebolla roja y* Bristolbar Chutney. A close-up of an ostrich graces the sign.

In front of a field abutting a house, I spot a curious-looking stone structure built onto a parapet.

"*¿Que este edificio?*" I ask Juan-Do. "*¿No es un palomar, por los cereales?*" What is this structure? Is it a shed, to store grains?

"*Es hórreo.*" Yes, it's storage. "*Para secar mais. Por pan. Por hacer el pan de mais.*" Corn is stored and dried here for baking bread.

When the rain clears up, the landscape glistens in its stillness, muros dangle—far beyond reach. Another swath of cornfield juts out of nowhere. When I stretch upward on tiptoes, grasping for a bundle of drooping figs above, my recklessness causes a gate to fling open, sounding an alarm. I make a quick and fig-less getaway.

Falling behind Juan-Do is a mixed blessing. On the one hand, there's no danger of him surprising me from behind, urging me to carry on another umpteen kilometers: *Un poco mas.* On the other, there's no telling when I might find him next—and, more to the point—what his state of mind might be. When I catch sight of him up ahead, standing still, hands off the Carrix and clasped overhead, I notice that his path is blocked by a *bullish* traffic jam. Cows are lined up, traipsing up the hill, elbowing the others out of the way. Their herder is missing. As each cow passes, it stops to stare and sniff out the Carrix. A species unknown to them. "What is this weird-looking creature?" I imagine thought bubbles forming above their heads. "Should we run for the hills?"

When they amble by me, I catch a whiff of an altogether distinct scent. Perfumed dung in the air. *Eau de Cow.*

❧

Chapter 56: To the Max

Ancient ruins flank both sides of a river that must be crossed to reach the grand stairway at the entrance to Portomarin. In case we have been misled, the sight of *flechas amarillas* confirms that we are on course. Those ubiquitous yellow arrows, are painted on markers, stones, pieces of wood, the road, columns, walls, bridges, surfaces everywhere. I envision a band of dedicated graffiti artists and hospitaleros, walking the Camino, their backpacks jam-packed with yellow paint and brushes.

Late in the day, this relentless uphill climb in search for a bed and shower, leads me to a fork in the road: A choice between the only two albergues remaining open in Portomarin, in this twilight of pilgrim season. One reeks of sweaty twentysomethings, damp laundry and beer. The other features a large empty room with an array of bunk beds and en-suite kitchen, oddly situated in a floor-to-ceiling glass enclosure (like an airport smoking lounge or a well-conceived prototype of the SNORP-dorm), as if space were at a premium.

An empty kitchen bodes well for my plan to make dinner. After picking up staples at a supermarket, I'm heading back uphill when I see Juan-Do walking down a side street, ostensibly in search of dinner. My instinct is to call out to him, share the food. Maybe, with nobody else in the vicinity, I can finally ask him: *What happened? Why don't you want to talk with me?* But I hold back. I still can't shake the feeling that he wants nothing to do with me—or perhaps he is just a recluse, tightly bound to his shell, hard at work.

Back at the albergue, I whip up a delicious, nutritious feast for one.

I'm lying in my upper bunk, tucked into my sleeping bag and reading, when Juan-Do returns from dinner. He sighs heavily, shuffling across the room to his lower bunk at the other end. He doesn't say a word. Minutes later, all movement and sounds have faded. The fluorescent light on the ceiling still buzzes above my head.

I wait.

Juan-Do asks if he should switch off the light.

"*Sí,*" I answer, "*por favor.*" Yes, please.

He gets up and fiddles with the switch for a few seconds. Mumbling inaudible words to himself, he gives up and returns to bed. The lights are still on. Perhaps he can sleep equally well, in the light and the dark; but I cannot.

"Juan-Do," I say, more calmly than I feel. "*¿Que pasa?*" What happened? An open-ended question, almost an invitation, that could be answered in any number of ways.

"*No puedo,*" he says. I can't.

I step down the ladder from my airy perch, switch off the light and climb back into bed.

My mind swirls with confusion and dead-end questions. Mani's words soothe me, when I feel entirely unsoothable.

He's just in his own world.

Let him be…

In the light of morning, I'm still in the dark. I can't gauge whether or not Juan-Do wants to eat before we head out. I prepare a breakfast of sliced fruit for myself, and leave a pan of boiled water on the stove, in case Juan-Do wants an infusion.

On the way out of Portomarin, the sight of cornfields strangely appeases me. Sunlight filters through apple trees, pine trees, their glimmering needles scattered on the ground.

Nature never lets me down, even when the weather is undecided, shifting without warning between hues and moods. One moment, I feel too thinly dressed; moments later, I'm overdressed and sweat forms on my brow. Rain falls. I pull up my hood. Rain abates. I drop the hood. It starts up again. It's cold. I zip up. The sun peeks out. I unzip. Oy, what a yo-yo.

We walk through a long chain of small but entirely vacated villages: Abandonada—to the max. The aroma of freshly roasted chestnuts mixed with cow manure is the only enduring sign of human life. By now, all corn is harvested, all grapes and chestnuts collected. At the edge of a crusty cornfield, two parked tractors, long unused, wait listlessly for a buyer.

Less than 80 kilometers until we reach the city of Santiago. A saint's city, looms ahead, only two digits away.

Chapter 57: A Serving of Corn… and Nadal

The drizzle starts up again. Two young Spanish guys dash by, their stride so confident it might outpace the rain. Without slowing down or skipping a beat, the tall one gives his *bastón* to the other, unhooks his backpack, shifts its full weight onto one shoulder, pulls out a poncho, slips it over his head, realigns the backpack into place, and turns to his friend to retrieve his *bastón*. A series of complicated maneuvers and he has not once broken out of step. An astounding feat, worthy of a Guinness Record, an Olympic gold medal, or at the very least, a mention in Brierley.

My own *bastón*, now embellished with a fragrant, herb-ringed string, has proven itself handy for other reasons; it is a blackberry-picker, par excellence.

A farmer stands at the edge of his field, watching his cows graze. I stop close enough to point to the structure a few steps away.

"*Hórreo*," he says, his pronunciation of the word—different than Juan-Do's—bringing to mind the chocolate and vanilla cream cookies that I used to split in two and slowly devour at summer camp. He gives me a basic lesson on these, yes, corn sheds. I learn that these vernacular structures, constructed mainly by stonecutters and craftsmen, are an important part of the Galician patrimony, dating back nearly two centuries. I also find out that the larger, ornate *hórreos*—mostly found in northern O Coruña—are greatly prized, with some valued as high as 2 million euros. These granaries once formed part of a bride's dowry; the prospective groom's parents would inspect the intended's hórreo and its contents, to determine whether or not their family would profit from the union.

Grateful for the illumination, I turn to leave. But the farmer shouts, then rushes after me waving his arms in the air. First there were tomatoes. Then, wine and mushrooms. And now: corn. So many gifts of food along my way; trail angels, showing me that nourishment and love takes many forms, including what grows in the ground. The farmer shaves off a few kernels into his palm, hands them to me and I take a bite.

"*No me gusta mucho*," I say, grimacing in disgust. "*Quiero mas con agua caliente.*" I don't like it; better if it's boiled.

He shakes his head, but the sharp taste of uncooked corn does not entice.

"*No*," he corrects me, "*en fuego.*" Better in the oven.

A few kilometers past my lessons in corn, I learn about the prominence of the letter "x" in the Galician dialect. In the names of villages, restaurants, menu items, the appearance of "x" is a dead giveaway that we are closing in on Santiago. The region of Galicia—in which Santiago is located—is steeped in Celtic heritage; X helps to mark the spot.

With that new detail in mind, I opt to stay in Airexe—partly to facilitate a slow transition into all things Galician, but also because I'm partial to the guttural sound of its X. Airexe is, much like Fonfria before it, another entry in Spain's corpus of micro-villages—though not nearly as memorable, its godawful dreariness mirrored in the rainclouds which are sunken onto road and rooves. From the doors of the municipal albergue, now sealed, the village seems to have fallen into hibernation. Fortunately, for us, the private albergue next door remains open, barely. There is one sparsely furnished room, with a handful of bunk beds.

The sole, grungy-looking bar across the street has even slimmer pickings: Only one item on the menú del día is available: fried and fatty dish. A morose-looking drunk is perched on a stool at the bar, spouting off much about nothing. A large flat-screen television draws me in, offering a front-row seat to the ATP World Tour Finals, with Nadal on serve. If the food falters (as it inevitably does), the tennis match makes up for it by sweeping me away, for nearly one hour, into the stands of London's O$_2$ Arena, where celebrities and royals rub elbows in the glorious sunshine, and where top-ranked players sidestep competition long enough to shake fans' hands and throw expired balls into the stands.

While crossing the empty stretch of road back to the albergue, a young Korean man with wavy black hair rides up on his bike; properly equipped with road lights, saddle bags and every serious cyclist's miscellany. We introduce ourselves and K.O. follows me inside. I lie down on my upper bunk and read, while K.O. unpacks his gear onto the bunk below mine.

Later that evening, we are hanging out in the foyer, where the hospitalera sits at the desk, looking bored, when I ask K.O. about his cycling voyage.

"Where have you been?"

"I started off from London," says K.O., now in flip-flops while he brushes mud off his cycling shoes. "Then I cycled around many European countries, until I reached Saint Jean Pied de Port." From there, he joined the Camino Frances.

"I left O Cebreiro last night," he continues, "and I'll be in Santiago by tomorrow." Our snailing pace is no match for his speed.

Later, in the stillness of the night, I will hear a quiet mumbling from below. It cannot be Juan-Do, who is already snoring loudly from the far end of the room. When I peek over the railing, a flashlight beam points towards a page, from which K.O. is reading. I squint to see if he might be reciting a psalm from Brierley, possibly the Kindle version. But no, it's a Saint James Bible.

There are no signs of rain in Airexe the following morning. With sunshine in the offing, and the Carrix still wheeling around with my backpack intact, all engines are go for today's stage leading to Palas de Rei.

"*Hola Otto*," I write.

"*Bien aqui*," I ramble on, noticing how effortlessly Spanish phrases now spill onto the screen, without a single word of Indonesian slipping in. "*Un poco mas viento y lluvia, creo que Juan-Do va bien tambien pero no se 4 sure… Dejamos de Eixere esta manana. Muy tranquil aqui!*" All is well here despite the wind and rain. I think Juan-Do is ok, except that I can't know for sure… We left Airexe this morning. It's so quiet here!

In Otto's absence, it seems only fitting that I dedicate today's portion to he who made my Camino possible, even if that gift included a long stint with a tree-hugging loner.

The green dewy and muddy fields of Galicia seem to be sprouting kingfishers and crows, so plentiful they are, soaring above my head. Pueblos are scattered around in the distance, dotted with the usual fields of corn and concrete. Wild blackberries are harder to spot. I am bundled up against today's low-sizzle chill: leggings, pants, a new and possibly waterproof rain jacket, scarf and a sunhat now smeared with forehead sweat. My hands are tucked into socks, while my rosy toes remain committed to the Tevas.

On our way out of Airexe, an elderly German pilgrim stumbles when she spots my naked feet. She opens her mouth and points at my sandals, searching for words now stuck in her throat. I try to explain in the most pitiful almost-German-sounding-Yiddish I can muster: "*Yoh, es iz a bissel kalt,*" I say, bewildered at just how badly I can butcher the tongue of poetry and wisdom that I learned in school for 11 years. "*Auber meine fees zayn zeier frid.*" Sure, it's a little cold, but my feet are very happy.

By the time we reach Palas de Rei, a farmers' market is in full swing. Not surprisingly, the ground swells with bushels of corn. Two ripe bananas and a flaky croissant later, I steal into a tobacco shop to purchase credit for my cell phone. Then I slip out of Juan-Do's sight and into a local bar, where I linger over a café con leche. When I'm done dawdling, I head outside just in time to spot the Man of Few Words trudging downhill with his back doubled over. I tail him, reluctantly, like a child trailing behind her parents' shared misery.

Chapter 58: Juan-Do Goes Missing

In Ponte Campaña, we are alerted to the presence of dogs by their incessant barking. Villagers hunch over a field of chestnuts, picking through this morning's offerings. A gully is covered by an overhang of trees. At the far end of the thick forest, a handful of molinos jut up from the hillside, their motionless propellers outstretched like hands reaching for thinner air.

At the 60.5 km marker, a single hiking boot sits on the path, as if in wait for a foot gone missing. If a pilgrim recently decided to temporarily ditch her boots in favor of sandals, she will be sorely surprised to learn she's left one behind. Losing a boot or two can lead to outright anguish; or, in some cases, awakening. Just ask Strayed.

On the way to Melide, the path is like a pit of silence. There is a mere trickle of pilgrims. The natural landscape embraces us in its high definition intensity: Trees. Molinos. A stone bridge spanning a stream. Falling leaves. Cornfields. Cows. Pastures. Castañas. A fence separating a young foal from its mother.

Before we reach the town, I see an old man carrying a rifle. Juan-Do stops to speak with him. When I ask Juan-Do later about the gun-toting man, he only says this: "*Jueves y Domingo.*" Turns out that, because of a dwindling population of wild animals, hunters are only permitted to legally hunt prey on Thursdays and Sundays. Saturdays are taboo.

Melide's municipal albergue is closed for renovations. Par for the course, our late-season gamble. But have no fear, private albergues are here—and open. We are first to arrive on the doorstep of a contemporary, six-month old albergue privado. Styled in Camino minimalism, stark white walls, and a forest of bunk beds, the décor is simple—except for a flat-screen TV and full-length leather couch, on which I will later rest to watch flamenco. Other than a snorer's low-key buzz, my sleep is long and undisturbed.

It is well past 9 a.m. when we bundle up and step outside. Today's flavor of cold is milder and less pungent than preceding days. Heading out of town, I see wall-to-wall cornfields, only occasionally interrupted by a lone house sprouting in their midst; or the front bumpers of cars parked in a mechanic's lot, crushing a whole row of stalks that run along the edge.

When we pass the fifty-kilometer marker, the rain resumes—as if testing our resilience and stamina. It shifts gears, swiftly escalating into a downpour. Juan-Do finds refuge in front of a house with a covered verandah, but he looks glum. He misplaced the large plastic garbage bag that has, until now, waterproofed his backpack. Low-tech, but it did the job. I fail to think of a solution. Without a word, Juan-Do unfurls his crinkly silver mat and spreads it over his bag, tucking its edges under the ropes of the Carrix. A quick fix; he does not let minor setback stop him from going on. As he turns towards me, I see that large droplets of rain drip from his hood onto his face. He looks beaten, sad, hapless.

If it pours any harder and if his silence gets any louder, I will come apart at the seams.

"Go on," is all he says. I feel drained of words, so I just walk.

Inside the forest, we seek sanctuary from the downpour under a canopy of trees. Juan-Do downs the last of his water and, as if he were channeling Harry Dean Stanton's gruff character with a red baseball cap, in the opening scene of *Paris, Texas*, he tosses the empty plastic bottle to the otherwise pristine ground.

"*¿Porque dejar esta botella aqui en natura?*" I ask as he walks away, appalled. Why are you leaving your empty bottle behind, here in nature? He loves trees, but then… this.

He rolls his eyes, doesn't utter a word, and turns away.

I pick up the bottle and walk on slowly, looking upwards to the tips of eucalyptus trees, through the tops of which I can almost see the sky. I feel a stifled scream in the pit of my stomach.

I'm shaken out of my silent reverie by a horde of pilgrims barreling by at record speed. No longer do I hear the traditional greeting of previous days and weeks. Cheerleading seems superfluous the closer we edge towards Santiago; done with the heavy lifting, everyone is heading towards the finish line. Everyone, that is, but Juan-Do. He is missing.

I wave down passing pilgrims and approach locals sitting at the roadside.

"Have you seen a man with a hat and blue cart behind him?" I ask, unsure in which direction to search.

Where in the world is Juan-Do? With no forks on the path, no place to err in direction, his disappearance is a mystery. Has he fallen into a cornfield? Maybe he met his soulmate—or he gave up, veering off the trail to unload for the very last time, my backpack onto the ground, unconcerned that it might one day in the future be excavated by crane from the bottom of a trash dump piled high with bocadillos, coffee grinds and pilgrim castoffs.

Puzzled about the whereabouts of the Man of Few Words, and feeling a deep ache rising, I step off the path and into a restaurant. No sightings. I kneel on a bench and sip on perhaps my hundredth café con leche in nearly as many days, pondering my next step. I feel all washed up—and out. Ready to call it quits. Juan-Do, if I ever find him again, will make a case for going on. I will push back. May the gentler one win.

Once I return to the path, a delicacy long forgotten pops into view: blackberries at eye level, as if dropped from heaven's limbs. No need for my bastón; I merely stretch out my hand and pluck them off a branch with ease. Great juicy sweets come to those who wait.

An older Galician man, a farmer perhaps, sits in front of his house, which faces the path.

"*¡Hola señor!*" I call out. "*¿Tu ver un hombre, un poco mas viejo, pasado par aquí, con un carrito?*" Did you see an older man pass this way with a cart on wheels?

"*Ay no,*" he says. Nobody has seen Juan-Do. Maybe he teleported himself into the universal cosmic field.

With some trepidation, I finally resort to sending him a text message. "*Hola,*" I write. "*¿Dónde eres tu? Yo paso un pueblo a 42 km, no te vistu… Si tu eres adelante por favor espera parami en Ribadiso. Obrigado.*" Where are you? I passed a village at 42 kms and haven't seen you… If you're ahead, please wait for me in Ribadiso. Thanks.

Intentionally, strategically, I thank him in Portuguese. Maybe it will please him, buoy him, compel him to reply. Just this once. Wishful thinking. Nada. On the far bank of the Rio Iso is the tiny village of Ribadiso. At the edge of the path, a low stone building houses an albergue and bar.

As I near it, there seems to be a glum-looking Juan-Do sitting on the front stoop, slumped over as if in defeat. He looks up and glares at me without a word. It would be futile to ask why and where and how. He stands up, hooks himself into the harness and veers onto the path. Without a word, we go on.

Chapter 59: Juan-Do Goes Missing (Again)

A cornfield at the edge of another village shows signs of being recently harvested and its stalks chopped down. At the edge of the field, a dog yelps while caged in to ward off trespassers and corn-thieves. But my attention is diverted to a tree limb that had snapped and toppled over a fence, inadvertently lowering a substantial mass of figs to mouth-level. But the real catch of the day happens under the largest leaves, where the juiciest figs are concealed. I restrain myself, lest I reprise my teenage experience of gorging on more cherries than my body could digest… leading to unfortunate results.

After close to three hours of relentless rain, I finally feel satiated from my big find of figs. Heading out of the forest, I see that the skin around my ankles is streaked with fruit fibers and dried weeds. Here at KM 40.0, with eucalyptus reaching skyward and crows swooping between trees and bushes, I look down at my feet, the left one clenched tight and claw-like from cold. Yet, they glisten.

A sign welcomes me into the town of Arzua—just as a niggling feeling takes hold. Again. Juan-Do is nowhere to be seen. No sign of man or cart. Oh, the *Juandering-Do*.

I look up at the sky and recognize a familiar weather pattern on the horizon. Grayness hints at imminent rain. I seek cover inside a café, ordering a bowl of soup, and standing at the bar from where I can easily slurp and scan the sidewalk for signs of Juan-Do.

I glance out periodically. Through the pelting rain, I look out just in time to see a stooped figure slinking into view, sheets of water bouncing off his hat and off the back of his two-toned jacket. The

Hunchback of Santiago, lost and found. Juan-Do stops in his tracks and glances sideways into the bar, peers at me intently, and fixes me with a menacing glare. Steely-eyed, he frantically waves his hand in front of his face, as if he were a mobster conveying threat through crosshairs. Jack Nicholson in *The Shining*, or Billy Bob Thornton in *Sling Blade*—take your pick.

I drop my spoon, grab my jacket, bastón and Shrek-pack, and quickly pay for my barely-touched meal. We slog into the municipal albergue and wait behind a burly American pilgrim who stands in front of the reception desk. I deliberately stand at a safe distance from Juan-Do, the air between us dripping with rumors of all that is unseen and unsaid.

Beds, in a spacious second floor room, are assigned by number. The bunk below mine is Juan-Do's. He hauls up both our backpacks, and sits down, sweeping his hand across the bed, as if cleansing it of bad energy. When I wake from a nap, I step down to the floor, careful not to wake my bunkmate. He turns over.

Arzua too abounds with signs of recession and poverty. Shuttered shops, along with the ubiquitous Al Vende signs are taped on many windows. A store selling over-priced house-wares looks sullen, as if on the cusp of closure—particularly when compared to its neighbor, a five-star restaurant. But the hair salon, here like elsewhere on the Camino, does brisk business, customers entering and spilling out of its front door in droves. Economic downturn be damned, these people will not sacrifice their cuts, curls and perms.

After checking emails in the town library, I cross the street to the supermarket to get ingredients for dinner. The produce section boasts a vast selection of imports: Oranges grown in Portugal. Red plums from South America. Pineapples from Costa Rica. Apples from Chile. Bananas from Portugal, Belize and Cameroon. Strange fruit. Where are the Spanish grapes? Figs? Blackberries??

Back at the albergue, I shower, change into t-shirt and a pair of clean long johns, and climb up onto the top bunk—where I can breathe clean, sweat-free air. My body needs to stretch. A few yoga poses should do. I contemplate leaning over the side, and letting my head and arms dangle, reaching towards the ground; among my most-favored resting poses, when the bunk below mine is unoccupied. But Juan-Do is down there, and I cannot imagine that he will take too well to seeing my face inches from his, upside down. Although, who knows: it might make him laugh. Taking no chances, I lie on my back, with legs straight and arms to my side. Savasana. Corpse pose.

Chapter 60: A Vow of Silence

A posse of pilgrims is up before the crack of dawn, shooting light beams along the walls, as if to announce their imminent departure. I hear rustling below, signs that Juan-Do is stirring too. No doubt thrilled at the possibility of reaching Santiago today—in time for mass. No chance; I need another go-slow day.

In light of Juan-Do's recent disappearances, this penultimate day demands that I get through it with my sanity intact. A strategy for self-preservation is called for: I will take a vow of silence. No use telling Juan-Do. He is not likely to notice.

I walk out of the forest and straight into the solid, outstretched stalks of a cornfield. A sudden burst of gunfire reminds me that it is Sunday. Galician hunters are on the loose. May all pilgrims be out of stray bullets' way.

A lack of clear signage, coupled with the sight of other pilgrims crossing over into the forest—Juan-Do among them, means that I almost bypass my next stop of choice: O Pedrouzo. *No possible!* The next albergue is at least fifteen kilometers away. Temporarily breaking silence, I yell out to Juan-Do, imploring him with exaggerated gestures to backtrack.

Inside the Refugio de Xunta, I approach the counter with one finger to my lips. To the perplexed hospitalera seated on the other side, I mouth the word *silencio*—and indicate with hand signals a preference for a top bunk. She nods approvingly, and takes my credencial. As soon as my backpack hits the ground, I leave in search of hot tea.

***

The girl could not have known that one day, far off in the future, as she lay on a beach of white sand, she would think back to her earliest memory, of looking out the back window of her father's dark blue late 60s model Oldsmobile convertible while on a family road trip, and a drive through a forest, and while becoming transfixed by a little child, caked in mud, sitting and playing in a clearing where the driveway leading to the family home meets the road, but where the child should not have been left alone, and as if the girl herself was a Wonder Woman in disguise and of her own making, she would fast forward herself into her life two decades on, while telling her to stand up and brush off the mud, turn right at the road and keep walking until she found herself on the way.

***

As I sip and drift off into a calmer headspace, I wonder what became of a flat bit of tinsel that, along with the shells, I had brought from Bali and forgot about. Until now. I dash back to the albergue, and like the Korean guy with the misplaced watch, rustle madly through my backpack. Wedged in among my hiking boots and long unused paraphernalia, I catch a glimpse of glitter—stuck between pages of the now-spineless Brierley. I draw it out carefully and tuck it into my Shrek-pack. Before falling asleep, an image of the tinsel hanging from a bramble or vine comes to mind, as if it were waiting for the rains to breed more of its kind.

Though I'm heavily sleep-deprived the following morning, and feeling slightly groggy, I head out the door with Juan-Do on my tail. He looks utterly spent, skulking behind me in his rain jacket, its collar upturned until he looks buried inside. A half-finished concrete structure near the refugio stands like an architectural skeleton, one more example of an economy in tatters. Weeds grow out of wood planks and tarps crackle in the wind. Grandeur does not live here.

Under a sky now smothered by stubborn fog, we disappear into a forest—and I disappear, away from Juan-Do, as if standing outside of myself in order to merge with my surroundings. Forest bathing.

I crave the grace and solace of trees as badly as some pilgrims need Camino candy.

Stopping in the forest, I reach down to un-strap my sandals and plant my chilled feet on sod. Barefoot walking on anything other than grassy or uneven terrain is unthinkable; in moments, pain spikes up and into my sacrum. But standing, or moving about gently on soil, is another story. My feet touch the ground whenever possible. Pieds a terre. Soles to the earth.

We are still in the forest, enveloped by a grove of eucalyptus trees, their limbs piercing cloud formations, when I hear indistinct sounds. I stop to focus my senses. Airplane engines revving. A muted thrum of cars. City noises already encroach upon us, splicing through the receding purrs of nature. I am not prepared for a return to urban life. Juan-Do walks by, his figure dwarfed by eucalyptus, looking so small and insignificant by comparison. I look over at the closest tree, and feel a sudden urge to lace my arms around its skinny trunk. I don't, but it's not the first time that I understand his penchant for clasping bark. Still earthbound, it's the closest he gets to heaven. Tree-huggers, largely misunderstood, are intermediaries; straddling worlds, they tap into heaven's sap.

I am skirting muddy puddles on the gravel path when I spot a young woman sitting alone on a large stump, her poncho concealing the entire contents of her backpack and body—except for her head, that cranes upward while marveling at the crowns of majestic, duo-toned eucalyptus trees.

Alegria is from Andalucia, the country's southernmost region. I break silence.

"What do you know about these trees?" I ask her, mesmerized by their height, and how they scrape the sky.

"They are not native to Spain," Alegria says. "They're imported and planted in large numbers because they grow very tall in a very short time." Planted, grown, cut down and sawed off—for the sake of manufacturing furniture. Even here, on the outer edges of Santiago, nature is appropriated.

As Alegria and I walk together and gaze upwards, the sky is intermittently visible, through a latticework pattern of limbs and leaves. At the roadside, I kneel to empty out the last of my shells—tucking them behind rocks, under large mushroom caps, on top of a hardened, frozen berry.

Chapter 61: Santiago

Fifty-three days on the path. More than 700 kilometers walked. No more O Cebreiros, no Poio de Altos. Santiago is a short and easy stroll away, mostly downhill.

Emerging from the forest with mixed feelings, I step onto a path that skirts the far end of a runway at Santiago International Airport. Crosses are jammed into the chain-link fence by passing pilgrims, in commemoration of their arrival—by foot rather than on wings.

On the periphery of the city, with Santiago in full view, stone houses are boarded up; their roofs decrepit, paint peeling, windows cracked, locks broken and hinges rusted. With markets and super-mercados a stone's throw away, the last bits of nature's bounty, primarily figs and apples, free and fresh for the picking, entice me still. For the first time, I do not know for whom I am walking today.

We reach Monte Gozo—the last vantage point offering a bird's eye view of Santiago, before arriving. Unlike high season, when Gozo's humungous albergue overflows with pilgrims, today there is but a trickle.

"*Hola Mario!*" I text a local who agreed to host me for a few days. "I will arrive in SdC a la tarde. Is there room for Alegria to stay too?" Mario readily agrees.

At the first busy intersection, we reach a stoplight—my first, since leaving Pamplona. The pathway across the street leads waves of pilgrims into the Casco Historico (old quarter), and directly to the Cathedral of Santiago—ground zero for most pilgrims. The light is red. I look down at my left sandal. The bridge of my foot, directly under the strap is suddenly raw and red also—and there is blood. My own *stigmata*.

I limp behind Alegria and Juan-Do, who walks at record speed, an urgency mirrored in his body language. Without a word to Juan-Do, who marches on, Alegria follows me into a pharmacy, where the trainee hands over a package of Bandaids while laughing at the history of my wound. We reach the main Cathedral square, but Juan-Do is missing. Again. Alegria dumps her bag and collapses onto the stony ground. I crouch down beside her. Out of the corner of my eye, I see Juan-Do barreling towards us.

"*¿Dónde?*" he stammers. Where?

"*¿A Finisterre?*" I deadpan. By which I mean the next coastal village on a Brierley Stager's circuit; at least two days away for slower trudgers like me. But he is in no mood for a joke.

Alegria turns to Juan-Do with the pilgrim's perennial question. "*¿Ahora que?*" she asks, oblivious to all that has come before. What now?

"*¡A casa!*" he says. Home!

Alegria and I go off in search of a nearby bar, for food and temporary storage, from where I send directions to Juan-Do by text. That, he reads. I stand outside, watching him arrive, untie my backpack from the Carrix and dump it in front of the door. He hoists his pack onto his back, folds up the cart, grips it in one hand and turns. I can tell that he is anxious to leave and sever the shaky bond between us that somehow became a gulf. Juan-Do's mind is already focused elsewhere, the look in his eyes as distant as the day we met; as if he has boarded a homeward bus, already lost me to memory.

"*Por favor*," I say to Juan-Do, "*espera un minuto.*" Wait a minute, please.

I untie my daypack and fish out the small plate of tinsel. It is a cherub-shaped ornament, hand-crafted in Bali. I present it to Juan-Do, expecting him to recoil. I don't realize until then, that, all along, the angel was meant for him. I reach out my hand, and Juan-Do shakes it as reluctantly as he did in Logroño. "*Muchas gracias*," I say, looking him in the eye, searching for the light. Nada. No reply. No kindness. No chance of a hug. Turning on heels now far scruffier, but looking ever so slightly more erect, the Man of Few Words walks away and vanishes into the dizzying tangle of tourists and pilgrims. And just like that, nearly two months after shuffling into my life, Juan-Do, a man of unbridgeable silence and mystery, backs out. At which point, what may be the most time-consuming, patience-testing, mystifying and accidental blind date in history comes to an entirely uneventful and anti-climactic end.

Chapter 62: The End of the Earth (and Beyond)

It does not take long for me to switch gears.

Alegria and I duck through a low-ceilinged entryway into a café thick with the scent of spice and sweat. We store our backpacks—mine tied to the little carrito—behind the bar, and order two glasses of vino. If nothing else, it is time for a celebration. Satiated, we lug our bags a short distance away, along cobblestones and sidewalks, in search of Mario's house. He would be away for a few days, so he left instructions. I unlock the front door and we gasp in unison: this is heaven.

Like a pair of hobos gone Hollywood, we land in a chic, post-Camino refuge unlike any other. An all-white, sleek and spotless three-storey dwelling, worthy of an architectural magazine cover story. Over the coming days, Alegria and I will luxuriate under the rainfall shower, where I scrub off layers of meseta and bocadillos and tomatoes and bramble thorns and frost and loneliness. We will linger and laugh over café con leche and croissants at Café Tertulia, receive our Latin compostela at the Camino office, and dine with other pilgrims at the elegant Parador hotel.

While I stroll among the hubbub of churches, plazas, and people, Alegria goes off to attend mass in the Cathedral, shop for souvenirs and meet up with the Czech guy she fell for. After less than one day in the city, I feel overwhelmed: Too much grim and grime, not enough green.

I plan a quick escape to the city's periphery, dotted as it is with voluminous parks and gardens, where I can once again walk about. Among the greener pastures, I discover the natural wonders of Parque Alameda and others like it; San Domingo de Bonaval and Parque Belvis. I marvel at the elegant swans of Parque de Musica, and I roam among the palm trees of Parque Vista Allegre. If I'm due for penance, it happens at nature's altar, *en plein air*, far from the confines of any man-made edifice.

After each of my strolls through gardens and forests, I explore a range of Galician cuisine—including the best empanada in town at Mercado Abastos, where the shopkeeper urges me to try one stuffed with *bacalau* fish, curry and raisins. Mouth-watering. There is space still for one more menu item, so I head over to the nearby La Radio, where I guiltily indulge in a plate of chocolate con churros—dishing up a flawless mix of crunch and creaminess.

Most pilgrims end their Camino in Santiago de Compostela, its cathedral their symbolic end point. But I'm not done. My next destination is Finisterre on Galicia's northwestern coast, a.k.a. the end of the earth as it was once known to be. With yet more walking on the horizon, Santiago is merely an interlude for me; a time carved out for transition, rest and reflection, hovering between my Juan-Do breakup and all that lies ahead—including the imminent (and long-awaited!) arrival of my friend Charlotte. This state of limbo allows me to reground myself, re-energize my lagging spirit, anticipate the next stage of my westward journey.

Feeling refreshed from my stay at a deluxe retreat, I decamp to an albergue around the corner from Mario's home. Here too, I claim an upper bunk featuring a priceless view of the cathedral's (scaffolded) façade, roofs and steeples. I peer outside. Charlotte is lumbering up the road, her backpack hanging off sturdy shoulders. I leap off the bunk and sprint downstairs to greet her.

A British expat who has for more than a decade called Andalusia home, Charlotte deliberately reared her son on farm that is off-the-grid; she did all the heavy lifting, chopping and fixings herself. I had met Charlotte years ago in Nepal, when we both lived in a village at the edge of a jungle. Even then, I knew she had extraordinary character and strength.

It is the frozen tail end of the season for backpack transport services. Charlotte suggests—and I, guiltily, yield to—an outrageous commingling of our gear. The entirety of our belongings (mine slimmed down to the absolute bare essentials) is tightly stuffed into my backpack, which—except for the first day, when we pay for taxi delivery—is glommed onto Charlotte's back for the coming week. I become unbearably self-conscious about the optics of this imbalance—until that monster-mochila becomes fodder for many jokes. I yield to the hilarity.

Over the next couple of weeks, we will sleep on paper-thin mats piled on the floor of an unheated albergue—on a blistering cold night. We will meet a young Venezuelan cyclist who will share his woeful tale of a thief pilfering his bike with all of his gear, while he stepped inside the pilgrim's office to register. We will gorge on local delights such as *pimientos padrone, pintxo de patatas, caldo gallega*— paired up with plenty of café con leche. And Charlotte will wait impatiently for her *gambas a ajo* (red peppers with garlic) and arm herself with the occasional "rocket fuel" (aka Coke), while I continue to forage for the very *very* last figs and blackberries. We will marvel at the sight of twin rainbows close enough to touch, wade through cornfields and hórreos, and climb a mountain where we stand within a few meters of molinos. Wind sentinels. Trail angels too.

When we reach the Atlantic coast, while scanning the horizon for dolphins that remain unseen, we will notice a young man dressed in red down by the water, putting finishing touches on a large heart that he carved in the sand—as if timing its completion with our arrival. I will think of the mythic but still-faceless Frank, and wonder if his heart might have seared wide open by the time he reached this shore.

After a one-night pit stop in Finisterre, Charlotte and I will keep in step while heading on to Muxia—as if to prove that life exists beyond the end of the earth. On the way, I will apply my new wood-tracking skills towards finding a custom-made bastón for Charlotte.

We will learn that this mystical town, population 5,000, owes its name to the *mojas* (monks) who disembarked here on pilgrimage long ago. And that one of the boulders, called Pedra de los Cadris—located at the edge of the sea and in front of a church known as Sanctuary of the Virgin of the Boat—is thought to be a remedy for back pain and kidney ailments. According to legend, people who clamber 9 times through its lowest opening will heal themselves of spinal problems. Enough said. I will fall to my knees and, claro, crawl through.

By the time we reach Muxia, I will have clocked just shy of 900 kilometers. By the time I leave the country, I will have… lost count.

"How can I stop walking?" I will ask Charlotte, bringing a look of glee to her face.

"No idea," she will say. "Maybe we should go on." I couldn't agree more. Neither of us will be ready to call it quits. Besides, there will always be another road to travel. So we will… go on.

We will meander through forests until we reach the Fox House, a small stone structure in a quaint village and billed as a post-Camino retreat for pilgrims; where we will be welcomed with open arms, hot tea and cake, treated to hot showers, laundered sheets and British fare. But, the promise of clean, fresh sea air will soon lure me back to Muxia while Charlotte will stay behind, loath to leave a new gardening project behind.

The return trip to Muxia will mark the first time I ride in a vehicle since landing in Pamplona months ago.

Over the coming windblown but sunny days, I will spend time exploring the fishing village; waiting for the boats to return with crates of *pulpo* (octopus); and making a labyrinth on the beach— using the niblets of corn gifted to me by the farmer. Seagulls will soar high above, then dive into the harbor for a strategic catch. Planes will pass overhead, leaving a vapor trail in their wake. And, in the corner top bunk of a near-silent dorm room, alone with myself and the diffused light from a solitary streetlamp, I will break down into a soft sob of tears, as if all the rains of the past weeks had somehow managed to seep deep into my gut through all the wicking and impermeable fabrics and pores of my skin, and wonder why I failed so miserably to connect with another human being.

I will buy a bus ticket to Santiago, a train ticket to Madrid, and yet another to Granada. Before I leave the Muxia albergue, I will place my dependable bastón into a bin where others are bunched together, awaiting pilgrims who, like the Frenchwoman, the peripatetic troubadour Carlos and Señor Poppi before them, choose to walk against the tide—and into the sun.

On my one day in Santiago, I will buy a few postcards and souvenirs, then make a beeline to the Convent of San Paio de Antealtares, where I will procure the most prized gift of all: Tarta de Santiago—from cloistered nuns who serve up each pie through a revolving window so as to remain hidden from view. The sweet aroma of the renowned almond delicacy will accompany me on the overnight return journey to Madrid.

I will detour to the south for a week's visit with friends, in Granada and at their family beach house—where we will gorge on oranges plucked from trees in their garden. I will walk through brightly lit Christmas markets and the glorious Alhambra. On the way back to Madrid, I will squint out the window to marvel at three old-fashioned windmills, relics from another century, their blades inert.

Señora Elena will again host me for a few days, and we will together enjoy the last crumbs of Tarta de Santiago. On my final evening in Spain, while a frosty chill sends Christmas shoppers into a frenzy, Elena and I will meet in the center of a busy plaza, the Puerta del Sol—door to the sun. She will guide me to a spot where a small crowd gathers. Etched into the ground, I will read: 0 km. Ground zero. The epicenter of Spain.

I will stand in its center, rubbing warmth into my fingers—stuffed into a newly washed pair of wool socks—and realize that there is only one thing to do when you think that you've reached the end of a road—or your rope: Go on.

Epilogue

A couple of years after walking the Camino, and buffered by the immense physical distance between Canada and Bali, I began asking my mother questions about her life. After the initial hesitation, her floodgates opened, until she almost came undone.

One morning, a dreary Sunday on which I would normally be leafing through *The New York Times*, I was lying under a duvet in my parents' home, when my mother walked in. We were both in pajamas, folds of cotton crumpled from sleep. She sat beside me, an unfamiliar awkwardness lining her face. She asked if I had more to say or ask. I did. She listened closely, as if for the first time, hanging on my every word; visibly moved. But she could not remember. I drew out the rescued, faded-yellow notebook, its pencil markings still decipherable, and handed it to her.

The morning sun, rising above the eastern flank of St. Joseph's Oratory, was already heating up the room, its blazing rays dappling the tips of the blue shag carpet.

"I'm sorry. I didn't realize how cruel I was to you…"

The world surged to a sudden stop and silence—but a silence in every way unlike that which had suffocated me in Juan-Do's presence. In that gap of nothingness, her words cleaved to the wall, then reverberated and seeped through my pores until they etched themselves into my mind's archive; while tiny little breaths, bound for decades like glue to every cell of my body, dared to detach and exhale.

In that moment, it struck me as virtually impossible to gaze into a face awash in regret, unaffected.

I could not have known when I scribbled in that Hilroy as a little girl in pigtails and polyester pants, that it would make all the difference in the world.

Dayenu. It was enough. Later that day, I ripped the notebook into shreds.

Acknowledgments

A special note of appreciation goes to my Indiegogo supporters. Without your backing, the Camino might have remained a distant dream.

High-fives to Lee Constantine and the Publishizer team, for *disrupting* my life in Bali at the right time, and guiding me along the virtual path of crowd-publishing.

I'm grateful to each and every one of these people, who on faith alone (or led by crazy impulse) pre-ordered a copy of my book: Aarin MacKay, Adi & Gili Golan, Alan McWilliam, Alissa Stern, Amit Erez, Andrey Ruchin & Ida Rucina, Anna Fraenkel, Arlena Mourier, Bali Silent Retreat (Patricia Miklautsch), Barbara Soesan, Bernard & Shirley Herman, Carmela & Amos Yudan, Cheron Long-Landes, Cindy Krupka, Cristina Raczkowski, Tammy & David Paynter, David & Leanne Matlow, Debbie Dankoff, Deborah Korn, Denny Creighton, Elissa Kline, Eva Virago & Dave Hirschheimer, Eve Kundycki, Eyal Pavell, Frances Dines, Graziella Benenati Costanzo, Hadassah Kingstone, Harriet Grunvald, Hayley Weatherburn, Hayley Grace, Heidi & Adi Levite, Jan Ameen, Jenny Byrne, Jesse Rubenovitch, Jules & Ellie Samson, Katie Chase, Leo Kaklamanos, Liane Wakabayashi, Liliane Kandel, Linda Bunch & Patrick Matthews, Lisa Bowen, Liudmila Leuckaja, Maile Ellington, Michelle Katz, Mindy Shapiro, Mooh Hood, Ayu Mandala, Nancy Anello, Neville Katz, Nora Bednarski, Orit Janco & Hagai Golan, Orna Rotbart & Yoni Nitsan, Penelope Ward, Peter Wall, Rachel Samson, Rhoda Kagan, Robert Primavesi, Robin Lim, Sam Coppola, Simon & Mary Jane Ginsberg, Stephanie & Wayne Firestone, Sujata Dayal, Susan & Jimmy Gutman, Susan Railer, Tara Murff & Odeck Ariawan, Tracey Howard, Wouter Lincklaen Arriens, and Yu Onodera.

Mulțumesc foarte to Danny Janco, who pre-ordered enough *naches* copies to last him several lifetimes.

Huge thanks to: Rachel, Monica, Ines, Linda, Mary Jane, and Marc for nudging me towards emotional honesty; I love you all. Kate and Ruby, for helping me to reframe. Deborah, for listening with a trained ear and understanding heart. Sue Kenney, for that very first Second Cup. Suzanne Kiraly and Susan Gutman, for beta reading inexcusably amateurish drafts. Joel, for all the films, music and hospitality. Shelley Kenigsberg, for her sharp and sensitive editing; and for steering me towards the end of my book (*un noch veiter*). Joanne Haskins, for patiently navigating me through the wilds of book-making.

To all those who provided quiet havens, while I cobbled together one messy and gap-filled draft after another—in Israel, Singapore, Bali, Australia, and France—thank you for your kindness and generosity: Lola, Carmela, Orna, Judith. Aparna, and Tété. Jero and Gusti. Ashlea. Sophie.

To Dr. Helen D., who long ago stood out from the crop by reading what could not yet be spoken.

To family and friends, in Bali and around the world: You continue to scaffold my life's journey, in so many ways. *I love you. I'm sorry. Please forgive me. Thank you.*

Tattoos of gratitude—via invisible Sharpie—go to: M.S., for keeping me afloat, sane and trusting in the holiness of nature, friendship and laughter. Orit, Hagai, Adi and Gili Golan, for always making their home, mine. My mother, for the apology. My father; for reasons I cannot fathom, he still lets me *dance* on the tips of his shoes…

Resources

CAMINO DE SANTIAGO

Sue Kenney, *My Camino: A True Story About the Spiritual Journey of a Woman Confronting Her Deepest Fear.* White Knight Publications, 2004.

Sylvia Nilsen and Greg Dedman, *Your Camino: On foot, bicycle or horseback in France and Spain.* Pilgrimage Publications, 2013.

John Brierley, *A Pilgrim's Guide to the Camino de Santiago.* Camino Guides, 2019.

Camino de Santiago Forum – https://www.caminodesantiago.me

Camino Guides – https://www.caminoguides.com

Camino Guidebooks – https://www.caminoguidebook.com

INVISIBLE IMPAIRMENTS and ILLNESSES*

Invisible Disability Project – https://www.invisibledisabilityproject.org/

Disabled World – https://www.disabled-world.com/

Invisible Disabilities Association – https://invisibledisabilities.org/

The Mighty – https://themighty.com/

*Also: Diffabilities / Diffabled. Inabilities. Invisabilities.

C-PTSD (Complex Post-Traumatic Stress Disorder)

The ACEs Study (Adverse Childhood Experiences) – https://www.cdc.gov/violenceprevention/acestudy/

ACEs Too High – https://acestoohigh.com/got-your-ace-score/

Harris, Nadine Burke, M.D., *The Deepest Well: Healing the Long-Term Effects of Childhood Adversity.* Mariner Books, 2019.

Nakazawa, Donna Jackson. *Childhood Disrupted: How Your Biography Becomes Your Biology, and How You Can Heal.* Atria Books, 2016.

Levine, Peter. *Waking the Tiger: Healing Trauma.* North Atlantic Books, 1997.

Miller, Alice. *The Drama of the Gifted Child: The Search for the True Self.* Basic Books, 1997.

Miller, Alice. *The Body Never Lies: The Lingering Effects of Hurtful Parenting.* W.W. Norton & Company, 2006.

Redford, James. *Resilience.* https://kpjrfilms.co/resilience/

Van der Kolk, Besser. *The Body Keeps the Score: Brain, Mind, and Body in the Healing of Trauma.* Penguin Books, 2015.

Walker, Pete. *Complex PTSD: From Surviving to Thriving: A Guide and Map for Recovering from Childhood Trauma.* CreateSpace, 2013.

About the Author

A lawyer by training, Amit Janco is a writer, artist, serial walker, and yoga practitioner who splits her time between Montreal, Canada, and Bali, Indonesia. She's also been a media producer, teacher, and public investigator who tracked down missing heirs around the globe. Amit has contributed to *Travel + Leisure*, *Journeywoman*, and *Inspired Bali*. She has trekked in the Himalayas, ridden horseback through the Mongolian steppe, and floated in the Dead Sea. After surviving a precipitous and devastating drop from a bridge in Cambodia, she discovered the benefits of an *upright* life—including improved posture, a heightened search for truth, and easier access to dangling fruit.

Amit blogs at healingpilgrim.com and dabbles in social-mediaesque pursuits at @amitjanco.

(Un)Bound, Together is her first book.

www.amitjanco.com

Made in the USA
San Bernardino, CA
12 April 2019